HOW TO WRITE PLOTS THAT SELL

HOW TO WRITE PLOTS THAT SELL

F. A. ROCKWELL

Foreword by Ray Bradbury

Contemporary Books, Inc.
Chicago

Contents

Foreword

For more years than we can pretend to acknowledge, I have known F. A. Rockwell, whom I have admired for just about all those years. The admiration had to wait, of course, until I could see that not only could F. A. speak writing and think writing but do writing. And F. A. has done writing of many kinds. The latest example lies here in your hands at this moment.

Without my telling you, leaf through and see for yourself how bright this author-instructor is without hitting you over the head with it, how intelligent without using it as a weapon as if to prove superiority over your automatic inferiority. I have always found F. A. to be at ease with a high I.Q. and in control of a good store of knowledge.

F. A. is a hard worker as a human being teaching others how to write. I have watched it happen. F. A. is a hard worker at putting together a book that can help the poor bewildered beginner, as well as the professional writer, make it through the next twenty-four hours, then the next week, and, hopefully, the next year.

This book is packed with insights, information, hints, revelations, and ways to think and do things. It must have taken forever to write, yet it does not show signs of being overworked or overthought, and thank God for that.

This book serves its purpose if it only offers us a few shortcuts through the wilderness, crying out: not that way, *this!* but not insisting on it, merely suggesting it. F. A. Rockwell does not shout but talks to us with quiet thoughfulness about a literary life spent gathering the kind of information we all might need, early on in our careers as writers, to make a start.

I hope that F. A. goes on teaching person-to-person, as has been the case for more than half a lifetime, and that more books like this will be forthcoming.

What more can I add?

My Foreword is short because F. A. has a long book here, which, in the reading, seems very short indeed.

F. A. has much to say. Listen.

Then . . . get to work!

Ray Bradbury
All Hallows Eve, 1974

The Roots of the Rainbow

*"From things that happened and from things as they exist and from all
the things you know and all those you cannot know, you make something
through your invention that is not a representation but a whole new thing
truer than anything true and alive, and you make it alive, and if you make it
well enough, you give it immortality.*
That is why you write and for no other reason that you know of. . ."

Ernest Hemingway

*"The blossoms of today draw strength from the roots of 1,000 years
ago."*

Japanese proverb

To be an author you must be an archeologist.

The work is similar: probing into the past, excavating
and evaluating so that the digging will enrich mankind. Only
the tools are different; archeologists use concrete utensils like
picks, hoes, shovels, broadblade knives, crowbars, sledge-
hammers, trowels, and fine brushes to dig into the past,
whereas authors' tools are abstract words and ideas. Yet
writers often dig deeper!

"We archeologists seldom dig for the roots of rainbows,"
said a digger at South Cadbury, England, where excavations
are under way to find and restore King Arthur's Camelot. On
the contrary, clever authors *always* dig for the roots of
rainbows!

Whenever you are dazzled by the bright rainbow success of a professional story or drama, be sure to dig to its roots. Study them and the soil they flourished in as well as the spectrum of colors that make up the rainbow itself. The colors come from different sources: from reading, real experiences, and people and from many other roots that will be discussed in the following pages. You will learn to graft onto these sources in order to build successful scripts, and by doing so, you'll never run out of ideas.

The primary colors of the fiction rainbow are:

Characterization
Plot action
Premise
Setting or X-plus factor
Style

All writers borrow some (consciously or unconsciously) and invent others. Even if you borrow most of the elements of your stories from "received structures" as pros often do, your own synthesis and addition of timely factors will make your rainbow your own thing! Goethe said: "All truly wise thoughts have been thought already thousands of times. But to make them truly ours, we must think them over honestly until they take root in our personal experience."

Readers and viewers like the glint of recognition and the reappearance of a familiar story in a fresh new way, preferably with relevance to their own lives.

Many titles proclaim the sources or "roots" of scripts that are nonetheless original works. *Androcles and the Army, The Four Musketeers, Dr. Jekyll and Sister Hyde* (a doctor experiments with hormones and transforms himself into a woman), *Joe Macbeth, Cleopatra Jones, Jezebel, The Resurrection of Eve, Mistress Pamela, Geronimo Rex, Sweeny Agonistes, Jesus Christ Superstar, The Gospel According to Joe*—these are merely a beginning. How many more can you list?

Blacula, Scream, Blacula, Scream, Blackenstein, and *Carmen Jones* use famous frameworks for dramas about Black characters; *Cinderfella* transposes sexes to a male hero, fairy godfather and stepbrothers. *Cinderella Liberty* refers not just to the sailor's pass that expires at midnight but to the patient, good, lonely, and love-hungry gob who does everything "good" including marrying a pregnant hustler and befriending her mulatto son and who is eventually rewarded by being freed from confining duty when he stays ashore to enjoy civilian life and sends a navy-loving buddy back to his ship to replace him.

Romanoff and Juliet, Romeo and Julietta, and *West Side Story* are all based on Shakespeare's greatest love story with different settings and details. There are, of course, many other borrowings; for example, *Robinson Crusoe on Mars* and *Swiss Family Robinson.* A clever title trick is to use a common denominator title that throws light on the author's meaning by bridging different eras or ideas. That's why Joseph Wambaugh called his novel about contemporary policemen *The New Centurions.* He pointed out parallels to Roman centurions who were "unsupported and unhonored by their countrymen. They are like the men who held the frontiers of Empire until Rome was finally overwhelmed by the Barbarians."

Authors acknowledge their debts to earlier works by referring to them subtly or obviously. In *A Touch of Class,* scriptwriters Frank and Jack Rose show their adulterous lovers watching an old movie on television, *Brief Encounter,* about an extramarital affair that could have inspired the newer film. In *Thieves Like Us* (an admitted updating of Ed Anderson's mid-thirties novel *They Live by Night*), the fugitive lovers are a shantytown Romeo and Juliet who play out a love scene against a radio broadcast of Shakespeare's classic. The hero of the movie *Honeypot* sees the play *Volpone* and patterns his behavior after that phony fox-like character who pretends to be dying and promises to will his fortune to others in order to get theirs. In Neville Smith's *Gumshoe,* the Liverpudlian amateur detective is hooked on *The Thin Man* and claims to owe much of his technique to the earlier private eye.

The Happy Hooker, Xaviera, and *Letters to the Happy Hooker,* all fictionized memoirs of a former Manhattan madam, Xaviera Hollander, are called "the Scheherazade of male adolescent fantasies." So are similar works dating from and before *Fanny Hill*, whereas the real Scheherazade of *Arabian Nights* fame is charmingly resuscitated in John Barth's *Chimera*.

Because conflict is the essence of drama and plot and Big Conflicts make Big Dramas, there has always been and always will be fiction about the threatened destruction of humanity. In H. G. Wells' *War of the Worlds* Martian invaders are destroyed by earth's bacteria, an idea reversed and technologically updated in Dr. Michael Crichton's *Andromeda Strain*. Earth's takeover is threatened by human-sized pods in Jack Finney's *The Body Snatchers*, by "possession" of children in *Village of the Damned*, and by mushrooms in the Bradbury horror tale "Boys, Raise Giant Mushrooms in Your Cellar." Bradbury's *Post* story and movie *The Beast from 20,000 Fathoms* is in the classic tradition of murderous sea monsters (popular all over the world).

A common variety of this destruction theme can be seen in certain movies: ants are the threat in *Phase IV* ("an ecological suspense tale") and also in David Seltzer's *Hellstrom Chronicle* in which insects set out to inherit the earth. Thomas Page's *The Hephaestus Plague* repeats the fear of earth's grisly destruction by super-bugs. If you're deceived into believing in the innocence of "the birds and the bees," you'll change your mind after studying Hitchcock's *The Birds* (based on a Daphne du Maurier story) and Arthur Herzog's *The Swarm*, which is advertised as "a masterpiece of chilling adventure—that just could come true." How many other plots can you think of that stress the man-destroying danger of rats (*Willard*), bats, and other creatures? What new variations could you develop along the line of this perennially popular format?

Any best-seller or box office success is followed by many imitators like a huge ship with smaller boats riding along its waves. The *Bonnie-and-Clyde*-killers-who-are-chased format keeps appearing with different trimmings in dozens of movies like *Badlands* and *Thieves Like Us*. Reviewers enjoy pointing out these parallels. *Playboy* says the movie *The Pyx* "is frankly derivative, as if *Klute* and *Laura* had mated to produce a sibling for *Rosemary's Baby.*" *Electra Glide in Blue* is described as "a bastard son of *Easy Rider.*" "*Night Watch* is the *Rear Window* bit about a rich, high-strung lady who sees—or thinks she sees—terrible things in a deserted mansion across the garden from her London townhouse." (Both are, of course, reminiscent of an older movie, *The Window*, in which an imaginative little boy reports seeing a man kill a woman. He is disbelieved, and later the murderer chases and tries to kill him. The many plots along this line probably go back to the old folktale "The Boy Who Cried Wolf.")

Sometimes critics and reviewers are sarcastic about literary look-alikes, exhibiting an "If you've seen one, you've seen 'em all" attitude. One wrote of Gore Vidal's *Weekend*: "If you saw *Guess Who's Coming to Dinner?* and *The Best Man*, you can skip this. It's a rehash." Arthur Knight called *The Devil's Brigade* "sort of *Dirty Dozen* multiplied by 200." John Reed wrote: "*Clown of Bombay* [by Aaron Judah] is a kind of mini-*Catch 22*. I say mini because it is . . . one-third the length of Joseph Heller's wildly comic book. On this smaller scale it is just as dazzling a performance."

Movies are always accused of carboncopying each other. *Everyman's Woman* was panned as "a disappointing counterfeit *Never on Sunday*"; *Therese and Isabelle* is advertised as "making *The Fox* look like a Sunday school picnic" (the same thing said about *Doctors' Wives*, by Frank Slaughter, following Mary McCarthy's *The Group*); *Will Penny* echoes *Shane*; and *Newsweek* said that *How to Save a Marriage and Ruin Your Life* should be titled *Son of Pillow Talk*.

These critics do not realize that *everything* derives from some previous origin. Hemingway may have oversimplified it when he said, "All American literature comes from one novel by Mark Twain called *Huckleberry Finn*," but, on the whole, literary works, like people, descend from previous ancestors. It's no secret and it's no disgrace. The most brilliant object in the world, the diamond, has no light of its own but shines by reflected light. Likewise, the most brilliant fiction reflects a dazzling array of previous lights. ·

Producer Joseph Strick worked eight years as a laser physicist to earn enough to make movies, which he proudly claims "pirate the classics," including Zola, Proust, Durrell, Henry Miller, and Joyce. The latter's *Ulysses* has its roots in many other odysseys-into-maturity going back to Homer's ancient classic, but Joyce's work forms the roots of subsequent novels like Anthony Burgess's *Enderby* and Tom Kristensen's *Havoc*, which changes the backdrop (setting) from Dublin to Copenhagen.

William Golding's *The Spire* owes a debt to Ibsen's *The Master Builder* insofar as the protagonist's pretended spiritual aims become egotistical, materialistic, exhibitionistic, and even phallic. Damon Runyon's *Guys and Dolls*, about a Salvation Army lass and a gambler, has roots in G. B. Shaw's 1905 drama *Major Barbara*, in which the Salvation Army girl is wooed by a suitor who pretends interest in the organization to win her, as does gambler Nathan Detroit in Runyon's story.

Almost everyone knows that *Oklahoma!* was taken from Lynn Riggs' *Green Grow the Lilacs* and *Carousel* from Ferenc Molnar's *Liliom*, but they aren't aware of other rainbow roots. *Hello, Dolly!* is from Thornton Wilder's *The Matchmaker*, which he borrowed from his own short story "The Merchant of Yonkers" based on an old German farce by Johann Nestroy. The same clever, charming, fun-loving, matchmaker, Mrs. Levi, stars in all of them!

No matter how freshly sensational any current best-seller appears to be, a little sleuthing will prove that its plot is not an original product of its author's imagination but that it is a recombination of several sources that the writer has studied and blended in his own unique way.

William Peter Blatty's *The Exorcist* is based on the real life case of a fourteen-year-old Mt. Rainier, Maryland, boy. In 1949 his body suffered torturous writhing and devilish behavior similar to that which seize the twelve-year-old Regan in the recent novel and movie. The boy was eventually cured by specific priests who were not physically harmed or killed as are the fiction priests.

When he was a student at Georgetown University, Blatty learned of the case from Father Eugene B. Gallagher, a Jesuit priest who lectured on exorcism. Blatty was drawn to the subject because throughout his Jesuit education he had always been haunted by one line from the Liturgy:

> . . . Satan and the other evil spirits who roam through the world, seeking the ruin of souls . . .

He researched the true story thoroughly as a class project. Decades later when the public's interest in the supernatural increased and fantastic success rewarded such works as Ira Levin's *Rosemary's Baby*, Blatty's thorough research, dramatized with his own premises, style, and additional characters, resulted in the most discussed novel and movie of our time.

Supernatural "possession" was not an original discovery of Blatty's. In Miami, Florida, alone, Jackson Memorial Hospital's Crisis Intervention had been treating thousands of "possessed" patients long before Blatty dreamed of writing *The Exorcist*. The Director, Dr. Hardot Sukhdeo, says, "Usually we treat 600 to 700 a month." Florida has many superstitious Jamaicans, Haitians, Bahamians, Cubans, and Puerto Ricans who insist that they hear voices and feel spirits within them.

Exorcism goes back much farther . . . in fact, throughout pagan and ancient Hebrew lore exorcism abounds. In the Bible, young David acts as an exorcist to drive evil spirits of depression from King Saul with his harp-playing. Later in Jewish history, demonic possession was stressed in the Kabala (a theosophic system developed by these rabbis from the seventh to eighteenth centuries based on a mystical method of interpreting scriptures). The Kabalists taught that the rebellious builders of the Tower of Babel were punished by being thrown down to earth and transformed into *shedim* and *mazzikim*—evil, destructive spirits who restlessly roamed the earth, clung to the living, and formed a *dybbuk* or attachment to a live person.

Shin Ansky's play *The Dybbuk*, written in 1913, predated *The Exorcist* by over sixty years, using rabbis instead of priests who exorcize demonic spirits from a young bride-to-be whose body is "possessed" by the vengeful spirit of a young man (now dead) to whom she had been promised by her father before she was born. This old play was Ansky's recombination of many earlier real-life stories of ancient Hebrew folklore.

Spirits of the dead have "possessed" many living women throughout literature, which of course gave motivation for the persecution of witches. The phenomenon appears in many recent scripts like *The Invasion of Carol Enders* and television plays like "She Waits," in which a sweet, shy bride becomes a vixen as her body is invaded by her husband's bitchy first wife. Men aren't immune. In *The Possession of Joel Delaney*, the mild-mannered hero is possessed by the violent spirit of his dead Puerto Rican friend Tonio through "Brujeria." Even in Edward Albee's play, *A Delicate Balance*, Mother says we sleep "to let the demons out."

An entirely different plot with a seemingly unique and "new" idea is Philip Roth's *The Breast*, in which Comparative Lit Professor David Alan Kepesh is transformed into a gigantic breast. He is shocked to find himself immobilized in a hospital sling, deprived of all faculties except feeling, hearing, and speech. Previously he had admired and then envied his mistress' bosom and also studied Kafka, Gogol, and Swift. Thus Roth acknowledges the sources for his "unusual" idea. In Kafka's "Metamorphosis," the hero, through no fault of his own, turns into a cockroach; Gogol's protagonist becomes a nose (the nose was always Gogol's sex symbol). No mention is made of Eugene Ionesco's *Rhinoceros* in which people are mysteriously transformed into these beasts, but surely they all have a common denominator and theme: **Man's helplessness to control his fate.**

Let's look at the best-selling novel that enjoyed the greatest prepublication success in literary history: Book-of-the-Month Club selection, movie sale, over $1 million in subsidiary rights, and major ad-promo before the public had access to it! See how many roots you can recognize in the brief synopsis of the plot rainbow of Peter Benchley's *Jaws*.

Story

A great white man-eating shark has veered out of its

normally deep waters and threatens the beach at Amity, Long Island, killing a young woman swimming alone at night. When bits of her body wash ashore the next day, there's no doubt about what happened, and Police Chief Martin Brody wants to close the beaches to protect the populace. But the town's civic leaders, including a prosperous real estate man and a powerful newspaper editor, persuade him not to because it's the beginning of the tourist season, which will bring in lots of money; rentals are lagging and the beast will probably mosey off to Patagonia or at least East Hampton. But the shark continues to menace Amity, killing more victims, until it is pursued and destroyed by our hero plus an oceanographer and a grim fisherman.

Roots
(1) In 1965 a 4,500-pound killer shark was caught off the coast of Long Island, making big headlines.
(2) *Moby Dick*. Here, too, the action drama becomes an allegory, as the chase becomes a search for "catharsis," "personal expiation," and triumph of good over evil.
(3) Jonah (from the Bible) and Pinnochio were both swallowed by a whale.
(4) In Ibsen's *Enemy of the People*, the righteous hero tries to combat mercenary opponents who choose profit over safety.
(5) Benchley's strong knowledge of the sea and skin diving.

William Golding's *Lord of the Flies* shocked readers with its portrayal of the primitive savagery of children (choir boys at that) in an emergency situation without adult supervision. The same premise appeared two decades earlier in Georg Kaiser's *The Raft of the Medusa* in which a liner taking children from bombed England to Canada is sunk by a German sub. Some of the ten- to twelve-year-olds escape death in a lifeboat. The natural leaders are Allan and Ann; the latter soon points out that they number thirteen—a disastrous number ever since the Last Supper. She wants to get rid of one child and selects as useless a much younger, redheaded mute called "Foxy" who is too little to row. Although Allan loves Ann, he objects to the murder. She proves to him that Christians do kill when there's a just cause. Allan builds a makeshift tent to protect Foxy, but it does no good. After the children have disposed of the child, a seaplane spots and rescues the poor, sweet innocents, much like the end of *Lord of the Flies*.

Playboy was profusely congratulated on the "originality" of George Byram's story "The Chronicle of the 656" about a World War II battalion on maneuvers in Tennessee. Suddenly the men find themselves in the middle of the Civil War with modern weapons that could change already-past history. Agonizing decisions must be made by the Southern C.O. who must aid in the defeat of his beloved South so as to avoid prolonging her losses and to preserve the United States.

Original? Yes, insofar as the magnificent suspense, characterizations, action, research, and motivation are concerned. Even the cause of the phenomena is explained by the little-known A-bomb experiments in Tennessee that preceded those in New Mexico. But the time-transport idea has many roots in past literature, including Mark Twain's *A Connecticut Yankee in King Arthur's Court* (1889) in which a Bridgeport shop foreman is transported thirteen and a half centuries backward into King Arthur's England; John Balderston's *Berkeley Square* (1929) in which American Peter Standish living in London finds a diary of an ancestor bearing his name and moves backward in time to 1784 to become that man; and numerous science fiction stories about time travel.

Charles Webb's *The Graduate* has had the most fantastic success with American youth since J. D. Salinger's *Catcher in the Rye* because it exposes the immorality and phoniness of adults who corrupt idealistic kids. The seduction of a twenty-one-year-old boy by his girl friend's mother also appears in another "new" and "now" novel, Sigrid de Lima's *Oriane*, which seems to carry on where *The Graduate* left off. A middle-aged woman elopes with her son-in-law on the eve of his marriage to her daughter, planning to live in Sophoclean sin in Italy.

New? Now? This plot is a rainbow with roots that go very deep and back over 2,300 years, as we shall see in the chapter "Plotting from the Classics," which will examine some of the hundreds of versions of the Phaedra tragedy since Euripides wrote *Hippolytus*, in which an older woman was passionately in love with a young man.

As you study the roots of rainbows, think up your own clever embellishments and gimmicks, but don't think you must have a brand-spanking-new plot before you start to write a story.

No matter what color they paint the Eiffel Tower—red, blue, gold, orange, brown, or blue—it will always maintain its structural majesty beneath the outer coats of paint. So will a strong plot.

Editor Tom Congdon is right when he says, "The whole nation is like a child that climbs up on his father's knee and says 'Tell me a story.' " Everyone wants a *really good* story, agreeing with the old adage: "A good tale twice told is better than a poor one once."

The secret of the pros will help you enrich your fiction and your bank account. Use it! Quit wasting time trying to dream up new plots or waiting for inspiration to strike. Once you have mastered and elaborated a basic structure, it may work over and over again for you as in the case of Gothic novels or the works of many writers including Mickey Spillane, Ian Fleming, Agatha Christie, P. G. Wodehouse and other perennial favorites.

John Masefield credited this anonymous quatrain with his success:

> Sitting still and wishing
>   Makes no person great.
> The good Lord sends the fishing
>   But you must dig the bait.

Marvelous catches await you if you learn to dig the proper bait.

Happy fishing!

2

Where Do You Get Plots?

"Where do you get all your plots?" is the most frequent question asked of professional authors.

"Everywhere" is the most frequent answer—an answer that is frustratingly incomplete. The would-be writer is assured that there is a plot in everyone he meets and in everything he does, sees, reads, hears, feels, dreams, and thinks. Of course it's true. There *are* "tongues in trees, books in the running brooks," and "sermons in stones" as Shakespeare said. But how to *differentiate* the worthwhile from the worthless ingredients and how to blend and build them into full-bodied fiction are secrets most professionals will not reveal, but this book will.

Most successful authors acknowledge the wide range of sources of their plots. Many get ideas from the news.

Here are just a few of many films based on news events:

Motion Picture	True Incident
Rage	Army nerve gas killed sheep.
The Day the Fish Came Out	Bomber dumped two A-bombs in ocean—Spain.
What a Lovely Way to Die	Florida wife killed husband for lover.

Harold and Maude   "80-Year-Old Widow Weds 17-Year-Old Boy!"

A newspaper squib about the population explosion inspired William F. Nolan to write *Logan's Run* in which there's no more room in the overpopulated world for a man over forty so he must kill himself or be eliminated. Then Mr. Nolan changed the situation to a "death at twenty-one" level and sold it to the movies for $100,000. The same or similar clippings could have sparked other popular fiction like Kurt Vonnegut, Jr.'s "Welcome to the Monkey House" (originally published in *Playboy*) about the future world in which Earth's seventeen billion people are compelled to take ethical birth control pills and encouraged to commit ethical suicide in ultra-plush Suicide Parlors. Or Dr. Bernard V. Dryer's novel *The Torch Bearers*, which is concerned with overpopulation's impact on religion, medicine, politics, and war. Or Edmund Cooper's novel *Five to Twelve* about the gruesome twenty-first century in which women enslave men whom they outnumber twelve to five.

Inspired by such examples, the would-be writer starts a clipping file of news items that are surely more exciting than population statistics:

(1) CRYONICS SOCIETY'S FACILITY FOR "FROZEN DEATH" OPENS.
(2) ARAB TERRORISTS KIDNAP OFFICIAL . . . (or SKYJACK PLANE).
(3) CANNIBALISM ENABLES PLANE CRASH VICTIMS TO SURVIVE.
(4) VICTIM KILLS MUGGER WITH JUDO.
(5) RUNAWAY WIVES INCREASE 40%.
(6) ZODIAC KILLER STRIKES AGAIN.

The novitiate writer is confident that any headlines as dramatic as those will make better plots than an overpopulation statistic. Too shy to aim at the $100,000 movie jackpot, he modestly writes stories for the $100 markets, then waits for checks that never come because *ideas* do not make *plots*.

In this book you will learn how to develop successful fiction from many other sources besides headlines. You will be made aware of the fact that there is a wide cross-country stretch of terrain between getting an idea and writing a publishable script. You may think of it as the Wilderness you must traverse to get to the Promised Land—a Wilderness you can jeep through if you learn and apply the technical skills of writing.

The up-to-date tips and techniques in the following pages will help you bridge the distance between wanting to be a writer and being the star of those sparkling champagne autograph parties.

When James A. Garfield was president of Hiram College he told his students: "Things don't turn up without someone turning them up." Maybe it was this philosophy of learning-how-to-do and then *doing* it that enabled him to become the nation's twentieth president. It is the key to success in any field—even writing.

Let's take a hypothetical trip from idea to plot that could have started from the previous six headlines, realizing that in each case the professional author(s) created *original* works due to their unique blending of characterization, plot action, premises, setting, and individual style.

1. CRYONICS SOCIETY'S FACILITY FOR "FROZEN DEATH" OPENS

How many different ways have you seen the idea of cryogenics used to freeze a dead person so that he can be resuscitated in the future when, hopefully, a cure for his illness can be perfected?

A satirical slapstick science-fiction comedy was developed in Woody Allen's movie *Sleeper* (co-author, Marshall Brickman), which also has similarities to Washington Irving's *Rip Van Winkle*. This hero, part-owner of a Greenwich Village health food store and clarinet player with the Ragtime Rascals, enters a hospital for routine exploration of a peptic ulcer. Complications set in, he never regains consciousness, and a cousin gives permission for him to be admitted to a cryogenic immersion program. Discovered and revived 200 years later, he is pursued by selfishly motivated doctors, scientists, and police through hilarious sight gags and Chaplinesque mayhem.

Quite different in style, characters, plot, and setting is the television horror play "Live Again, Die Again" by Joseph Stefano, which opens in the present from which *Sleeper* takes off into the future. It begins with the revitalization of Carrie Carmichael who died of rheumatic fever thirty-four years ago and was "frozen." She soon realizes that being young and beautiful thirty-four years after one's "death" isn't as euphoric as it sounds. She's much too young for her too-old husband and friends—even younger than her son and daughter. The latter was always Electra-ishly jealous of her prettier mother and was unbalanced enough to want to kill her to gain her father's whole love. The entire Oedipus-and-Electra plot is evident in the gruesome, murderous action, which unlike the ancient Greek tragedy, ends with mother and daughter becoming reconciled after several deaths.

Science fiction seems to be using cryonics or cryogenics to replace the time capsule in transporting characters from the present to the future. It is the springboard for Gene Rodenberry's television pilot *Genesis II* and Pierre Boulle's *Planet of the Apes* to explain how and why a young man from the present can still be young and vigorous decades or centuries later (as *Sleeper* does).

2. ARAB TERRORISTS KIDNAP OFFICIAL . . . (or SKY-JACK PLANE)

This headline could have been the spark to ignite many recent plots including that of Eric Ambler's *The Levanter*. In this novel, Michael Howell, director of Agence Commerciale et Maritime Howell (a trading firm in Syria founded by his English grandfather) and his Italian mistress are forced into guerrilla terrorist activities and must extricate themselves.

Although terrorist kidnap plots are ubiquitous, each is developed somewhat differently, but, due to the grim nature of the subject matter and the usual victimization of innocent people, comic treatment would be inadvisable.

3. CANNIBALISM ENABLES PLANE CRASH VICTIMS TO SURVIVE

This concept of people eating human flesh shocked

everyone at the time of the Donner party tragedy in which the remaining members owed their survival to cannibalism, but the idea is frequent in today's literature. It has appeared in such short stories as the one in *Playboy* by Henry Slesar in which the newsman narrator tracks down a plane crash survivor years later, eats dinner with him in a conventional restaurant, and now disbelieves the rumors that condemned him for the fact that he didn't even lose weight whereas his fellow passengers had died of starvation. After the reporter leaves him alone with his deaf-and-dumb servant, he plunges into his favorite food—guess what? (It has been planted that children have recently disappeared, one at a time.) Savoring his meal and smiling, he says "Once one has acquired the taste . . ."

As food shortages become more of a world problem, cannibalism appears in many motion pictures and novels about the future like Richard Fleischer's *Soylent Green* and *The Bridge* by D. Keith Mano. Mano's novel opens with a religious ceremony of human sacrifice and cannibalism. It is a celebration of life by the descendants of the last survivor of our civilization, a man named Priest who resisted mankind's collective death wish and refused to die. He is now a savage who meets the last Christian and learns just enough to start his own religion: a perversion of Christianity that is accurate in the superficialities but anti-religious in the spirit. Here the sacraments used are real flesh and blood instead of bread and wine.

This could have been inspired by the news article, "Cannibalism on the Cordillera," about the sixteen survivors of a crashed F-27 turboprop in the snow-capped Andes who warded off starvation-deaths by eating the dead. *Time* reported that after they were rescued "Roman Catholic moral theologians agreed that the act was justified under the circumstances. A few . . . even likened the situation to the central act of the Eucharist where the faithful consume the body and blood of Christ under the species of bread and wine."

And of course these same never-new elements reappear in

a later best-seller, *Alive,* by Piers Paul Read. Never ignore a subject because it's been done before. You just work hard at doing it better!

4. VICTIM KILLS MUGGER WITH JUDO

At this writing there is a plethora of martial arts films and an increasing popularity of judo, karate, and other Eastern forms of self-defense, perhaps spurred by the television series "Kung Fu" and/or the increasing rate of violence. You can think of many different ways this headline could be developed.

In Richard Deming's "Black Belt," the effeminate owner of a Fifth Avenue beauty salon takes up residence in the dope-mugger area of the Bronx. Mugged three times, he kills all his assailants since he is a Japanese-trained Black Belt. The police try to persuade him to move out of this dangerous area, but he insists on living where he wants to. Actually he considers his "set-up" ideal for business, realizing that more and more women will come to his beauty parlor, knowing their hair will be done by a real killer!

5. RUNAWAY WIVES INCREASE 40%

This is such a contemporary problem that it appears in many ways, running the gamut from tragic fiction involving rape, murder, drug-addiction, and other crimes to comedies and "straight" happy-ending stories in which the wife-mother, longing for liberation, comes to appreciate the blessings of wifehood and motherhood and learns that marriage is better in spite of its limitations. The television Movie of the Week "I Love You, Goodbye" by Diana Gould is a typical example. The same multilateral development is true of plots involving runaway children and teens—another relevant problem.

6. ZODIAC KILLER STRIKES AGAIN

The public imagination was intrigued by this criminal who sends colorful tip-off notes to the San Francisco police boasting of his murders and who keeps getting away with it. Obviously many fiction characters have been patterned after him. One of my students, Ray Cantrell, had no trouble selling his original screenplay *The Zodiac Killer,* and of course this clever crook is dramatized as the villain against whom San

Francisco's "Camelot cop" is pitted in the film *Dirty Harry* by Harry Fink and his wife R. M. Fink. Pauline Kael, *New Yorker* reviewer, explains how this characterization becomes the bedrock of the plot:

> . . . The variety of his perversions is impressive . . . no depravity is foreign to him. He is pure evil: sniper, rapist, kidnaper, torturer, defiler of all human values. . . Harry cannot destroy this walking rot, because of the legal protection, such as the court rulings on Miranda and Escobedo, that a weak, liberal society gives its criminals.

This gives you a good idea how all five "Musts"—characterization, plot action, premise, setting, and style—must be effectively synthesized and blended into a dramatic whole. This blending is the only possible originality.

Most fictioneers agree with John Cheever who says a writer should never be a cryptic (auto)biographer even though some story elements can be taken from life. The true facts must be manipulated and changed in order to make full-bodied fiction, as Kurt Vonnegut, Jr. supplements his P.O.W. life in Dresden, Germany, during World War II with fully developed characters, planned incidents, black comedy and science fiction in his novel *Slaughterhouse Five, or, The Children's Crusade.*

How can professional writers be so prolific and versatile?

The answer spotlights another major difference between authors who sell staggering amounts of fiction, plus perhaps a television play every week or two, and the amateurs who mistakenly think they must have world-shakingly *original* plots before starting to write. While the former produce several fiction works, the beginner stares at blank paper, racking his brain trying to conjure up something "different." It is impossible as well as egotistical to think you can invent any plot that has not reverberated throughout literary history hundreds of times.

Absolute originality is impossible. The same basic plots appear over and over as they always will. Some experts attribute this to "ubiquity of ideas," while others realize that there are only so many possible plot combinations. Georges Polti sums them up in his book, *The Thirty-Six Dramatic Situations*, but other authorities reduce all different plots to seven. Fitzgerald said there were only two, and Hemingway claimed that all American literature comes from one novel by Mark Twain called *Huckleberry Finn.*

Do not delude yourself into thinking you must have a brand new plot for each story you write. The only original ideas are those you haven't yet discovered, but the well-read editor has! Originality was defined by Voltaire as "judicious imitation," whereas Dean Inge dubbed it "undetected plagiarism," and T. W. Higginson wrote that "originality is simply a fresh pair of eyes." (There is even similarity in definitions.)

If you read extensively, you'll observe identical plots occurring in the folklore of cultures that have had no contact with each other. There is no evidence that ancient Chinese authors had access to our Old Testament, but they had similar plots. Just one example is the ancient Chinese play *The Chalk Circle*, in which a dispute between two women claiming the same child is settled using the same method described in the Old Testament story of King Solomon. Lovely Haitang becomes the second wife of childless Ma Chun Sing and bears him a son, incurring the jealous wrath of his first wife. The villainess and her lover poison the husband, frame Haitang as the murderer, and claim the baby in order to get the inheritance. Haitang is tortured into a false confession, condemned, and dragged on a bitter, snowy journey to a higher court to be sentenced. An honest judge determines to learn the truth as to which woman is the real mother. He puts the baby inside a chalk circle from which only the real mother will be able to lead him out. The first wife snatches the boy from the circle, but Haitang refuses to maim him by tearing at him. This proves her motherly love, and her enemies are condemned to public execution.

In I Kings, chapter 3, Judge Solomon settled the women's conflict over the baby by calling for a sword and announcing that he would cut the child in two and give half to each woman. Although the false mother agreed, the real mother was willing to give up the infant rather than let him be harmed. This proved her claim and she won him.

Bertolt Brecht borrowed the situation and Chinese title in his play *The Caucasian Chalk Circle*, adding fresh reversals. Azdak is a drunken rascal instead of a wise, just king and the real mother is a vain, selfish clotheshorse who abandons her child in her hurry to pack her dresses during a civil war, while the adopted mother is a lowly servant girl who has loved the boy and protected him from danger.

It's not difficult to renovate and graft your original ideas onto other Biblical plots because of their universal truths, strong characterizations, suspense and conflict. For a further exploration of the use of Bible stories, see Chapter 9.

Patterning Is Not Plagiarism

When Professor Brander Matthews and Nicholas Murray Butler were discussing plagiarism, Matthews said: "In the case of the first man to use an anecdote there is originality. In the case of the second there is plagiarism, with the third it is lack of originality and with the fourth it is drawing from a common stock."

"Yes," agreed Dr. Butler, "and in the case of the fifth it is research!"

Most professionals who use this technique of building on other structures think of it as *patterning*. The professional tailor can make several different-looking garments from the same pattern, using varying materials, details, and accessories. If you have ever built or observed houses, you know that great variety can be achieved even when you use the same floor plan. The exteriors may deviate to Cape Cod, Hawaiian, modern, Colonial, ranch style, or rustic, with materials ranging from brick, flagstone, wood-frame, or stucco. Seemingly different on the outside, many "tract" houses are identical inside.

In fact, all houses have certain basics in common: walls, floor, roof, living room, bedroom(s), and kitchen. The same is true of all fiction. Even though you consider yourself exceedingly creative, always teeming with "fresh" ideas, you *must* copy something that has been done before. But no matter how much you copy it, it won't be plagiarism if you saturate the writing with your own individual thinking and stamp it with your hallmark. When Wordsworth conceitedly told Lamb, "I believe I could write like Shakespeare, if I had a mind to try it," Lamb replied, "Yes, nothing is wanting but the mind."

Shakespeare's genius produced the greatest plays of all times and all languages even though there wasn't an "original" plot among them! Emerson reminds us that when Shakespeare was charged with plagiarism (Robert Greene called him a "crow beautified with our feathers with his tiger's heart wrapped in a player's hide"), Landor added: "Yet he was more original than his originals. He breathed upon dead bodies and brought them into life." Using this and other examples, Emerson wrote: "It has come to be practically a sort of rule in literature that a man, having shown himself capable of original writing, is entitled thenceforth to steal from the writings of others at discretion."

Just as houses have certain basics in common, so do all plots. "The Plot Skeleton" is an excellent term for story structure because it emphasizes the fact that the bony framework of normal people is essentially similar even though the people may be quite different in age, size, color, character, appearance, and personality. Likewise stories can be excitingly different even though they have one or more of the same basics:

> Characterization
> Action line from problem to solution
> Premise or theme
> Setting or X-plus factor (time, place and background)
> Style and mood

If you borrow one or more of these from another source and blend it imaginatively with *your own ingredients*, you won't be plagiarizing. Your *creative* blending will make it your own just as the winners of the several thousand dollar annual Pillsbury Bake-off win with recipes that recombine already-prepared ingredients. A $25,000 prize went to one that merely added canned cherry pie filling to brownie mix, and another prize was awarded to a recipe that spread canned corned beef hash over rolled-out refrigerated biscuits that were then shaped into attractive meat pies. In writing as in cooking, invention is the clever recombination of what already exists.

"We can say nothing but what has been said," wrote Robert Burton. "Our poets steal from Homer, our story dressers do as much. He who comes last is commonly best."

When you do your best to *improve* upon any classical structures and when you *embellish* them with fresh, timely touches, backgrounds you know well, a philosophy you believe, your own unique style, and reader identification, you will enjoy standing on the shoulders of giants.

Warning: Never copy any story exactly as you read or hear it without recombining elements and adding your original characters, action, premises, or setting and style. If you hear a catchy anecdote, try to track it down to the source and always change it drastically.

Don't ever try to get away with a variation of one of the perennial "oldies" that turn editors off. Here are some examples:

1. *The pawn-ticket-mink joke.* A married businessman wants to give a mink coat to his secretary even though his wife doesn't have one. To avoid gossip and her finding out, he buys and pawns the mink, planning to give the secretary the ticket the next day so that she can redeem it, claiming a friend found it and gave it to her. But that night the wife goes through hubby's pockets, finds the ticket, gets the mink, and wears it to her husband's office, telling everyone she found the ticket.

2. *The doubtful-food-and-dead-cat yarn.* In a hurry to cook company dinner or party luncheon, the housewife has doubts about some food item (usually fish or chicken). She

tries some of it on the cat. He eats it eagerly and begs for more. Convinced that it's O.K., she cooks it or puts it in the salad and serves it to her guests. After dinner she is horrified to find the cat dead on the lawn or the back porch. She confesses all and there's a Big Crisis. Doctors are called or everyone is rushed to the hospital to have stomachs pumped. Later a neighbor or delivery boy comes to apologize for having run over the cat. There are a variety of reasons for the delay in admitting it.

3. *Lone-woman-followed-by-truckdriver story.* She is frantic as he pursues her, gesticulating. The surprise twist is that he isn't really being "fresh" or a threat—he is trying to warn her of the real culprit hiding in the back of her car.

4. *The obstetrician-protects-his-predictions anecdote.* A new mother accuses the o.b. of being wrong about predicting the sex of her baby even though he has a reputation for faultless predictions. He claims he was right and shows her his little notebook in which the correct sex is written. Twist: he always tells each mother-to-be the sex she wants the baby to be, then writes the other sex in his book. If she gets what she wanted, she tells everyone how right he was. If not, she calls him on it and he shows her the book.

There are many such exasperating "cuties" that come off like practical jokes to readers seeking well-developed characterization and real story values. The following pages will suggest some of the more reliable sources that pros use as bases for their original works.

3

Jokes as a Goldmine of Plots

While amateurs develop ulcers trying to think up an original plot, professionals write and sell prolifically using a technique that I've been teaching my Hollywood writers for years: Build a story on the foundations of a joke that has universal values and a specific market slant.

Leonard Wibberly's *The Mouse That Roared* was inspired by a true anecdote that occurred in 1948 when Israel became a nation but had little chance of surviving since it was unarmed, untrained militarily, and outnumbered by hostile Arabs who surrounded her and who were determined to push her into the sea.

"There's only one thing to do," Ben-Gurion told Parliament. "Declare war on the United States."

This was met with an uproar and the unanimous objection: "But the U.S. is our only friend! How can you say that?"

Ben-Gurion replied, smiling, "Look at the world today, gentlemen. The only flourishing nations are those that lost a war to the U.S.: Japan, Germany, Italy, etc."

Wibberly's genius with satire, characterization, and plotting enabled him to build this anecdote into a hilarious comedy in which an impoverished, pipsqueak mouse of a country attacks the world's mightiest nation in order to reap the benefits it grants its former enemies.

The joke about the henpecked husband who was afraid to tell his pregnant wife that he's sterile could have sparked a sequence in the B.B.C. television series *Upstairs, Downstairs,* in which a wife seeks a divorce on the grounds that her husband is impotent, then discovers that she is two months pregnant!

You can have fun guessing the jokes that may have sparked such "original" plots as Neil Simon's movie *Heartbreak Kid* in which a newlywed man falls in love with another woman on his honeymoon or Harry Crew's novel *Car* in which a man eats his auto, a bit at a time.

Such movies as *Harry in Your Pocket* or *Thieves Like Us* are reminiscent of the joke about the pickpocket brought before the same judge for the sixth time. His Honor asked him: "Aren't you ashamed of yourself? What have you ever done for humanity?"

The pickpocket replied, smiling, "I've kept a couple detectives working regularly."

You've probably heard the after-the-nuclear-holocaust joke about the male and female monkey who were the only survivors. One looked at the other and said, "Do we have to start the whole thing over again?" This is said to have triggered the idea for Pierre Boulle's *Planet of the Apes* and could have sparked other plots like *The Omega Man* and Robert Merle's *Malevil*. In Merle's novel, the survivors' leader, Comte, dies of appendicitis (there are no M.D.s), and the others determine to reinvent civilization giving priority to guns!

Here's one of many jokes I have assigned my writers to see how many different ways it could be developed:

Two fighting Irishmen were such bitter enemies that they disturbed everyone, everything, and every place they knew with their constant quarreling.

Finally an angel came to earth and told Murphy: "You're so cruel to Clancy that it must stop! The Lord will give you anything if you'll let Clancy have two of them."

"You mean if I'm head of one labor union, he'll be head of two?"

'That's right."
"If I win the Irish Sweepstakes once, Clancy wins twice?"
'Yes."
"And if a brass band follows me, he has two?"
"Correct."
Murphy thought for a moment, then said: "O.K., angel. I'll take
a glass eye."

Look what Robert Shekley did with this oldie in his
Playboy story "The Same to You, Doubled." He changes the
belligerent Irishmen to peaceful members of ethnic minority
groups. The protagonist is an amiable bachelor, a rather self-
conscious Jew named Edelstein, who is offered three wishes by
a Black man who magically walks *through* his double-locked
door and introduces himself as Charles Sitwell, field man for
the Devil. There are some very updated, satirical descriptions
of hell, which, like U.S. Steel and ITT, is "a big outfit and
more or less a monopoly." Hell is also overloaded with
souls—what with all the wars going on—so there won't be a
Faust pitch. Edelstein can have any three wishes granted on a
thirty-day offer, but his worst enemy will get twice as much of
everything. Edelstein insists he has no enemies, but soon
learns otherwise.
    Each thing he wishes for, his friend, Manowitz, gets
double. The aggravation of someone else profiting so richly
from *his* wishes curdles the protagonist's fondness for his
former friend. His first wish is for $20,000 and the other man
gets $40,000. His second wish, therefore, is a spiteful one. He
wishes for 600 pounds of chopped chicken liver, eats some,
stores some, and sells the rest at half price, making $700. He
enjoys the thought of Manowitz up to his neck in chicken liver
. . . enjoys it until he learns that the other man stores some
and sells the rest to the tune of $2,000. Edelstein now hates
not only his ex-friend but also himself, saying: "I'm the
world's prize imbecile. I gave up a million dollar wish, and all
I got was two pounds of chopped liver!" His third
wish—you've guessed it—is one designed for his pleasure and
Manowitz' destruction: a voluptuous wife!

Sheckley has added increased characterization, timely satire, and the *Playboy* slant to the old joke about human spite.

Irvin S. Cobb said that the surest evidence of a good joke is that the theater claims it for its own. "If a yarn is very good, it should be in refined vaudeville within two weeks after its appearance, in musical comedy before the month is over, and inside of six months it ought to be serving as a tag-line to bring down the first act curtain of a fashionable farce."

Of course, today there are many more markets for renovated, plottily developed jokes, including voracious television as well as the magazine and book field. It's almost inevitable since a joke often contains such plot ingredients as characterization, conflict, problem-situation, solution, premise, suspense, and that element that everyone loves: a surprise punch line.

The Best Jokes in Life Are Free

Another reason anecdotes often burgeon into complete stories is the fact that they are marvelously available. As the old saying goes, a joke is the only thing you can borrow these days without paying interest. Of course you must add plenty of dramatic interest, which means incorporating as many original variations as possible.

Develop the habit of reading, listening to, and scrutinizing jokes and anecdotes in your quest for plot material. You'll not only hit exciting jackpots as far as writing stories is concerned, but you'll find the comic relief therapeutic, especially when you've been working on serious or depressing ideas. There's an apt lesson in the anecdote about the ancient king who was criticized for telling and laughing at jokes. His critics insisted that he should sit soberly on his throne, the symbol of dignity. He replied: "When an archer goes into battle he strings his bow till it is taut. When the shooting is over, he unstrings it again. If he did not unstring it, it would lose its snap and be no good to him when he needs it."

There's plenty of snap to jokes and humorous true incidents. Look for ones that have reader identification and some tie-up to today's problems, which is very possible even in the ancient ones. In our time of longevity, gerontology, and geriatrics, oldsters are sometimes exploited by younger people, even their children. Therefore what happened to Sophocles 2,500 years ago has timeliness today:

> When Sophocles was an old man he was always so preoccupied with thinking and writing that his sons summoned him to court to pronounce him incompetent on the grounds of senility. They tried to get possession of his properties by proving him too senile to manage his estate.
>
> In court Sophocles recited the whole play he had just completed, *Oedipus at Colonnus*, and asked the judges if that were the work of a man in his dotage. He won his trial.

The situation of selfish children trying to push an older parent out of the way is a frequent theme today. In the movie *Kotch*, the father is committed to a "rest" home from which he escapes. Subsequently he proves himself to be more sprightly, ingenious, and efficient than many younger people and in no way ready to be retired to pasture.

In Ruth Gordon's play *A Very Rich Woman* (which became the motion picture *Rosie*), the protagonist is a spirited widow who enjoys her money by giving away "diamonds, paintings, and taxicabs . . . and buying an oversize yacht as if it were a boat for the bathtub." Her two mercenary daughters (who are as Regan and Goneril were to Lear) commit her to a mental institution that cannot hold her. She enlists the aid of friends, including her granddaughter, to prove herself "unincompetent," gain her freedom and control of the fortune she helped her husband earn. Equally independent and active as a spy is *The Unexpected Mrs. Pollifax* (novel by Dorothy Gilman).

Another could-be descendant of wise old Sophocles outwitting avaricious youth is Mrs. Savage of John Patrick's comedy *The Curious Savage*. This widow has inherited $10 million in negotiable securities from her late husband and plans to use it altruistically to help others realize their hopes and dreams. Her stepchildren try to get the money by committing her to a sanitorium to bring her to her senses. Here she meets various social misfits who cannot adjust to harsh realities and she helps them. They all love her for herself, not her money, and she is so happy with them that she doesn't want to leave even after the doctor says she's fine. However, she must be on the outside to help masses of needy people with her fortune. In the final fantasy scene, a farewell dinner party, each of her asylum friends realizes some hopeless dream that was unattainable before. Throughout the play the all-giving Mrs. Savage is happy and unruffled, whereas her self-seeking stepchildren are thwarted and frustrated.

The ungrateful-children plot isn't always a comedy. In Ray Bradbury's Gothic horror story "The Screaming Woman," which became a television Movie of the Week, a rich woman returns home from a mental institution only to be pressured by a money-hungry daughter-in-law and weak son into selling her beloved estate to a land developer. While walking on her property she hears a woman screaming from under the ground, and the antagonists use this ridiculous impossibility to prove her still insane (and ready to be sent back). After the widow risks her life in many suspenseful scenes, the still-alive buried woman is unearthed, her would-be murderer exposed, and the heroine's sanity established.

The novel *The Eye of the Storm* by Australian Nobel Prize-winner Patrick White is also grim, even tragic. When wise old fiesty Elizabeth Hunter lies dying in her Sydney mansion, her greedy children, actor Sir Basil Hunter and Princess Dorothy de Lascabanes ("heartless as attack dogs"), come to dismantle her property, fire her servants, and pen her up in a nursing home to save expenses and increase their inheritance. Throughout the novel their ill-mannered uptightness contrasts with Elizabeth's peace of mind and good relationship with her devoted servants.

In pointing out such parallels between an anecdote (old or new) and a recent script, we are not saying that the professional author took his idea from the specifically mentioned source. He may not even know the "original." In such instances you can chalk it up to "ubiquity of ideas." Oliver Wendell Holmes described this phenomenon when he wrote:

> Literature is full of coincidences which some love to believe are plagiarisms. There are thoughts always abroad in the air which it takes more wit to avoid than to hit upon . . . Honest thinkers are always stealing unconsciously from each other. Our minds are full of waifs and strays which we think our own. Innocent plagiarism turns up everywhere.

If you read omnivorously and listen intently you can use other ideas and pattern your own plots, adding such original variations, reversals, or fresh highlights that they will become your own. Whether you plan comedy or tragedy, fiction or drama, be on the lookout for jokes that have one or more of the basics:

> Characterization
> Action Line from problem to solution
> Premise
> X-plus factor
> Style or mood

Some seem to contain *all* so completely that they are practically encapsulated "instant" plots. Here is an example of an old gag and a similar story written by Jesse Stuart. This will show you how to expand a brief joke into a full story with the necessary pluses and minuses, cause and effect, and additional characters.

How to Blueprint a Full Plot Based on a Joke

> A tourist driving through the uninhabited Idaho mountains saw a lonely shepherd, stopped and asked him what he did to amuse himself.
> "I hold up motorists and rob 'em," he explained.
> "But aren't you afraid you'll be arrested and sent to jail?"
> "Nope, I do it this way. Ye see this hairpin bend in the road? Well, that's where I hold 'em up, and when they go on I duck over the hill, take off my mask, put on my badge, an' meet 'em down at the bend. 'I jist caught that fella that robbed ye,' I tell 'em. 'Here's yer valuables.' There's no danger in it and it's kinda exciting."

This joke has all the major elements of a story: clearly defined character (mischievous and ingenious); with a goal (excitement and adventure); an obstacle to the goal (dull, lonely life); a problem (boredom); a solution (robbing travelers, then paying them back); and a premise (imagination and ingenuity can make a dull situation tolerable, even fun—a man enjoys exerting power over others, and if he can do so in a harmless way it does him a lot of good and others no harm).

Compare the above joke with Jesse Stuart's quality story "Clothes Make the Man," which has a similar character, goal, obstacles, problem, solution, and premise. Here is a simplified plot blueprint:

Problem   Eife wants excitement and relief from bore-
              dom.

—   He's a logger in a dull job where nothing
      ever happens.

+   He decides to stir up excitement by becom-
      ing a wild man and taking off his clothes.

—   Suffers the discomforts of thorns, cuts, and
      bruises.

+   Achieves success by screaming and acting
      like a madman, scaring all the people who
      drive by in cars.

—   Some of the drivers, convinced he is a mad-
      man, shoot.

+   Returns safely to his friend Burgis (who's in
      on his secret). They have a good laugh
      while Eife buries the huge bone he fright-
      ened folks with; also other "wild" acces-
      sories.

— Sheriff and his men come looking for the wild man.

+ They divert their attention, sending them in a false direction, after being warned to be careful. Eife enjoys teasing the sheriff.

— As his exciting exhibitions continue, all of Eife's personal glory in his scheme is eclipsed by many weird tales of different townspeople who report their encounters with the monster-man. Others steal his thunder for wonder!

+ Eife has the satisfaction of knowing he started it!

Crisis As things worsen, the Sheriff doubles his efforts to catch the Wild Man and sell him to a circus. Combing the area, the lawmen close in on Eife's mountain hiding place before he is completely and respectably dressed after one of his scare binges.

Solution-
Climax Quick-thinking Eife trembles as he tells Sheriff the Wild Man attacked him, took his clothes, roughed him up, disheveled his hair, etc., as he fought him off. His story is believed, he is hospitalized and heroized as he achieves his goal of stirring up excitement and gaining attention.

Evaluate Each Joke from the Standpoint of Slanting

The women's slant

How could you work out a plot blueprint for a woman's slick magazine of the marvelous ingredients in this joke:

Three women were having tea when one said, "I'd hate to think of trying to get to heaven without first confessing my cardinal sin. In this nuclear age we can all be destroyed without having a chance to clear our consciences. So I will confess now, if you'll all do the same."

They agreed.

"Now, here is my sin. You know all that money I've been collecting for charity. I've stolen all of it and play cards with it. That's my sin."

The second woman said, "You know that red-haired butcher at the market? He's been my lover for years and my husband hasn't an inkling. That's my sin."

The third one said, "My sin is gossip—and I can hardly wait to get out of here and tell everyone about this."

This gag already has a splendid punch line, good characterization, and reader-identifiable subject matter for the ladies. You should build up cause and effect and motivation. Perhaps the gossip sets up the whole situation and stimulates the confessions for purposes of blackmail. You could increase the number three to four in order to have a bridge game. The gossip is an "outsider" to the usual bridge foursome with whom she wants to get "in." Maybe she learns to be a good bridge player, wins a tournament, or (?) so that when one of the foursome is away or ill or for some reason can't play, they ask her. She could use props: perhaps she has the game at her house and serves truth serum in the refreshments, gets them tipsy on cherry Kiafa with vodka (this often makes women garrulous), or she might even use hypnotic powers or ESP or a ouija board. It's easy to think up probable sins for a fourth person—she could have had an illegitimate child long ago or have been a member of a subversive group or you-name-it. The gossip's subsequent hold on the group, her being "accepted" or else—or her husband's promotion—can be her goal. For a mystery, of course, she could be murdered and the details of their group "confessional" be supressed until the end of the story.

Writing for general slicks

A slight variation of the "group confession" situation occurs frequently in television sitcoms, including "All in the Family." For amusement, one character suggests they all say what they don't like about the others. As a result, friendships curdle into enmities until the suggester reverses the game so that they'll say all the nice things they like about each other. Echoes of Blaise Pascal's words: "I lay it down as a fact that if all men knew what others say of them there would not be four friends in the world."

This might inspire you to write an entirely different piece of fiction, but be sure to work out a complete blueprint before writing the story.

What could you do with the knotty situation in this joke?

> The town nuisance was a cheat, a chiseler, and an all-around no-good bum. He died but nobody wanted to go to the funeral. Finally one citizen came to another and said, "You know his family. Why don't you go to the funeral and say something good about him?"
> The second man agreed, saying, "I'll manage to say something good about him if you insist."
> Thousands came to the funeral just to see what he could say good about the bum. He started his eulogy: "The man that's lying there was a cheat, a crook, a grafter, an all-around, no-good phony bum. He has six brothers, and compared to them, he is an angel."

The excellent short-short "No Pockets in Shrouds" by the late comedian Eddie Cantor is obviously a descendant of this old gag. Characterization is beautifully developed as the no-good bum is changed to a misanthropic miser, Ezekiah Tucker, who is rich but hatefully stingy, always sneering, "The Salvation Army is a fake . . . Who knows what the Red Cross does with their money? Did they ever render a statement? . . . Why should I contribute to underprivileged children? If parents would learn to be thrifty, hard-working, and conservative there would be no underprivileged children."

When he finally dies, leaving his unliked, lonely widow, Reverend Higgins has the suspenseful decision as to what to say about the hated Scrooge "waiting to be ushered into the kingdom of heaven." Quoting scriptures throughout, he tells the curious crowd that Zeke seemed unfriendly in life because he was working constantly to leave worthy bequests after death. He tells them that the rich miser's wish was to clear the church mortgage, to leave $10,000 to the orphanage, $5,000 to the Salvation Army, $2,000 to the Boy Scouts, $2,000 to the Girl Scouts, and other donations. After the funeral, his widow, Sarah, is surrounded, invited to many homes and, for the first time, loved by the townspeople. Later she tells the minister:

> "Thank you . . . for making Zeke beloved in death as he never was in life. The entire fortune will be turned over to you!"
>
> They looked deeply into each other's eyes, their glances locked in mute agreement. For they both knew that Ezekiah Tucker had left no will.

Springboards for stories for men's magazines

> Just as a congenial group of sportsmen were starting on a hunting trip into the wilds of northern California the cook they'd hired to accompany them fell ill. On such short notice the expedition couldn't find a substitute so they decided to go ahead anyway.
>
> After they pitched camp they fixed on this emergency plan: Every second day they'd play a round of poker hands face up, and the member with the lowest hand had to be cook for the next two days with the proviso that if anyone complained about the cooking, the cook would be relieved and the kicker made to cook instead.
>
> The first man stuck with the cooking job was a prominent attorney who had never boiled a potato and the meal he concocted was so terrible that hardly anybody could touch it.
>
> "This is the worst stuff I ever ate," one victim said in an absent moment. Then, remembering the penalty, he added, "But I like it. Gee, how I like it!"

What ideas do you have for developing this into a story? First, of course, you'd build strong characters with contrasts and conflicts between them. It could be a whodunit with the cooking set-up an opportunity to poison one or more victims (far from the city and sophisticated crime-detection methods). If the men have discovered a treasure, a secret, or a silver, gold, uranium, or (?) strike, you have motivation for a fatal fight. Perhaps you could write a farce, where the cook makes the meals worse and worse so that someone will complain and have to replace him. Because of the dreadful food, the men could lose weight. Perhaps the characters are all prominent bachelors who don't want to "get involved." They argue

"Who needs a wife?" since there's such a splendid variety of restaurants, laundries, maid service, and available dates. Introduce the character of a girl who wants marriage, either singly or with the men's other girl-friends, she could have kidnaped or lured away the cook at the last minute so that the guys will suffer enough from their own cooking to appreciate the girls'. How many other plots can you develop from this joke?

Many full-length, high-priced stories in *Playboy* and other magazines are so similar to jokes that they might have been inspired by them. You've probably heard several jokes about girls who cling to their mid-Victorian principles until "the price is right," like the golddigger who was willing for a big check but complained, "I've been attacked!" when the check bounced. The subject matter plus the theme of man-outwitting-woman and the golddigger-getting-her-due combine to make fresh variations of the following joke popular with the men's markets:

> A man took a buxom blonde to the furriers where she chose the most expensive mink, which he agreed to buy for her. Since it was Saturday and the banks were closed the manager explained he couldn't verify the man's credit or cash the check until Monday.
>
> "I understand," the playboy said. "We're going away for the weekend anyway, so we'll leave the coat here and pick it up later after you've cashed the check."
>
> On Monday when the man returned to the store alone the manager explained that the check and his credits were no good and they couldn't let him have the coat.
>
> The man smiled and said, "Oh, I know all that. I just dropped in to thank you for a perfectly marvelous weekend."

The more changes and additions you make, the more original your story will be. "Would You Do It for a Penny?" by Harlan Ellison and Haskell Barkin is about Arlo, Great White Hunter, a rather shiftless, bored, conniving Hollywood wolf who uses a coin collection and a sob story about his dear, dead father's tribulations in collecting the "priceless" pennies to lure girls. When he gives a hard-to-get chick an old penny with a "fabulous" history and value (all fictioneered by Arlo), it works and she yields. But the next morning she takes it to a numismatist, learns it's worth only a penny, phones and cusses out Arlo who puts on an act of injured innocence and grief that poor dear Poppa had been dupped. His act is so convincing that the girl's cursing melts to compassion and she suggests coming over again to comfort him. The story ends with his consenting: "I guess so. Yeah, OK. Why don't you stop off at a deli and pick up some corned beef and pickles and we can . . ."

Ken W. Purdy's *Playboy* yarn "Testimony in the Proceedings Concerning Edward Darwin Caparell" has for its chief ingredients slingshots, kookiness, fanaticism, and a mental institution reminiscent of the following gag:

> An inmate at the funnyfarm was being examined for possible release. "What are you going to do when you get out of here?" the doctor asked.
> "I'm gonna get a slingshot and come back here and break every window in this place!"
> He was kept for six more months of psychiatric treatment and observation, then reexamined for dismissal. When asked the same question about leaving, he said "I'm going to get a job."
> "Great," said the doctor, "then what?"
> "I'll rent an apartment."
> "Good," encouraged the doc.
> "Then I'm going to get a girl and take her there."
> "Sounds very normal."
> "Then I'm gonna steal her garter, make a slingshot out of it, and come back here and break every window in this place!"

Mr. Purdy developed more characterization and a personal feud between two rivals who were working in the same advertising agency but who had been enemies since the eighth grade at St. Ignatius, a tough school. The story opens with Ed Caparell on trial for a not-immediately-revealed crime. The first witness (Lucas Stiver) says that Ed was considered by all to be "a real stable fellow, steady, even-going, you know; but I think now I was just a victim of the common delusion that the stolid, quiet type of character never goes off the track."

For suspense purposes Ed's crime is withheld until the end, but we are told that throughout boyhood Ed and his ears that stuck out were favorite targets of Angelo Salzman's deadeye slingshots. Years later when both men work for the same advertising agency, Angelo continues to persecute Ed until, because of their constant fighting, Ed is fired. He sends his wife away on a visit and sits nights drinking and staring at Salzman's place through a spyglass. Then he orders lumber and tools, chipping away at stones and building a huge machine, a giant mechanical slingshot from which he bombards Salzman's property, shattering the chimney and smashing his roof and car.

When the constable and his men are called to the scene, they're attacked by rocks twice as big as baseballs. He testifies:

> . . . It was a very big slingshot mounted on a timber framework with old automobile wheels under it . . . It was a slingshot using ten full inner tubes for power with a very ingenious electrically driven compound pulley arrangement so that Caparell could pull the pouch back almost immediately after shooting and shoot again. It had a telescopic sight. The balls were hand-chipped round stones and they all weighed exactly six pounds.

The hearing terminates with the psychiatrist's diagnosis that Ed is a hopeless schizoid who must remain at Merrylegs Farm (the mental institution). He is kept happily busy building bigger stones for his project. Each weighs 100 pounds and he wants to make 250 before building his new slingshot.

How much more complex and complete is the full story with its augmented cast of characters, dramatic cause and effect, strong personal motivation, and pointed premise that, just as the child is father to the man, childhood experiences can be the mainsprings of adult behavior and accumulated grudges can unhinge the mind. The author's originality exaggerates the drama, as is symbolized in the gigantic slingshots built to avenge damage done by tiny ones so long ago and by the increasingly large stones. Supreme style and suspense also contribute to the story's success.

The kernels of juvenile stories

Most joke-books contain contents pages and/or indexes

to help you look up gags on special subjects or of appeal to specific readerships. If you want to write for children, the trick of developing stories from jokes still applies. A smart-aleck who wants to show up a teacher could "lose face" with the gang through a prank that backfires:

Two little boys caught a butterfly, a centipede, a beetle, and a grasshopper. They glued together the centipede's body, the butterfly's wings, the beetle's head, and the grasshopper's legs to make an original insect, which they took to a naturalist (or teacher, if you wish).

"We caught this bug in the field, sir," they told him. "What is it?"

He examined it solemnly, then asked, "Did you notice whether it hummed when you caught it, boys?"

"Yes, sir," they answered, concealing their mirth.

"Just as I thought," said the man. "It's a humbug."

Or maybe you'll get ideas from more "different situation" jokes like this one:

A little boy was caught stealing candy in a candy store. When the police called the father he told them to put the child in jail.

"We can't put an eight-year-old kid in jail," said the cop.

"That's the only way you'll cure him," insisted the father.

"OK," agreed the officer.

In jail, the child met a hardened criminal who asked, "Whatcha do, kid?"

"I stole some candy from a candy store."

"Why didn't you rob a bank?" teased the criminal.

"I couldn't. I don't get out of school 'til 3:30."

Like all juvenile fiction, the subject matter must be of interest to certain age groups. As the age advances, interests include sports, adventure, more complex school activities and studies, and, for the burgeoning teen-age girl markets, the boy-girl relationship. There's a plot in the cartoon of the homely girl in the charity booth advertising "Kisses $1." A meek man stands lipstick-marked as she says, "Thank you, sir. Here's your $1!" An excellent plot lies in the joke about the G.I. who received a "Dear John" letter from his girl, in which she asked him to return her picture. To squelch her as she had hurt him, he sent her a batch of pin-ups, saying: "Please pick yours out. I've forgotten what you look like."

Slanting the joke for Western markets

There's good problem, solution, and characterization in this:

> A college grad inherited a ranch and went out to run it. He soon discovered his cattle were being rustled by his neighbor, a rough, tough killer who terrified everyone. Being a timid, "citified" intellectual he didn't want to fight, so he wrote: "Dear Neighbor: I'd appreciate it if your cows wouldn't sit down where I park my branding irons."

Add other devices to make the villain foolish.

Building fantasy and science fiction stories from jokes

For your fantasy file there are several goodies with conflict and expandability. Graft your original ideas onto ones like these:

> A fisherman pulled in his line and brought up a strange bottle with an odd cork. When he opened the bottle, a cloud of black smoke rushed out and turned into an angry, terrifying genie.
> "I will avenge myself for my imprisonment in that tight bottle!" he roared. "I'll kill everyone I see, starting with you!"
> The quick-thinking fisherman replied, "Go ahead and kill me, I'm tired of living in this rat race anyway. Tear down all the mountains, swallow up the sea! But I don't believe a big, fat monster like you could ever fit in that tiny bottle."
> "You don't, eh?" roared the insulted genie. "Doubters like you really burn me up. Look at this, you twerp!"
> Condensing himself instantly, he poured himself back into the bottle.
> "Amazing!" said the fisherman, as he replaced the cork and threw the bottle back into the sea.

(Remember the motion picture *The Brass Bottle?* Similar?)

Here's another joke that suggests an intriguing opening situation on which you can build fascinating developments:

Red-eyed and sleepless, a pop song writer told his lyricist: "What a nightmare I had. My God, I never want to go through another night like it! It was frightening!"
"Calm down and tell me what hapened," said the writer.
"I dreamt Beethoven came back to life with a smart lawyer!"

Religious fiction ideas in jokes

Humorous collections usually contain wonderful stories about ministers, priests, and rabbis, which often contain wisdom that can serve as a premise. I'm sure you've heard hundreds of versions of the controlled clergyman who played golf with a profane, temper-exploding golfer. In one account both are such bad players that the swearer asks the man of cloth how he can keep from cussing after a poor shot. The latter admits, "I do not swear, but when I dub a shot I spit, and where I spit the grass never comes up again." In another the minister tries to reform the other by saying, "I notice that the players who get the lowest scores are those who do not swear." To which the divot-digger answers: "What do they have to swear about?"

From Joke to Original Story

Seek suspense-situation anecdotes that can launch your original story into orbit with entirely fresh happenings afterward
Whether you develop the following for a Catholic magazine or not, it has marvelous drama and reversal that stimulates many possibilities of further development:

On the day a young priest was ordained, a man with a gun rushed up to him. The man's eyes were burning with excitement and the priest knew he'd need calmness in handling his first crisis. Trying to keep his cool and not look at the gun, he walked up to the man, smiled, and said, "Hello."
The man shoved the revolver at him and said, "Father, would you bless this revolver that I might use it only in the cause of justice? I was admitted to the police department today."

Isn't your brain teeming with hundreds of ideas already?

It's better to use a good joke as the *beginning* situation or foundation on which you construct an entirely different story. The editor will not have seen it so often, for one thing, and, secondly, your imagination will grow healthier from constant exercise. Furthermore, readers seem to like a familiar dramatic situation worked out in unexpectedly different ways.

The British theater sometimes has skits called "blackouts" between the acts of a play. One of the oldest and most popular starts with a man trying to commit suicide (almost always by trying to jump off a bridge) when another man comes along. There is a wide variety of reasons for the suicide attempt and varying endings. After the second man hears all the first's reasons for wanting to end it all, he might say "Wait, I'll give you a push" or "Let me join you" or "I don't blame you a bit" . . . all unexpected endings for the audience that thinks the second man will rescue the first.

Murray Schisgal developed this corny situation into the play and movie *Luv*, in which the second man, a go-getter, rescues the first, a square, for selfish reasons. He takes the would-be suicide home to attract his wife so she'll divorce him, leaving him free to marry a female gym teacher. After multiple crazy mix-ups, they all jump in the river.

John Collier's story, "The Right Side" has a similar beginning:

> A young man who was looking extremely pale walked to the middle of Westminster Bridge and clambered onto the parapet. A swarthy gentleman, some years his senior, in evening dress with dark red carnation, Inverness cape, monocle and short imperial, appeared as if from nowhere and had him by the ankle.
>
> "Let me go, damn you!" muttered the would-be suicide with a tug and a kick.
>
> "Get down and walk beside me," said the stranger, "or that policeman who has already taken a step or two in our direction will most certainly run you in. Let us pretend to be two friends, one of whom wishes for a thrill, while the other is anxious that he should not tumble over."

This opening situation leads to a series of adventures during the course of which we realize that the older man is the

Devil who takes the young man down a gigantic elevator to Hell where he sees the hideous fate of suicides, especially drowned spectres like Ophelia. He decides to keep on living.

As you collect jokes that suggest openings for full stories, see how many different ways you can work them out and how many professional fiction features might have been inspired by them. For example, Paul Gallico's *Mrs 'arris* books (*Mrs 'arris Goes to Paris, Mrs 'arris Goes to New York*, etc.) and the English movie *Ladies Who Do* (John Bigney's novel, screenplay by Michael Pertwee) about charwomen who become tycoons by playing the stock market tips they find in wastebaskets echo this old joke:

> A cleaning woman inherited a fortune of $50,000. Excitedly, the staff asked her if she was going to give up her job? travel? buy a house? car? clothes?
> "Of course I'm not giving up my job. I wouldn't know what to do with myself without it. But I'm warning you all—Heaven help them as gets in the way of me mop!"

For exercise, work out different plot blueprints starting with one or more of the following as openings:

> Two men were walking along and saw two women approaching. The first man said, "What'll I do? Here come my wife and my mistress."
> "Funny," said the other. "I was about to say the same thing."

Think plot. Think slant. The obvious thing would be for the Casanova-like husband to be angry at his wife's behavior at first, but he learns to appreciate her as her image is now changed from the "dishes-and-diapers" *hausfrau* to the desirable glamour girl. Perhaps dressed up, next to the other gal, she looks good! Since this is the obvious plot line, think out other developments—good advice for all opening situation jokes.

Here are a few more:

> A poor boy went to an expensive restaurant and gave the head waiter $5.

"I suppose you want me to reserve a table, sir?" asked the *maitre d'*.
"On the contrary. I'm coming back later with a girl and I want you to tell me there are no tables, so we can eat in a cheaper place."

A Hillbilly granny saw sky writing for the first time. She ran into her cabin screaming, "Hey, Paw, I knew it'd happen someday. One of them TV commercials got so loud it finally caught fire!"

What can happen to your skywriting pilot downed in a primitive area—Africa, South America, etc.—whom the natives consider a god or a devil?

Jokes often offer clever solutions that you can use to climax your story

Many jokes and anecdotes have such clever solutions they suggest successful plots if you add well-slanted and carefully developed variations. What fresh build-ups can you think of for the following:

No one could understand why X——— had such good luck with the used cars he bought. He never seemed to have any trouble with them. One day a friend asked how he was able to choose so wisely.
"After all, you know very little about cars."
"True. But I've got a system. You see I get a car on approval then drive it right over to another used car dealer and tell him I want to sell it. In the next minute he's telling me everything that's wrong with it."

On the Chile-Argentina border stands the Christ of the Andes statue, symbolizing a pledge made by the two countries. As long as the statue stands, it was agreed, there shall be peace and good will between Argentina and Chile.
Ironically, the statue itself caused dissension. When it was completed, someone pointed out that the Savior's back was toward Chile, which slighted the natives. But when indignation was flaring, a Chilean newspaperman saved the day. In an editorial he explained: "The Argentineans need more watching over than the Chileans."
His people were satisfied. They laughed and smugly returned to their daily tasks.

Several jokes give unique solutions to the problem of parking, solutions that might give your characters ideas:

> A woman, desperate to find a parking spot on a crowded street, found the only vacant space was in front of a fire hydrant. She drove off, returned soon after, stopped, looked furtively up and down, then, seeing that no one saw her, she took a trash can out of her car and inverted it over the fire plug and parked.

In another yarn, a man parks illegally, then puts a green ticket for illegal parking under the windshield wiper. This is similar to the killer's action in *Point Blank* (from Robert Stark's novel, *The Hunter*). Parking illegally on a bridge, he raises the hood and puts a red paper on the antenna (police signal for car trouble). Since these devices are dishonest, they should be used by unsympathetic characters.

If there's timeliness and reader identification in jokes, it doesn't matter how old they are—they're available and convertible to plots

As long as we have a navy, and surely as long as we have wars, there will keep cropping up a joke about a seasick sailor or one who's fed up and asked what he'll do when he gets out. He replies: "I'm gonna get a pair of oars and start walking away from the ocean. I'm gonna keep walking till I come to a place where a little boy points at my oars and asks, 'Pa, what are those things?' When I hear the dad answer, 'Son, I don't know'; well, sir, I'll stay there!"

Although it may be pawned off as a new joke on a future television program, it's as old as Homer, who wrote that Odysseus said: "For Tiresias bade me fare to many cities of men, carrying a shapen oar in my hand, till I should come to such men as know not the sea."

You can find many more examples that prove that the old can be ever-new if there's a timely tie-up. Humor can also contain serious human truths, so do not underestimate jokes as a source of plot material. Many jokesmiths use the glitter of laughter to embellish life-lessons and happenings, in the tradition of George Bernard Shaw who said: "My method is to take the utmost trouble to find the right thing to say, and then to say it with the utmost levity."

4

Plotting from the News

When best-selling author Irving Wallace was interviewed and asked, "How do you keep fit?" he answered, "I jog in place for fifteen minutes every morning listening to the news. We're news freaks."

With that brief reply he revealed a double-feature tip that can help you avoid the worst occupational hazards of authorship: a sedentary job's lack of exercise and writer's block or running out of the fresh, exciting ideas that are *relevant* and most wanted by readers, publishers, and producers.

Whether or not all successful writers actually jog to the news, it's a cinch they keep up with current happenings and scrutinize them for plot stimuli. You, too, should be an omnivorous reader, clipper, viewer, listener, collector, and a soaker-upper of all interesting items and ideas. As Wallace says:

> I am a great *blotter*. I soak up things. I overhear something at a party and immediately I want to know more about it. Afterwards I make notes . . . . much of what one sees and hears is stored away automatically in the mind's computer, and then it pops out five or ten years later . . .
>
> I'm never bored. Everything I read, every scene I'm a witness to, every conversation has some reward.

Overhearing men on a train say they'd love a night with
Elizabeth Taylor sparked the idea for his novel *The Fan Club*,
in which a group of businessmen kidnap a movie queen sex
symbol.

Formerly fact and fiction were opposites (antipodal).
Fact was what really happened down to the last letter of truth.
Fiction was pure fantasy—a fabricated concoction from the
fertile imagination of a writer.

Then life caught up with fantasy in drama, terror, and
irony. Some authorities blame it on the widening scope and
influence of sensation-stressing media, others claim that
relaxing law enforcement has increased crime and violence.

As each day and night proved more and more that "truth
is stranger *and stronger* than fiction," many general magazines published more nonfiction than fiction, which refused to
surrender to the new trend. In a grandiose gesture of "if you
can't lick 'em join 'em," fiction united with its former enemy.
Result: a hybrid of fictionized facts in a plethora of novels
with fancy names like the New Journalism, Autofictage (John
Gregory Dunne's term for his combination of autobiography,
fiction, and reportage), and Jan De Hartog's description of
his *Peaceable Kingdom* as Fictional Faction or Factional
Fiction because it dramatizes the lives of real Quaker heroines.

"Faction" is the blend of fiction and fact that James
Eastwood's author-hero Marcello writes. When he can't think
up a new plot, he commissions two of his female conquests to
commit real crimes, which he then uses as the basis for his
fiction. Gore Vidal's novel *Burr* topped fiction best-seller lists
even though this novel is about actual persons in our history,
and Norman Mailer's *The Armies of the Night: History as a
Novel, The Novel as History* is another example of the genre.
Stephen Lewis calls his *Housewife Hookers* a new form: "the
fictitious documentary."

"The Non-Fiction Novel" is the term Truman Capote
claimed to have originated for his *In Cold Blood*, but over a
century before that, Edgar Allan Poe used that phrase to
describe his fact-based fiction thrillers. When Poe was down
on his luck he enlisted in the U.S. Army for "three squares

and a flop." Stationed at Fort Independence in Boston Harbor, he was intrigued by the real-life happenings that had occurred there ten years before. In a hot-tempered card game a senior officer had accused young Lieutenant Robert Massie of cheating. Their argument exploded into a brawl and then a duel in which the man of high rank killed the young lieutenant. The lad's friends plotted a vicious revenge: They invited the officer to a bash, got him rip-roaringly drunk, took him to the lowest dungeon of the fort, forced him into a tiny casement, shackled him to the floor, and buried him alive by walling off the area.

Poe dramatized this true story in his famous *The Cask of Amontillado*, which begins: "The thousand injuries of Fortunato I had borne as best I could; but when he ventured up insult, I vowed revenge."

This fact-based plot has been used by many writers since Poe, even in "Usher II," a future-placed story in Ray Bradbury's *Martian Chronicles* that ended with the murderer telling the victim that if he had read Poe's drama he wouldn't have let this happen to him! You could write a plot based on a recent news item about Chicago residents near the University of Illinois campus who hired a bricklayer to build a wall around an illegally parked car.

More than 100 years ago Poe discovered a psychological trick that will help you sell: people are more fascinated by events that *really* happened than totally "made up" yarn-spinning. He proved this when as a plodding journalist he wrote a feature about an enemy invasion of the U.S. by balloon-borne enemies. It sold out several editions before it was exposed as the Great Balloon Hoax and Poe was fired. But his ahead-of-his-time victory of proving the public's love of fictionized fact makes millions of dollars for authors, publishers, and bookstores today.

A great majority of successful fiction today seems to "hug the headlines," thereby giving readers and viewers the all-important "shock of recognition" as Henry James called it. News stories and fiction plots seem to play a weird game of teeter-totter, taking turns as to which comes first. Real-life events follow fiction as often as fiction apes the news. A few years before the Hearst kidnaping, *Penthouse* published a story with great similarities. Rod Serling apologized for having written a television skyjack script that apparently inspired a real one.

There is irony on one page of a recent issue of the *Los Angeles Times*. In the left column is a negative review of the television movie *Mousey* by John Peacock, in which Kirk Douglas played a meek, mild teacher who had married a pregnant woman to give her unborn child his name. After years of loving and being a good father to the boy, he is told she will marry a rich man and the boy will take his name. Mousey's initial impulse to suicide transforms to homicide, which the reviewer called "incredible." On a far-right column is an item about a Carson, Nevada, man who killed his wife and fled with her son (same age as the television child!).

The love affair between fact and fiction is such a widespread phenomenon in today's literature that this blend may be your best way to break into the novel field via the *roman à clef*, and into television or motion pictures via the *cinema verité*.

Roman à clef is the French for "novel with a key." This means that the fiction characters are thinly disguised real people, often celebrities whose scandals and secrets the reader enjoys peeking into. His voyeur instinct is satisfied in this suspenseful game of "Guess Who I Am?" Pauline Kael calls it "the folklore behind the headlines, heat and immediacy, the richly familiar."

The Godfather (by Mario Puzo) relates true events in the war between rival Mafia families all the way to the severed-horse's-head shocker scene in the producer's bedroom. Rona Barrett's novel *The Lovomaniacs* is about Frank Sinatra; William Woolfolk's *Maggie* and Aldous Huxley's *After Many a Summer Dies the Swan* are both about Marion Davies and William Randolph Hearst; Simone de Beauvoir's *The Mandarins* dramatizes real French literary figures during and after World War II; and Willie Morris' *The Last of the Southern Girls* fictionizes the life of Barbara Howar.

Roman à clef is the specialty of many authors like Irving

Wallace and Harold Robbins, whose novels are always about real people. *The Betsy* dramatizes true facts about the Ford (auto) family as *Where Love Has Gone* tells the Lana Turner tragedy in which her daughter allegedly killed her lover; *The Carpetbaggers* is based on the Howard Hughes story and *The Adventurers* is about genuine jetsetters like Porfirio Rubiroso.

Knowing the surefire success of this formula, Jacqueline Susann used it for her novels, which instantly zoomed to the top of "Best Seller" lists and made Big-Money Movies. *Valley of the Dolls* was of course about real-life tragic figures of show business like Judy Garland; *The Love Machine* is the fictionized true story of Jim Aubrey, president of CBS (although the anti-hero is such a heel that many different men claimed to have been the model!); *Once Is Not Enough* is about Mike Todd; and *Dolores* concerns Guess Who? Story: The beautiful widow of a popular young U.S. president has a sister who is married to British royalty and who arranges (for payment of ten million dollars to each woman) for the widow to marry the world's richest man, who, after marriage, continues his affair with his former mistress; leaving his beautiful, frustrated bride alone on her wedding night, clasping to her bosom a sixty-carat diamond ring!

How does the author get away with exposing intimate details of the life of America's former First Lady all the way from out-of-marriage love affairs to the cold-blooded marriage contract? Of course the names are changed: the heroine is Dolores Cortez Ryan; the president was charismatic James (Jimmy) T. Ryan; his successor Elwood Jason Lyons; and his mother, the head of the fabulous rich and powerful Irish-American clan, is Bridget Ryan. The widow's sister is Nita (Juanita), married to Lord Nelson Bramley, who is unfaithful to her, while she is in love with billionaire Baron Erick de Savonne who insists on marrying the internationally famous-and-loved widow of the popular dead U.S. president to impress the world so that he can eventually become president of France. His mistress is transformed fictionally from opera star Maria Callas to internationally famous ballerina Ludmilla Rosenko. The sixty-one-year-old billionaire is

French instead of Greek and is tall and slim. Another protective device is the use of references to the actual people, with the implication "I'm not that somebody or I wouldn't refer to him or her in the third person." When planning her husband's funeral, Dolores says, "I want to know how President Kennedy was buried." Later Nita tells Dolores that Erick has "just bought a ship from the Germans—an ocean liner—and he's having it turned into a private yacht. It will be twice the size of the one Onassis has . . ."

Herman Wouk used such a disclaimer for legal protection in his *roman à clef* about Thomas Wolfe, *Youngblood Hawke*, when he has Hawke say: "The critics are going to compare me with Thomas Wolfe, I suppose, because I'm from the South and I write long books. Please don't think I'm crazy, but I think I can do better than Wolfe . . ."

If you plan to write a *roman à clef* be sure to change names, descriptions, locations, and some events and details— and use the above trick to protect your work from lawsuits. This is true whether you write of unknown or famous persons. In fact, it's a good idea to stay away from top celebrities, who are usually overexposed. The superdramatic lives of the superdramatic Kennedy family have inspired many blockbusters including *Executive Action* with its wild fictionizing of events leading up to the JFK assassination (Dalton Trumbo's screenplay based on a story by Donald Freed and Mark Lane, whose book *Rush to Judgment* disagreed with the Warren Commission's Report).

James Kamins' *The Cookout Conspiracy* is about Senator Bill Carlson, who had been involved in a situation that cost the life of a girl by drowning. It wouldn't surprise me to see a novel about a senator's child who has a leg amputated due to bone cancer, or better still and more in line with the current occult trend, a historical novel about a mid-nineteenth-century Irish witch's curse on a young Irishman who jilted her daughter, then went to America to build a fortune! This is a verified legend about the founder of the Kennedy clan!

Seriously, it isn't a good idea for an unestablished author to try to cut his teeth on a blockbuster. The "Biggies" are usually ordered from big name *roman à clef* writers. Such a book is a double feature for publishers and producers who plan to spend fortunes on promotion. Long before the Watergate case neared a conclusion, a book about it, *All the President's Men*, was sold to a major publisher and motion picture company by its authors, Robert Woodward and Carl Bernstein, who had won a Pulitzer Prize for their Watergate reporting for the *Washington Post*.

You still have many chances to cash in on the trick of writing news-based fiction. Develop an original plot with several of your own strongly-delineated characters, but with suggestive similarities to news events and/or real persons. When our POWs returned from North Vietnam there were many tragic stories. One of the worst was Air Force Colonel Theodore Guy's charges of misconduct and collaborating with the enemy brought against eight ex-POWs. After one of the men, Marine Sergeant Able Larry Kavanaugh, committed suicide, the charges against the other seven were dropped. While the tragedy was still fresh, Nicholas Meyer wrote the mystery novel *Target Practice*, in which his original private eye, Mark Brill, "stalks the grim secret behind the suicide of an ex-POW accused of collaborating with the enemy." The detective novel and movie *The Leavenworth Irregulars* by William D. Blankenship was obviously inspired by the big PX scandal rake-off by three ex-GIs a few years ago.

Television provides an omnivorous market for news-based fiction for many reasons. The programming can work closer to real happenings and seize viewer interest while the headline stories are fresh. Several more months are required for the publication of a novel or the production of a full movie (although some television plays later burgeon into full-length features and/or series).

So important and ubiquitous are these behind-the-headline television plays that most studios employ "documentarians" to research the details of real-life stories. Robert E. Thompson's *A Case of Rape* was initially inspired by a *Los Angeles Times* article by Bella Stumbo who attacked the injustice of our century-old rape laws. Ms. Stumbo's premise was:

> Ultimately, it is the burden of rape victims to overcome a tradition of myth and bias which has historically celebrated rape in song and poem and classical painting, equated rapists with red-blooded he-men, victims with seductresses and, in general, assumed time and again there is actually no such thing as rape . . .

The extensive article plus a plethora of news stories led documentarian Lou Rudolph into exhaustive research that proved that rape is the most common crime of personal violence in the country but that only ten to fifteen percent of the cases are reported either through embarrassment or awareness of the humiliating treatment our legal system allows. The original television drama is a smooth blend of horrendous details from four actual case histories, all of which dramatized the premise: "Rape is the only crime in which the victim is made to feel guilty." The harassed heroine, Ellen Harrod, suffers not only pain, trauma, humiliation, insults, and the suspicion of husband, neighbors and friends, but also a lost court case and the dissolution of her marriage.

Such well-done dramas have social significance and could lead to much-needed reforms. As actress Elizabeth Montgomery who plays Ellen says:

> It's a strange reversal of roles. It's as if Ellen is on trial, not the man who raped her. And she's guilty until she proves herself innocent. I have a line in the script about the rules of evidence in a rape case: "I'm open game. He's legally protected."

Her attorney, who tries to prosecute the liar-rapist but fails, later tells another lawyer: "Never prosecute a rape case unless it's a ninety-year-old nun with a minimum of four stab wounds."

"Owen Marshall" is but one of many television series whose scripts echo news stories but are nevertheless well structured, suspenseful, and *originally* developed. Not long after the wire services released a story about a Southern judge who ordered the sterilization of two retarded Black girls who had already produced illegitimate babies, this situation was dramatized here. Characters, motivation, and details were changed, but there was no doubt about the headline-source of the drama. In the television play, the two real-life retarded Black sisters were encapsulated into one sweet but slow-thinking woman whose boyfriend loved her as she was and wanted to marry her and have a family. The judge was not a man but an embittered woman whose own poverty background made her hate the poor and try to keep them from reproducing.

The true story of *Los Angeles Times* reporter William Farr who was jailed for refusing to reveal his sources of his feature about the Manson Family spurred the "Owen Marshall" script "The Ghost of Buzz Stevens" by Richard Fielder. The scene was changed from California to the Midwest, and the reporter, renamed Will Garner, who went to jail rather than reveal his sources, became a widower with two small children. Clever courtroom finagling caused singer Luann Daniels who'd loved Buzz Stevens (now dead of a heroin overdose) to expose the pusher and free Garner.

Motion pictures (sometimes developed from books) increase their reader appeal by advertising the fact that their stories are based on real people and events.

Here are just a few of many examples: Robin Moore's *The French Connection* is about New York detectives Edward Egan and Salvatore Grosso and Assistant District Attorney Frank Bauman, who were responsible for the exposure and destruction of a gigantic international drug ring. Real-life names were used for some leading characters in this and a sequel movie *Badge 373* by Pete Hamill, spotlighting the same Eddie Egan as hero. Another instance of the use of a real name occurs in *Serpico* (by Peter Maas, screenplay by Waldo Salt and Norman Wexler) about honest cop Frank Serpico who couldn't be bought, opposed the rip-off as a way of life, was shot in the face, testified before the Knapp Commission, and finally went to Switzerland to live.

More often the actual names are changed as in Joseph Wambaugh's police books and television series "Police Story" and in *The Super Cops* (by L. H. Whittemore, screenplay by Lorenzo Semple Jr.). The latter relates the heroic exploits of New York policemen Dave Greenberg and Bob Hantz who made more than 600 arrests in their super-tough Bedford-Stuyvesant section.

Mort Briskin's *Walking Tall* is about Sheriff Buford Pusser of McNairy County, Tennessee, whose wife was killed when they were both ambushed. *Conrack* is about Pat Conroy, the white teacher who brought knowledge and hope to under-privileged Blacks. *The Last American Hero* (scripted by William Roberts from Tom Wolfe's *Esquire* article) is about stock-car racer Junior Johnson, the independent hillbilly who became champ. Robert Merle's *Day of the Dolphin* is based on scientist Dr. John Lilly's work with dolphins. *Lady Sings the Blues* is about Billie Holiday; *Marjoe* is about the amazing child-evangelist; Clifford Irving's *Fake?* is about art-forger Elmyre de Hory; and *Papillon* recounts the adventures of Henri Charrière, the professional escape-artist who broke out of the world's worst penal colonies including Devil's Island.

Many movie anti-heroes besides Dillinger, Bonnie and Clyde, and the "Boston Strangler" are also plucked from news headlines. Lewis Carlino's *Crazy Joe* is about the colorful, intellectual Mafia gangster Joey Gallo who could fill a contract for murder in the morning, lunch with high society, and then quote Sartre, Camus, and Kafka at dinner. Terrence Malick's *Badlands* is about Charles Starkweather, the teenage killer of the 50s who took his fourteen-year-old girlfriend on a cross-country spree of robbery and murder that landed him in the electric chair.

Whether the film characters are heroes or villains, and whether they are identified by their own or fictitious names, viewers are fascinated by the ring of authenticity and the opportunity to delve beneath the headlines. The glint of recognition of truth appears in many best-sellers that are made into motion pictures.

Frederick Forsyth's *The Day of the Jackal* (screenplay by Kenneth Ross) is based on the 1963 attempted assassination of Charles de Gaulle by the hit man code-named Jackal who was hired by army dissidents after the liberation of Algeria, just as his *Odessa File* is based on fact. Constantin Costa-Gavras' *State of Siege* is about A.I.D. man Dan A. Mirione who was assassinated by Tupamaro guerillas in the Uruguayan revolution of 1970. Jorge Semprun's *Z* is faithful to the true story of a martyred Greek pacifist and the subsequent military takeover of his country, and Semprun's *The French Conspiracy* is about the 1965 political scandal in which Ben Barka, the leader of French Morocco's left-wing opposition party, was kidnaped and presumably murdered in Paris.

Any sensational, suspenseful, or action-filled happening in the news of yesterday or today is liable to be reflected in a movie, even when the plot is changed drastically into an "original." An entirely different angle on kidnapings or assassinations may appear as in the films *The Black Windmill* and *The Parallax View*. The same principle is used, and the author nurtures and recombines different "roots" to grow his own rainbow:

> Characterization
> Plot line
> Premise
> Setting or X-plus factor
> Style

If you are an unestablished writer without the experience, credits, and reputation to land an assignment to fictionalize the Big News, how will this trick of hugging the headlines help you? Here are some tips:

(1) *Dramatize your own version of a real-life drama for a minor market.*

For years the confession magazines have stressed relevance and have preferred news-related stories, often from the viewpoints of persons who have their own problems related to or behind the scenes of a big kidnaping, drug or jewel heist, or nation-shocking scandal or crime. A story with a news peg is one of the best ways to break into this market. After you become a "regular," you may receive assignments, for several editors in this field suggest a top headline to a few writers to develop and then they order the best-worked-out plot.

(2) *Start clipping and developing local human interest events that are not among the biggest national or international news events.*

Usually a local occurrence that has one region in a tizzy doesn't have such wide exposure that it is snatched and written up by top authors. Be on the constant lookout for the local happening that has conflict, suspense, action, characters with strong purposes and obstacles, perhaps even a chase or other visual activity.

One excellent example is the 1969 Texas incident in which ex-con Robert Samuel Dent and his young wife kidnaped State Trooper James Kenneth Crone and fled across the state in Crone's patrol car while local Texans, who love a maverick, cheered them on. While the rest of the nation was busy with other things, that local populace stayed glued to their televisions and radios, leaving them only to join the chase or somehow help the young criminals.

This regional event was written into an exciting story by Steven Spielberg, Hal Barwood, and Matthew Robbins and became the hit movie *Sugarland Express*. The authors added a great deal of contrasting characterization, motivation, and shoot-'em-up action. Both characters are criminals, with the wife, Lou Jean, out of prison before her husband, Clovis. When she learns that the State Welfare Board is going to give their baby out for adoption, she visits Clovis in a prison farm and threatens to leave him unless he helps her get their little boy back. She engineers his escape by dressing him in women's clothes (which she has worn over her own), then they kidnap a highway patrolman and force him to drive them in his squad car to get their baby and make an even exchange. Many exciting details are added to the news story.

The farmers in a Kansas locality were horrified when a respectable family (the Clutters) were brutally murdered. Truman Capote spent five years researching all aspects of this regional tragedy and transmitted them, along with his theories concerning contemporary violence, in his *In Cold Blood*.

Search for local happenings with writeworthy ideas. They

may not be as dramatic as those mentioned, but perhaps you can make them be by grafting on your original premises, characters, and plot action. Maybe you'll find material for a less ambitious market than a novel or motion picture. You may weave such items into a juvenile work or as a subplot in an original work.

In my neighborhood "throw-away" paper, recent headlines cry to be written into children's stories. A few are:

THE RIGHT FIELDER'S A GIRL—She beat 10 Boys to the Job!

10-YEAR-OLD GIRL FINDS $400 IN IVY

YOUNG FOSTER FATHER INVESTS IN KID POWER

COP HELPS PUNK KID BECOME CHAMPION BOXER

FREEDOM FROM SPANKING ADVANCED AS PART OF KIDS' "BILL OF RIGHTS"

VANDALS SLAUGHTER ANIMALS AT SCHOOL FARM PROJECT

8-YEAR-OLD SEEKS POST ON FT. WORTH PARK BOARD

STUDENT RECYCLING CENTER WORKS FOR BETTER WORLD

BOY SCOUT USES NEWLY-LEARNED FIRST AID TO SAVE SISTER

(3) *Write about long-ago events.*

Save clippings for years until "the right time" comes along for their development. Never be so involved with the one thing you're working on that you stop reading and seeking nuggets for future works. Sometimes a news event is too overexposed, painful, or taboo in some way at the time it happens but may be more acceptable later on.

It was almost four decades after England's King Edward VIII abdicated to marry American divorcee Wallis Warfield Simpson that Royce Ryton's play *Crown Matrimonial* appeared. After that hiatus of years, the British were ready for the royal family conflicts that had not been mentioned in their press at the time. Such contemporary censorship whetted the appetite of English audiences, and the play was a London hit as well as being a landmark, since it was the first to break the centuries-old tradition that no living or recently deceased royal family member could be portrayed on the stage. Then came Ralph G. Martin's book *The Woman He Loved.*

After the heat of the student uprisings of the late 60s simmered down, we had such novels and movies as *Strawberry Statement* and the French movie *To Die of Love.* The latter is a fictionalized version of the Gabrielle Russier scandal. This super-strict, thirty-one-year-old teacher-mother fell in love with the sixteen-year-old son of two Communist professors who acted in a bourgeois manner when they discovered the affair. They had Gabrielle arrested for seducing a minor and causing him to leave home. Harassed by her trials, imprisonments, and scandals, she committed suicide. (The scenario was scripted by her lawyer with author Andre Cayatte.)

It was a few years after the rupture of a pressurized oxygen tank crippled the spacecraft of Apollo 13 that the incident was the subject of a television drama, "Houston, We Have a Problem." Although astronauts were named and worried about, the real protagonists were the scientists at Mission Control, each of whom had a personal crisis to contend with in addition to the pressures of trying to save the hard-pressed astronauts and their vital mission. One was in danger of losing custody of his son, another was trying to conceal his condition of epilepsy, and the other was having severe wife-trouble.

Who says there isn't room for plenty of originality when you base a story on a news event?

War-related dramas have a strong fascination a few decades afterward, perhaps because they combine the perspective of history with the reader identification of personal remembrance. The 70s produced not only a plethora of works about World War II, but also reminders like Leon Uris' *QB VII* in which a Polish doctor (Adam Kelno) who had been in Jadwiga concentration camp sues author Abe Cady, whose book *The Holocaust* accuses the surgeon of having performed brutal experimental operations.

What long-ago news stories rattle around in your memory or your files, clamoring to be written about? It will be good research experience for you to check them out in newspaper morgues and libraries—perhaps adding interviews to your other legwork. Try to choose a story that you have a feeling for, preferably one related to a field you know well, and work out original additions, subtractions, and different details—whatever will make the drama relevant and readable today.

Long-ago headline stories are particularly good today in our Age of Nostalgia.

(4) *Reverse the facts for freshness and originality.*

You could make the seemingly guilty innocent and vice versa. Thievery is common newspaper fare all the way from house burglaries to bank robberies. Your character could break in to put money *back* as is done in the movies *Who's Minding the Mint?* (by R. S. Allen and Harvey Bullock) and *Sam Whiskey* (by William Norton). In this last-named film, a widow hires a saddle tramp to recover $250,000 in gold bars from a steamboat wreck and return them to the Denver mint before her late husband's theft can be discovered and his reputation ruined.

The principle of reversal can enable you to turn a tragedy into a happy-ending story. *The Neptune Factor* is based on a true incident in which the crew of a trapped sea lab all died, but in the movie, courageous rescue efforts save them.

In one gruesome news squib, a father is so worried about his little boy's disappearance that friends talk him into going fishing. His line hooks something and he pulls in . . . the blood-streaked corpse of his child. This is too painful and without justification. To fictionize the happening you could use this as the beginning of the man's actions to find the boy's murderer(s) and avenge the crime. Or you could change the relationships and build a plot along the lines of thinking that anyone who is inflicted with such a grim "catch" should deserve it. Your character could be a weak man or woman who is persuaded to give kidnapers some clues or help in abducting the child in exchange for money and the promise that the youngster will not be harmed. He or she could not only deserve the shocking assault on his conscience, but extreme nervous reaction could cause the "fisherman" to be accused of the crime. If you build a crime to fit such punishment, such a scene might be suitable for today's horror-loving audiences—especially with a touch of the occult.

(5) *Look for tiny fillers that other authors might overlook.*

Fillers such as the following may give you a gimmick for an original work.

> One tree native to Madagascar has seeds that can be lighted and used as candles.

They may even suggest a whole plot. Here are some nuggets:

> When police in Reading, England, painted their station drainpipes with greasy paint to stop people climbing up they didn't reckon with Joe _____. In custody at the station, _____ found the paint a big help in sliding down the drainpipes and escaping.

> Heirs of Mrs. Ida _____ were making an anxious search of files in San Jose area banks this week.
> She left a sizable fortune in stocks, bonds, savings and property and put most of it in a safe deposit box. But she forgot to tell anyone where the box was.

Start your own file of fillers and headlines that are plot-inspiring. Be sure to keep the entire articles, sources, bylines, and related items. Here are a few story-suggesters:

TV STATION SWITCHED OFF HIS PACEMAKER
GAL SKATER CRACKS THE ICE, PLAYS ON MEN'S HOCKEY TEAM
CHILDREN BUG YOU? JUST RENT SOME PARENTS

CRIME CASE WITNESS AND WIFE "RUBBED OUT"

RECORDING OF VICTIM'S TALK WITH SLAYER RULED EVIDENCE

FROM MADAM TO COUNCILWOMAN—A LONG FIGHT

PRISON CHIEF SUPPORTS BLACK EX-CON FOR COUNCIL

MISS WHEELCHAIR AMERICA INSPIRES OTHER CRIPPLES

LEGALLY BLIND WOMAN SCORES AT ART, PAINTING

YOUNG U.S. EXILE HAPPY BEING A SIKH

G.I. CROSSES E. GERMAN BORDER IN STOLEN TANK

BOY CALLED "BRAINS" IN EXTORTION PLOT

DEATH DURING SEX ACT HAS ITS REWARDS

KIDNAP VICTIM PITIES ABDUCTORS WHO WERE "BROKE"

5

Quotations—Rich Source of Plots

Like a strong building, a strong plot must be built on strong premises, for a story should be the parable that dramatizes a theme. Why not, then, seek fiction ideas from time-tried premises or wise quotations?

The best procedure is to weave a philosophy into your storyline, perhaps solving the problem as is done cleverly in *Hello Dolly!* Widowed Dolly Levi has been supporting herself by acting as matchmaker and finally wants to find a mate for herself. Her target is rich but stingy Horace Vander Gilder, the First Citizen of Yonkers. Her obstacles are his aversion to her aggressiveness and her loyalty to her late husband's memory.

After she overcomes Horace's hostility and he proposes, she still prays for a sign of permission from the late Ephraim Levi who always used to say: "Money is like manure. It's not worth anything unless it's spread around encouraging young things to grow." (He was so ultragenerous and extravagant that his death left her broke and needing to work, but they were always happy "living it up.") When miserly Vander Gilder asks her to marry him, she says she can't because she'd spend his money to help people, which is contrary to his penny-pinching character. She's really hoping for a sign from

Ephraim, which comes when the regenerated Horace tells her it's all right if she spends his money. He says: "I've always said money is like manure. It's not worth anything unless it's spread around encouraging young things to grow."

In this case, a philosophical line not only expresses characterization, but solves the problem and effects the climax.

Often you can guess the proverb that may have inspired a story. Many different cultures have a folksaying to the effect that "You cannot help someone else up a hill (or across a river) without getting there yourself." In the juvenile story "Farmer Frazer and the Too-High Hill" by Marilyn Kratz (in *Highlights for Children*), Farmer Frazer wants to trade his wheelbarrow-full of potatoes for Farmer Abel's apples so he can look forward to eating spicy apple pies all winter. But he can't push his load up the too-high hill to get to the other farm. After he forgets his self-seeking goal and helps several other characters push their loads uphill on top of his, he is surprised and delighted to find himself at the top within easy reach of Farmer Abel's apples.

When you find a quotation that you find expandable and appealing, study it from all angles. Try to learn what other writers have said about the values involved, how they developed their scripts to prove their point and viewpoint. Then work out your own plot with different characters and circumstances to express how you feel about the subject.

At some time everyone wishes for or prays for something, often something he'd be better off without. Many different quotations warn of the dangers of having wishes fulfilled. Just one example is from the ancient Greek:

> It is not good
> for all your wishes to be fulfilled.
> Through sickness you recognize
> the value of health;
> Through evil, the value of good;
> Through hunger, satisfaction;
> Through exertion, the value of rest.

Let's examine the fulfilled-wishes idea from all angles in much the same way as a landscape artist or photographer would study a scene before deciding how to picture it. In Ray Bradbury's "The Wish," Tom's Christmas wish is to see his dead father again. He walks to the cemetery where his dad is buried and gets what he wanted when he actually sees the old man walking toward him. But the crisis brings a double shock: His father is hideously withered and made miserably aware of his own death. Since, in a well-constructed plot, the crisis is the antithesis of the climax, this minus reverses to a plus when father and son are able to communicate now as they couldn't in life. Each says "I love you."

"More tears are shed over answered prayers than unanswered ones" is a quote from St. Theresa that inspired Truman Capote to write his novel *Answered Prayers*. He developed characters whose ambitions "are more or less material, but whose artistic ambitions are spiritual," and he worked out a plot that shows what can happen to four people who get exactly what they want.

That particular quotation isn't unique or original, but it has great reader rapport because most people do *not* get what they pray for, and it consoles them to know that they're better off than if they had.

Answered prayers causing grief

Many sages have uttered the same sentiment. Seneca wrote, "Nothing is so expensive as what is acquired by prayer," and Oscar Wilde believed that "When the gods wish to punish us they answer our prayers." Since a valid moral truth is the soul of a story, this idea has been dramatized by many writers.

More than a century before Capote, Edward Everett Hale used this premise in his patriotic classic "The Man without a Country." When Lieutenant Philip Nolan's hero-worship of Aaron Burr led him to treason, and he was proved guilty, he was asked at his trial whether he wished to say anything to show that he was faithful to the United States. He cried out in a fit of frenzy: "Damn the United States! I wish I may never hear of the United States again!" Colonel Morgan, who presided over the court, declared: "Prisoner, hear the sentence of the Court! The Court decides, subject to the approval of the President, that you never hear the name of the United States again." His wish granted, his prayer answered:

> ... He never did hear her name ... From that moment, September 23, 1807, till the day he died, May 11, 1863, he never heard her name again. For that half century and more he was a man without a country.

Philip Nolan shed many tears over his answered prayer as he lived out his isolated, ostracized life on a naval vessel on the high seas. Why not apply this formula to a U.S. draft-dodger in Canada or an Army or Navy defector?

Even greater tragedies result from answered prayers throughout literature: King Midas who wished everything he touched would turn to gold—and everything did, including his precious daughter, his food, his clothes; Macbeth, who wanted to be king and who helped his own prayer materialize, with miserable murderous results; and the unfortunate couple in "The Monkey's Paw" by W. W. Jacobs. In Jacobs' story, a couple with three wishes first pray for money, which causes a fatal accident for their son; they next pray to bring him back to life, but he is so horribly mutilated that their third prayer is that he be relieved from his agony in death.

You can think of many more professional examples. Such illustrations can be described as morally justified since the result of prayers that are materialistic, selfish, or harmful to others in the punishment of an unsympathetic character who uses prayer negatively. You might even add examples like Reverand Abner Hale in James Michener's *Hawaii*, who self-righteously and vengefully asks God to punish the Christianized natives who revert to Hawaiian customs and agonizingly sees his prayer answered in the wholesale destruction of the majority of the people plus his own personal miseries and losses that follow.

Answered prayers causing joy

In commercial fiction, satisfaction is achieved when good is rewarded and evil penalized. There are, of course, "miracle" and other happy-ending stories that follow such optimistic premises as Tennyson's "More things are wrought by prayer than this world dreams of" and the Bible's "What things so ever ye desire, when ye pray, believe that ye shall receive them and ye shall have them" (Mark 11:24) and "Ask and it shall be given you; seek and ye shall find; knock, and it shall be opened unto you" (Matthew 7:7). Throughout the Old and New Testament answered prayers cured the lame and sick, brought sight to the blind, life to the dead, and freedom to wrongly imprisoned believers. Answered prayers enabled Moses to lead his people from Egyptian bondage to the Promised Land, Joan of Arc to free her country, and the Mormons to convert barren desert into an oasis after seagulls appeared miraculously to devour the locusts that were destroying their crops. Every religion has its legends of prayers being the instruments of achievement, as do such personal stories as *The Wrong Man* and many other yarns of falsely accused persons whose praying led to their release and proved innocence. You can pattern your own story based on the "power of prayerful thinking" that enabled a cripple to walk again or a sympathetic character to win a worthwhile goal by using faith as a magnet. This can work in a juvenile or adult yarn and for commercial or religious fiction. Study professional examples, religious testimonials, and plan your own characters and plot-action, in accordance with your personal feelings and the market to which you want to sell it.

Middle of-the-road attitude toward prayers

Instead of believing that answered prayers lead to tragedy or miracles, you might prefer to follow a middle course along the lines of a "God helps those who help themselves" premise. Voltaire, known for his atheism, said, "I have never made but one prayer to God, a very short one: 'O Lord, make my enemies ridiculous.' " Of course his astringent wit and cleverness had much to do with his successful squelching of his opponents. Almost every language has proverbs that advise you to help the Deity help you, for example, the Russian "Pray to God, but row for the shore" and the Spanish "Pray to God, but hammer away."

Whichever viewpoint you choose to develop, it can be the overall premise for the whole story; or in the case of a novel, screenplay, or a work longer or more complex than a short story, you could juxtapose contrasting beliefs to create suspenseful conflict. For instance, in a war, adventure, or prison story, a cynical character could be anti-prayer or agnostic because of an embittered past in which everything he prayed for boomeranged and led to his crime and imprisonment. Another impractical, lazy man could expect prayer to accomplish results he should be working hard to attain. Dramatic action could reconcile these opposing attitudes into some compromise wherein both faith and action collaborate to solve the problem. For the men's market it would be even better to substitute luck for prayer—good and bad versus man's individual responsibility for his own fate.

Quotations May Give You Titles

Keep a file of quotations that intrigue you. Savor, ingest, and digest them and they may inspire an entire story idea. They may even provide you with a title: John Donne's poem "No Man Is an Island" inspired the subject and title of Hemingway's *For Whom the Bell Tolls*; W. B. Yeats' "Sailing to Byzantium" gave Seymour Epstein the evolution-of-a-new-life theme and title of his novel *Caught in That Music*; and Federico Garcia Lorca's lines: "The American girls carried babies and coins in their bellies/And the boys fainted stretched on the cross of lassitude" spurred Joan Colebrook's title *The Cross of Lassitude*. Thousands of best-selling titles come from biblical quotations, including *Lilies of the Field*, *Keys of the Kingdom*, *The Blood of the Lamb*, *Gone with the Wind*, *The Voice of the Turtle*, *The Tower of Babel*, *Comfort Me with Apples*, and *Inherit the Wind*. The film *Straw Dogs* takes its title from Lao-Tse: "Heaven and earth are ruthless and treat the myriad creatures as straw dogs. The sage is ruthless and treats the people as straw dogs."

Shakespeare's works are rich with quotable quotes that have provided thousands of authors with good titles. How many can you think of in addition to Knight's *This Above All* (from Polonius' speech: "This above all, to thine own self be true") and Clyde H. Farnsworth's *Out of This Nettle* (from "Out of this nettle, danger, we pluck this flower, safety")?

One word of caution: choose a title that throws light on the work's premise and subject matter. For example, *Out of This Nettle* predicts that out of its bloody wars of the past, Europe will move toward a unity comparable to that achieved by the United States of America.

Blending the Quotation with Other Story Factors

The better the quote you select for your theme and/or title, the harder you must work to synthesize it with well-developed characters, story line, style, emotion, and atmosphere.

Elliott Arnold attributes the success of his best-selling *A Night of Watching* to such a harmonious blending of ingredients. In a world full of hate, violence, man's inhumanity to his fellowmen, and widespread moral apathy and indifference to human suffering, his theme of "I *am* my brothers' keeper" is dramatized by Denmark's David-versus-Goliath courage in defying the mighty Nazis and saving its doomed Jewish population. The hopeful premise is combined skillfully with lifelike personalities, suspenseful action and emotions, carefully researched background, and appropriate style. He says:

> . . . the greatest statement of integrity, morality, what-have-you in fiction will go unread unless you tell a story. A book has to be entertaining, gripping; it has to have something to make you turn the page. You have to create people readers will react to . . . identification. Look, I don't know what makes a book sell, but I do know that if the reader doesn't sweat as he reads, the book is dead.

Most professional authors agree that the premise should be the basis of fiction and that the other vital ingredients must relate to it. In his N.B.A. acceptance speech, Bernard Malamud said:

> A mighty theme doesn't guarantee a mighty book. Some writers may chance upon one and not know they have it. And some who recognize such themes—indeed keep lists of them in their billfolds—once they try to make use of them, beat a hollow drum. . . .
>
> . . . A mighty theme is useful only when it inspires a good writer to symphonic response . . .
>
> Theme has an almost tangible quality—it has texture, visibility, flavor, but these differ from book to book and, of course, from writer to writer.
>
> . . . Art must interpret or it is mindless. Mindlessness is not mystery; it is the absence of mystery. Description of the world is not enough when it may be necessary to proscribe it.

One of the reasons Bernard Malamud's *The Fixer* won both the Pulitzer Prize and the National Book Award is because of the author's dramatic way of interweaving plot action and characterization with a powerful premise, in this case, man's sadistic and illogical inhumanity to man is often counterbalanced by man's nobility of character and altruistic endurance and integrity—or "adversities discover what we are."

Before writing your own fiction, formulate the theme or premise first, for your plot action, characterization, and style must build on it as any stable structure is built on its premises or grounds. Keep in mind Clayton Hamilton's words: "The purpose of fiction is to embody certain truths of human life in a series of imagined facts." Of course the "imagined facts" are not haphazard brainstorms or daydreams but cleverly fabricated incidents designed to prove your thesis and antithesis in such an intriguing way as to form the conflict, suspense, and dramatic power of your story.

Even though you borrow your premise from someone else's quote, the way you blend it with your own ideas of characterization, action, atmosphere, and timeliness will make it your original work.

Study Folklore and Proverbs of Different Nationalities

Every language has its time-tried aphorisms. Favorite proverbs are really short words embodying long meanings and may be short-cuts to plotting for you. Look for timeliness as well as timelessness. In a society in which there are more and more single women and an increasing amount of violence in the streets, there's a valuable premise in the old German proverb "A woman without a man is like a garden without a fence."

What sort of plot does this suggest to you? A successful woman-executive who feels incomplete, unprotected, and exposed without a man, for all her independence, fame, and fortune. A popular formula presents an attractive lady VIP in her thirties or forties whose life is, as always, full, rich, and happy without marriage. Suddenly and surprisingly she marries a rather plain, nondescript man whom everyone considers her inferior. In this case you'd highlight suspense and motivation. After registering the disbelief of her friends and/or fellow-workers, the motive could be revealed as a bombshell from the past, a woman's need for protection, or perhaps as a result of some petty yet symbolic event such as having been refused admittance to a ritzy restaurant, nightclub, or bar that requires a male escort. Or the frustrations of a heroine like Sarah Porlock (in Marian Engel's *No Clouds of Glory*) who decides that a PhD and memories of two messy love affairs aren't enough for a woman of thirty.

Helen Hudson's story "Don't Make a Sound" opens: "Something happened to Miss Early one night on Prescott Street. She never talked about it, even to Bartley Hobbs, whom she married one month later." You've probably guessed the plot already. Yes, Miss Early has been a happily unmarried librarian who enjoys her freedom to travel, to attend theater, concerts, and other cultural pursuits, and to avoid dull people—even Bartley Hobbs, who wants to marry her. Her prize possession is a large Greek bag given her by an Italian when she visited Greece. When the bag is snatched by a hold-up thief, she realizes it contained everything she needed for her independent life: all her credit cards, keys, and her new glasses. Only after this scare does she give up and marry Bartley, merely to have a man's protection. Starting with the same German proverb, you might go the way-out route of a woman *pretending* not to be single by wearing a wedding ring, propping up a male dummy in her car at night to deceive would-be attackers, or carrying a tear-gas pen or police whistle. All, of course, much more innocent and practical than the gruesome husband-substitute in William Faulkner's "A Rose for Emily," in which the old maid kept a male corpse in her bed!

An entirely different, more upbeat development of the theme "a woman without a man is a garden without a fence" could be the heroine's wanting a husband for his sake not hers, for joy in sharing not selfish need. Several widow stories in the womens' slicks show the lonely heroine wanting to cook Thanksgiving or Christmas dinner for others—preferably a man, of course. In this formula we see such premises as: Elbert Hubbard's "One can endure sorrow alone, but it takes two to be glad"; John Ray's "A joy that's shared is a joy made double"; or Mark Twain's "Grief can take care of itself, but to get the full value of joy you must have somebody to divide it with."

Part of the motivation for the independent single woman's sudden marriage could be fear of old age and loneliness. If so, you could interweave Aristophanes' words: "A man, though he be gray-haired, can always get a wife. But a woman's time is short."

If she marries impetuously and unwisely, the sad-story ending could dramatize Congreve's couplet:

> . . . grief still treads upon the heels of pleasure.
> Marry'd in haste, we may repent at leisure.

You could build a neurotic-reaction hate marriage situation like Edward Albee's *Who's Afraid of Virginia Woolf?*, Georges Simenon's *The Cat*, and Hitchcock-like yarns in which one spouse wants to murder the other from quotations like:

A bad marriage is like an electrical thrilling machine:
It makes you dance, but you can't let go. (Ambrose Bierce)

Oh! How many torments lie in the small circle of a wedding ring.
(Colley Cibber)

. . . man and wife
Coupled together for the sake of strife.
(Charles Churchill)

Wishing each other not divorced, but dead,
They live respectably as man and wife. (Byron's *Don Juan*)

You might plot a story of a disillusioned, degenerating marriage based on either of these anonymous quotes:

Love is the star men look up to as they walk along and marriage is the coal-hole they fall into.

It begins with a prince kissing an angel. It ends with a baldheaded man looking across the table at a fat woman.

From many languages and authors you can find quotes for and against marriage. Already you have an excellent conflict, and what is plot but the working out of conflicts and characters whose opinions are diametrically opposed? How many different ways can you work out plots from a clash of matrimonial cons and pros? Because a woman usually wants marriage and a man usually wants freedom, you might reverse the situation for freshness as Max Shulman does in his play *How Now, Dow Jones?* At any rate, select opposing proverbs then see how many original accessories you can add to the conflict.

Against marriage:

"Marriage is the tomb of love." Russian

"Wedlock, woe (*Ehestand, Wehestand*)." German

"Marriage is fever in reverse: it starts with heat and ends with cold."
German

"Marriage is the hospital of love." German

'Marriage is a school in which the pupil learns too late." German

"When God wants to punish a man He makes him think of marriage." German

"If you marry at all, marry last year." Irish

"Love makes passion, but money makes marriage." French

"Marriage puts everyone in his place." French

"Marriage is the only evil man prays for." Greek

"Age and wedlock lame man and beast." English

"Needles and pins, needles and pins,
When a man marries his trouble begins." English

"A young man married is a man that's marred." Shakespeare

"It is hard to wive and thrive both in a year." Fuller

"He that hath a wife and children hath given hostages to fortune, for they are impediments to great enterprises either of virtue or mischief." Bacon

For marriage:

"Two consorts in Heaven are not two, but one angel." Swedenborg

"Love is the flower; marriage is the fruit." Finnish

"Marriages are made in Heaven." John Lyly

"Marriage is honorable in all." Hebrews

"Marriage is the life-long miracle,
The self-begetting wonder, daily fresh." C. Kingsley

"The joys of marriage are the heaven on earth
Life's paradise, great princes, the soul's quiet,
Sinews of concord, earthly immortality,
Eternity of pleasures." John Ford

"It is not good that the man should be alone. I will make a help meet for him." Genesis

"He that said it was not good for man to be alone placed the celibate amongst the inferior states of perfection." Boyle

You can find many more quotes for and against this and any other subject you choose for the theme of your plot. Furthermore, many proverbs actually contain solutions to the conflict created by antipodal attitudes. How many happy-ending-to-marital-discord plots occur to you as you read the following:

"The happiness of married life depends upon making small sacrifices with readiness and cheerfulness." John Selden

"I will fasten on this sleeve of thine;
Thou art an elm, my husband, I, a vine." Shakespeare

(The wife gives in and feeds the man's vanity . . . irresistible!)

"Where one is wise, two are happy." H. G. Bohn

"Keep your eyes wide open before marriage, half-shut afterward." (said by Fuller and Ben Franklin)

In *Love's Labour's Lost*, marriage is called "a world-without-end bargain," and Elbert Hubbard wrote: "Of all the home remedies a good wife is best." Your heroine, of course, can do fascinatingly helpful things to change the thrifty or hypochondriacal bachelor and land him! She could even quote statistics about a wife's worth!

OTHER SOURCES OF QUOTATIONS FOR PLOTS

Chinese sagacity had a 3,000-year head start over Western wisdom and includes many idea-starters, often whole plots, like "The best cure for drunkenness is, while sober, to see a drunken fool."

Here's one that I assigned to my writing students for development that resulted in a wide range of sales from nutrition features to a conflict-filled television script: "All of man's diseases enter his mouth and all his mistakes come out of it."

A few of the thousands of other Oriental gems that might give you plot ideas are:

"Do not be ashamed of mistakes and thus make them crimes."

"Behave towards everyone as if receiving a great guest."

"Sweep the snow from your own door before you complain of the frost on your neighbor's tiles."

"The glory is not never in falling, but in rising every time you fall."

"Doubt is the key to knowledge."

"Even your own ten fingers are unequal."

"Fishes see the worm, not the hook."

"The best horse cannot wear two saddles."

It is also possible to get a plot idea from an epitaph on a tombstone. Merrill Joan Gerber's title story of her short story collection, *Stop Here, My Friend* shows how parent-dominated Kate, who at thirty-one has never lived her own life, is spurred on to make the break for independence by reading the epitaph of a forty-year-old spinster:

> Stop here, my friend, as you pass by
> As you are now, so once was I
> As I am now, so you must be
> Prepare for death and follow me.

You might develop a different humorous story from a comic epitaph like the one in Irvin Cobb's story about Simeon Ford who was never able to find comfortable dentures. He wrote his own:

Here lies Simeon Ford.
Came into the world on _____
Bit the dust on _____
It was the first decent bite he'd had in years.

There's no limit to the quotation sources for plotting, as long as you choose ideas that mesh with your philosophy and fit a particular market. Although we have been discussing adult subjects, you can use the same system for a juvenile market, selecting contrasting quotes then working them out to a philosophical conclusion. Here are some slogans chosen for *Boys' Week*:

"Defeat is not bitter if you don't swallow it."

"You can't expect to be a lucky dog if you spend all your time growling."

"When you can be yourself, why try to be a ghost of someone else?"

"A little intelligent foresight will put hindsight out of business."

"The test of your strength is the knowledge of your weakness."

When you go plot-hunting in books of quotations, you will find ideas for every market. No wonder so many collections of quotes are subtitled "Treasury of Quotations." They contain a priceless wealth of plot seeds for you to nurture, cultivate, and develop into full-bodied stories!

You'll never run out of ideas if you keep books of choice quotes nearby and read them, seeking characters, premises, and plots for your original works. What can you do with some of the following? What professional fiction might have been inspired by them?

"The essence of courage is not that your heart should not quake, but that nobody else should know that it does." E. F. Benson

"We all should be concerned about the future because we will have to spend the rest of our lives there." C. F. Kettering

"To weep overmuch for the dead is an affront to the living."

"Beware of little expenses: a small leak will sink a great ship."
Franklin

"There are no such things as incurables. There are only things for
which man has not found a cure." B. M. Baruch

"What splendid heights many people attain by merely keeping on the
level." J. N. Baker

"Coming together is a beginning;
keeping together is progress;
working together is success." H. Ford

"Some people are making such thorough preparation for rainy days
that they aren't enjoying today's sunshine." W. Feather

"To put alcohol in the human is like putting sand in the bearing of an
engine." T. Edison

"There is no reward for finding fault." A. Glasgow

"Everyone is a moon and has a dark side which he never shows to
anybody." Mark Twain

"The only man who makes money following the races is the one who
does so with a broom and shovel." E. Hubbard

"Minds are not conquered by arms, but by love and generosity."
Spinoza

6

What Bugs You?
Plotting from Irritations

"The world is full of cactus," wrote Will Foley, "but we don't have to sit on it." Nor should you ignore its possible uses. The creative Mexicans see beyond the cactus' prickly surface and convert it into food, drink, candy, needles, thread, and cloth, as you should be able to develop plots from irritations when you train yourself to use all facets and possibilities.

"I always see the truth in duplicate or triplicate," says the hero of Johan Daisne's novel *The Man Who Had His Hair Cut Short*. So do all professional writers, who realize that each misfortune contains a fortune of plot material if you adapt ideas to fit the market requirements and keep up with the newest trends. Timeliness is necessary, for things have reversed since Longfellow said, "To write these days you must divorce yourself from your environment." On the contrary, you must be in and of your environment today, expressing insights into current gripes to turn them into profit for your readers and yourself.

Ray Bradbury's best stories are inspired by things that irritate him. He says, "I have to get the hairball out of my system." The following is only one of many examples of such irritation-inspired stories. After the assassinations, he was so furious at the way the mass media celebrated and enriched the murderers that he wrote "Downwind from Gettysburg" in which he analyzes an assassin's motives and offers a logical solution. A computerized replica of Abraham Lincoln (symbol of love and national unity) is shot by a nonentity named Norman Llewellyn Booth, who, when asked why he did it, explains:

Coward . . . that's me. Always afraid. You name it. Things. People. Places. Afraid. People I wanted to hit but never hit. Things I always wanted, never had. Places I wanted to go, never went. Always wanted to be big, famous, why not? That didn't work, either. So, I thought, if you can't find something to be glad about, find something to be sad about. Lots of ways to enjoy being sad. Why? who knows? I just had to find something awful to do and then cry about what I had done. That way, you felt you had accomplished something. So, I set out to do something bad.

He admits his jealousy of the accomplishment of others while he's incapable of doing anything, of learning anything, of being "in."

The hero punishes him by depriving him of "worldwide TV-radio-film-magazine-newspaper-gossip-broadcast publicity." He takes away Booth's identity and notoriety, promising:

No pictures. No coast-to-coast TV. No magazines. No papers. No advertisements. No glory. No fame. No fun. No self-pity. No resignation. No immortality. No nonsense about triumphing over the dehumanization of man by machines. No martyrdom. No respite from your own mediocrity. No splendid suffering. No maudlin tears. No renunciation of possible futures. No trial. No lawyers. No analysts speeching you up this month, this year, thirty years, sixty years, ninety years after, no stories with double spreads, no money, no.

This same principle can work for you. Start a Gripe File of all the things that irritate you and be on the constant lookout for others to add. Of course merely writing them down is not enough, neither is "sounding off" emotionally, even if these methods make you feel better temporarily. You are a creative professional who has the power to transform "frustrations into fulcrums" (as Sidney Cox put it). You are seeking surer, more solid cures for your troubles and, perhaps, for society.

Test the fiction possibilities of each peeve from all angles as a test pilot tries out a plane before it is put to commercial or military use. Ask yourself the following questions:

1. Do I have a constructive, analytical attitude toward it?
2. Even though this is an Angry Idea, can I avoid bitterness?
3. Are there worthwhile lessons to be learned from it?
4. Can I work out a strong story line or plot blueprint before starting to write the story or book?
5. Can I develop convincing characterization and general (not just personal) human interest, since I realize readers are not interested in *what* happens unless they care about *who* makes it happen and *to whom* it happens?
6. Have I planned the most effective style to put my ideas across in a specific serious or humorous vein?
7. Will I write with a definite market in mind (men's, women's, children's, sophisticated, or popular)?
8. Can I give sufficient motivations for the peeve? Why it came about? Why it is wrong? How it affects the reader?
9. Will I present solutions?

When you can answer yes to these questions about your peeve, you are ready to build it into a worthwhile plot. As you examine each point of the test, adjust the discussion to your own original ideas.

1. *Do I have a constructive, analytical attitude toward it?*

Instead of ranting, raving, and simmering about something or someone who gripes you, welcome this peeve as a necessary part of a future plot. There's no story without conflict and no conflict without opposition or irritation. Be glad for the challenge adversity affords.

Centuries ago, the long-suffering Greek slave-philosopher Epictetus wrote:

> Difficulties are things that show what men are . . . remember that God, like a gymnastic trainer has pitted you against a rough antagonist. For what end? That you may be an Olympic conqueror. No man . . . has a more profitable difficulty on his hands than you have, provided you will but use it as an athletic champion uses his antagonist.

As the athlete uses his antagonist to bring out his own strength and skill, you can use your peeves to bring out your plotting skill and strengthen your writing success.

2. *Even though this is an Angry Idea, can I avoid bitterness?*

During the McCarthy era in the 1940s, successful screenwriter Dalton Trumbo was sentenced and blacklisted for not cooperating with the Un-American Activities Committee. He was forced to take his family to Mexico, where he kept writing harder and for much less money than before, but he says: "There's no point in bitterness because it frustrates everything you have to do. You have to sit and brood." His Mexican exile inspired many worthwhile works, including his Academy Award-winning screenplay for *The Brave One*, about a Mexican boy's love for his bull, Hitano, and his desperate efforts to save the bull's life.

The mere act of writing out what irritates you is therapeutic, and when you write constructively, professionally, and salably, you'll probably feel a sense of gratitude for whatever or whoever bugged you and spurred you on to making that sale!

3. *Are there worthwhile lessons to be learned from it?*

Every experience has value, and even the most niggling peeves and irritations can be usable as barriers in a plot or as a means to drive home a philosophical premise. What good can possibly come from exasperating plumbing problems? In addition to putrid puddles of water caused by backed-up plumbing, the heroine of Kay Boyle's short story "The Astronomer's Wife" has a super-intellectual unreachable husband who lies uselessly in bed while the crisis worsens and she calls the plumber, who teaches her a lesson. Mrs. Ames has always been a practical, down-to-earth woman who doesn't quite understand the fanciful, dreamy conversation of her astronomer husband. She considers their lack of rapport due to a basic sex difference between woman, who is earthy, and man, who is ephemeral. But as the plumber explains the pragmatic facts of plumbing life, she understands and is thrilled by the clarity of communication now that the subject deals with comprehensible concretes rather than the lofty abstractions with which her husband confuses her. The astronomer's wife understands that differences are individual, that: ". . . men were then divided into two bodies now seemed clear to Mrs. Ames. . . . Her husband was the mind, this other man the meat of all mankind."

4. *Can I work out a strong story line or plot blueprint before starting to write the story or book?*

By now you have zeroed in on your peeve, developed a constructive attitude toward it, siphoned off bitterness as you realize its plot possibilities, and developed the premises to be learned from it. Your next step is to work out a plot blueprint that starts with the protagonist's goal, which is unobtainable because of several obstacles, each of which he overcomes, only to meet a new challenge in a progression of minuses and pluses.

Keep in mind Jim Bishop's definition of good writing as "architectural semantics striving toward art" as you blueprint a crescendoing teeter-tottering of actions from the initial statement of the hero's goal on through a crisis and to the final climax. Continuity is maintained by the character's attitudes toward the peeve that sparked the story idea.

Cigar smoking can be a peeve to a nonsmoker, whereas a person who gripes about (and forbids) it is a peeve to the cigar lover. Already you have a good conflict for your plot, especially if the cigar smoker must win the approval of the antismoker for a particular purpose, and in so doing must deny and submerge his strong habit.

With a timely awareness of current hullabaloo about

smoking and lung cancer, P. G. Wodehouse uses this conflict of peeves in his *Playboy* story "A Good Cigar Is a Smoke." He builds it into the clear-cut, old-faithful general formula he has used in his best-selling stories and novels for over sixty years. In this specific case, his cigar-smoking artist-hero wants to marry a girl but needs the approval of her uncle who is dead set against smoking. The following is a blueprint of the major action of the story (you could use this same blueprint device to work out the format of other published stories as well as to work out your own before writing it):

P. G. Wodehouse's
"A Good Cigar Is a Smoke"

Protagonist and his Goal   Lancelot Bingley, rising young artist, wants to marry Gladys Wetherby immediately.

—   She refuses to marry until Uncle Francis, who holds her inheritance until her wedding, approves of her mate. He's sure to object to an artist on moral grounds.

+   Uncle Francis, a hunter, wants his portrait painted to present to the Explorers' Club. Lancelot will go to his home, win him over in the two weeks it will take to paint him.

—   Belonging to the ultra-modern school "expressing himself most readily in pictures showing a sardine can, two empty beer bottles, a bunch of carrots and a dead cat," will he be able to do a job good enough to please Uncle?

+   "All explorers have weak eyes from staring at the sunrise on the lower Zambesi. They don't notice a thing."

— Lancelot worries about meals, since hunters eat strangely.

+ Gladys assures him that Uncle Francis is a gourmet, with a divine cook.

— Lancelot, who loves smoking cigars, is told Uncle Francis objects, so he must knock off for the two weeks.

+ Prepared to please Uncle, Lancelot goes to his home at Bittleton down in Sussex. Takes forty cigars along. Impresses Uncle Francis since he enjoys the marvelous dinner, and makes a hit by saying he doesn't smoke.

— Overeating makes Lancelot need a walk, but when he returns to the house, the door is locked.

+ Breaks a window to enter, but does it noiselessly.

— Mistakes host's room for his and jumps into bed, on Uncle Francis' ample and sensitive stomach. Uncle is furious, won't even discuss the portrait.

+ Seeks solace in his cigar on a walk through the grounds, hears people coming, hides behind a bush, dropping cigar.

Crisis Uncle and cook are shocked to find the dropped cigar, lock it up to have it fingerprinted.

+ Lancelot sends for Gladys. They go to den to get cigar—to find that Uncle is smoking

secretly since cook objects. Lancelot
and Gladys threaten to tell her if he
doesn't okay their marriage, which he does.

5. *Can I develop convincing characterization and general*
human interest?

The plot value of your peeve depends upon human involvement. Virginia Woolf defined a writer as "a person who
sits at a desk and keeps his eyes fixed, as intently as he can,
upon a certain object: human life." This applies, whether the
actors are the victims of the peeve, as Yakov Bok is the
tortured target of anti-Semitism in *The Fixer*, or as James
Baldwin's, John A. Williams', Julius Horwitz's, and LeRoi
Jones's protagonists are the sufferers of racial prejudice, or
whether they are the peeves themselves.

Epictetus would probably call people peeves the most
"profitable difficulties" there are, since every plot requires an
antagonist who generates plot action through his conflict with
the hero. How could Ben Hur, Billy Budd, or Fletcher
Christian be spurred to heroic heights without the instigating
sadism of Messala, petty officer Claggart, or Captain Bligh?
Just as all sunshine makes a desert, all goody-goody characters add up to an arid, unsalable story. There is no saint
without a sinner to test and prove his sainthood. Your people
peeves can be converted into the most valuable ingredients in
your fiction if you preplan the various ways in which an unsympathetic character can be used.

A. *Kill them off in whodunits.* Many mystery story
writers actually develop their plots from the germ of someone
they hate enough to want to kill! Gwen Bristow and her
husband, Bruce Manning, were so peeved by a loud, radio-
playing neighbor that they kept thinking of ways to murder
him, which inspired their novel *Invisible Host*, which became
the successful play and movie *Ninth Guest*. When you feel like
blowing your cool over the endurance-talker on your party-line,
polish her off in a story like Henry Slesar's "Party Line" in
which the telephone-hog won't release the line to a man

wishing to call the doctor to save his wife's life, then later (after the resulting death of his wife), when he comes to kill her, she cannot break through her own phone-hogging party-line to call for help. Or use your creativity to build a stronger story like Frederick Knott's *Dial M for Murder* or Allan Ullman's *Sorry, Wrong Number.*

B. *Have their villainous traits trip them up.* Cold, selfish, emotionally impotent Yank Lucas in John O'Hara's *The Instrument* uses people for his writing purposes, then discards them, uncaring about the havoc and destruction this causes, until this playwright who plays wrong suffers from this same emotional boomerang. Almost any villain-is-foiled or biter-bit plot follows this format, which is popular because of the rightness of the retribution demonstrated.

C. *Use them to show up the evils of the society in which they live.* David Newman and Robert Benton's *Bonnie and Clyde* stresses the fact that the Depression contributed strongly to the development of criminal personalities; Truman Capote's *In Cold Blood* and Joan Colebrook's *Cross of Lassitude* show the results of our society that is senselessly violent, apathetic, and immoral. One of current literature's most repulsive characters is Eric Ambler's Arthur Abdel Simpson, reptilian Egyptian-British half-caste swindler, smuggler, pimp, and pornographer, whose life is "nothing but a long, dirty story," which gives the title to one novel in the series: *Dirty Story. A Further Account of the Life and Adventures of Arthur Abdel Simpson.* No matter how vile his villainy is, it's never as evil and far-reaching as the crimes committed by industrial cartels, whose international intrigue corrupts and manipulates nations and men. The irony of the immoral antagonist shocked by criminals far worse but more respectable and respected than himself and his search for identity in a world dominated by unscrupulousness and mercenary non-values emphasizes the symbiosis between the character and his environment. Obviously, Ambler juxtaposes two peeves—character *and* the international cartels—effectively enough to produce a popular novel series, including *The Light of Day*, which became the movie *Topkapi.*

D. *Have them appear to be all-bad, but with a cleverly hidden nobility within them.* The hardened convict risks his life in a medical experiment or to save a child; the "tough" guy performs tender acts; the Jekyll-Hyde person alternates between good and evil or passion and compassion; or the character pretends evil to camouflage his mission. One of my people peeves was a loud-mouthed man who dated a sweet, quiet girl, whom I pitied because of his loudness, which I attributed to uncouthness. In fact, the girl was hard-of-hearing and too vain to wear a hearing aid but too curious to miss what was being said. His loudness was a result of consideration not boorishness. A more dramatic example would be Eric Erickson, a Swedish businessman who was ardently pro-Nazi, thus hated and ostracized by many of his countrymen. But he was a courageous and valuable Allied spy who used his experience as an oilman to learn of and pinpoint German refineries for aerial bombing. His story is told in Alexander Klein's *The Counterfeit Traitor*, an excellent story of a person leading two lives and wearing two faces.

E. *Have them regenerate and reform, with the negative trait converted into goodness by convincing dramatic events.* Dickens' misanthropic Scrooge and Dr. Seuss's equally bitter Grinch turn into people-lovers and people-helpers. This character regeneration plot is popular in juvenile stories, confessions, and slick features.

Children can be particularly irritating around the rebellious age of twelve, often creating havoc that makes strong plot conflict. For example, study Lillian Hellman's play *The Children's Hour,* Enid Bagnold's *The Chalk Garden,* Maxwell Anderson's *Bad Seed,* and short stories like Joseph Whitehill's "Bobby." In this yarn, the twelve-year-old Bobby Sands dominates and exasperates his bachelor uncle John and his girl friend so much that John comes to realize that the brat is actually splitting up his own parents. The peeve of Truman Capote's childhood was bully Odd Henderson, "a bony boy with muddy-red hair and narrow yellow eyes" who appeared in "The Thanksgiving Visitor." He enacted unforgettable torments on young Capote:

.. he used to wait for me in the shadows under a water oak that darkened an edge of the school grounds; in his hand he held a paper sack stuffed with prickly cockleburs . . . There was no sense in trying to outrun him, for he was quick as a coiled snake; like a rattler, he struck, slammed me to the ground and, his slitty eyes gleeful, rubbed the burrs into my scalp. Usually a circle of kids ganged around to titter, or pretend to; they didn't really think it funny; but Odd made them nervous and ready to please. Later, hiding in a toilet in the boys' room, I would untangle the burrs knotting my hair; this took forever and always meant missing the first Bell.

The story doesn't show a regeneration, but he does teach the sensitive narrator unforgettable lessons about life and deliberate cruelty. Odd Henderson also illustrates the dichotomy of a personality with opposite traits, for in addition to brutality and even dishonesty, Odd is hard-working, responsible, and helpful to older people. He seems to prove Lord Acton's words, "good and evil lie close together. Seek no artistic unity in character."

As you construct character sketches of people who irritate you, decide on their relationship to contrasting personalities in possible fiction, and whether you'll make each an antihero, non-hero, villain, victim, or regenerated good guy.

6. *Have I planned the most effective style to put my ideas across in a specific serious or humorous vein?*

Since most king-sized, significant peeves are Angry Ideas, the temptation is to stress the tragedy involved, but you will be wise to consider other approaches to the subject for maximum effect. My candidate for the greatest peeve is man's inhumanity to man. However, any specific injustice always presented in a tragic light would be repetitious and perhaps not reach as many readers, but a sharply satiric treatment might. In the case of mistreatment of the Indians, there have been a variety of styles from James Fenimore Cooper's portrayal of Indian treachery and cruelty in his *Leatherstocking Tales*, to honorable Indians cheated by White duplicity in novels like Armand Lanoux's *Broken Arrow*, and to sentimental tragedies like Helen Hunt Jackson's *Ramona* and

Paul Wellman's *Apache*. Geared to attract a wider audience (moviegoers as well as readers fed up with bedroom-boredom-and-bloodshed who seek pure entertainment) is Clair Huffaker's satiric novel *Nobody Loves a Drunken Indian*. In a comic but effective style, the Paiute braves, fortified with homemade booze and ancient, dishonored treaties, try to capture Phoenix (their rightful property) by using paleface medicine—public relations. Humor sharpens its message and reviewer Martin Levin calls it "the first slapstick novel of protest," while Wes Lawrence admits that:

> It is more than funny. It is also a telling blow at the government and white people of the U.S.A., who take pride in observing their treaties—unless the treaties were made with those native American nations from which we stole our land.

Many more people will "get the message" because of the humor, which may be more successful in tackling your peeve than tragedy. Sugarcoating the pill lures more people into swallowing the pill, and often the sugarcoating is shockingly tart and pungent, as in Tadeusz Borowski's *This Way for the Gas, Ladies and Gentlemen* (about the coldly efficient madness and horror of concentration camps) or Jonathan Swift's *A Modest Proposal Preventing the Children of Poor People from Becoming a Burden to their Parents or the Country and for Making Them Beneficial to the Public* (about Irish starvation in the eighteenth century and the horrible solution of selling 100,000 one-year-old children for ten shillings apiece and using them for food!). Ugh! But the best prophylactic against cruelty and injustice, claims Dr. William Sargant, is laughter. Even black humor!

In preplanning the presentation of your peeve, consider its nature and your own talents when deciding whether the style should be straight, tragic, sentimental, shocking, or satiric. The last is popular today if you have the stuff to become a satirist, defined as "a lone, unsheltered artilleryman at the bottom of a hill, lobbing mortar shells upward at the great fortresses of established government, religion and social organizations." Satirists have exerted a strong influence on societies from ancient Greek and Roman literature up to the present. They've caused reforms ever since Aristophanes' *Lysistrata*, a satire on war that actually ended the Peloponnesian War; other satirists killed off the Victorian era by making people laugh at the stuffy, dumpy queen, and Alice Longworth helped shatter Tom Dewey's chances for the presidency by saying he looked like the little groom on a wedding cake. Laughter is the best way to pulverize a peeve and prick pomposity, and the literature of any age includes contemporary satire that is analytical, corrective, and fair in its milking of sacred cows and demolishing of targets like phoniness, conformity, Freudianism, momism, permissiveness, politics, materialism, and rationalized war—all of which are attacked in recent fiction.

Study the works of successful satirists: Peter de Vries, who ridicules all facets of our society from suburbia to the stock market in his entertaining novels, *Comfort Me with Apples, Vale of Laughter, Tunnel of Love, Through the Fields of Clover, Mackerel Plaza,* and *The Cat's Pajamas*; Terry Southern, who skewers irresponsible leadership in our nuclear age in *Dr. Strangelove*, pornographic literature in *Candy*, and the corrupting power of wealth in *The Magic Christian*; and Kurt Vonnegut, Jr., who lampoons misdirected philanthropy and extravagant grants to the unworthy in *God Bless You, Mr. Rosewater* and many of our phony values in *Welcome to the Monkey House*. For years Vonnegut has been such a farsighted satirist and social critic that his earlier acerbic novels are often reprinted years later. One example is *Player Piano*, which spoofs the shooting army for making the world so safe for technocracy that they can sit around lazily swapping stories while human values vanish.

Try a satirical style for your peeves. Perhaps you can join the satirists who, claims Malcolm Muggeridge, should attend summit conferences to "save us from being bored or bombed."

7. Will I write with a definite market in mind?

People are primarily interested in their own problems and peeves rather than those of the opposite sex or a different age, race, and background. Examine your peeve with this thought in mind, asking: "Who else shares my peeve?" "How can I clarify the material to help others cope with it?"

If you are griped by the American woman's domination and emasculation of the male, you'll beam your story to the men's market and write in a vigorous, virile style. If, on the contrary, your peeves include Mrs. Average-Wife-Mother's frustrations, boredom, and the "tired housewife syndrome," you'll write in the style of women's publications.

8. *Can I give sufficient motivations for the peeve?*

In the case of the housewife-frustration peeve, you might add specific, fresh motivations to the rather familiar facts of labor- and time-saving devices, the children's growing up, the husband's seeming to have outgrown his wife as he worked up into higher circles, and endocrine imbalance. A quite different example is Truman Capote's *In Cold Blood*, the carefully researched, emotionalized "non-fiction novel." This cold-blooded murder of the innocent Clutter family is blamed on our society's inadequate methods of detecting and treating mentally ill prisoners and their release before they are cured. Capote agrees with Dr. Menninger who maintains that we are all in danger because of our inefficient penal system that frees incurables to commit murder, and then, as an impossible would-be-deterrant to crime, murders the murderers.

9. *Will I present solutions?*

You should have several possible solutions in mind, whether you actually state them in your story or not. The frustrated-housewife's boredom can be solved by specific creative outlets in study, artistic endeavors, charity work, helping handicapped children or oldsters, or perhaps by doing something absolutely crazy to flush the boredom from her system. She may even cooperate with something crazy someone else does, like the bored wife who is kidnaped in Murray Shisgal's play *The Tiger*, which became the movie *The Tiger Makes Out*.

In some serious cases, pat solutions are avoided, since

they may oversimplify the problem and reduce its impact and tragedy. Many social satirists like playwrights Albee and Pinter merely present the evils in a stingingly dramatic way, hoping the audiences will be spurred to action. Often solutions are implied rather than evaded or stated. *In Cold Blood* and other novels about aberrated violence make us aware of the need for improved medical care for the potentially violent neurotics and psychotics among us, just as Joan Colebrook's *The Cross of Lassitude* points out the inadequate provisions for hellbound delinquent girls, even though she gives no set solutions in the book.

As you apply these techniques to turning your peeves into plots and profit, you'll also achieve emotional catharsis and therapy, whether you write farcical satire, like Jules Feiffer, who says he was born depressed but has cured his depression by externalizing his peeves. Or tragedy like August Strindberg, who wrote: "I find the joy of life in the hard and cruel battles of life and to be able to add to my store of knowledge, to learn something is enjoyable to me."

Your crucial peeve can be even more valuable in plotting if you can build it into the Crisis or Super-Obstacle to the hero's progressive action to achieve his goal, as we shall see in the next chapter.

7

Crisis—Vital Part of Plot

After you have learned to be objective-subjective about things, people, and situations that irritate you, you are ready to make them work *for you*. If you do it right, this can be one of the greatest advantages of being a writer: the trick of turning your gripes into gold.

Select readers who share your viewpoint, then work out a plot that will use the irritations as obstacles. They can appear anywhere in a story, but be sure to save the Worst for the Super-Crisis that precedes the end and is the protagonist's main challenge.

Look at this *Redbook* opening with which young housewife-mothers can identify (Judith Viorst's "Single Wasn't So Swell"):

> It was one of those weeks when all three kids had come down simultaneously with a stomach virus and the chicken pox, and my husband kept pointing out dust on the blinds and the baseboards, and my four-year-old drove his tricycle over my wristwatch, and my husband remarked that my dinners were quite uninventive, and my in-laws phoned to tell me I never phoned them and I said to myself, "For this a person gets married?"
>
> What, I asked myself, am I doing here with all these crabs and complainers, instead of lying in the arms of an ardent lover? Why am I stuffing potato peels down the garbage disposal when I could be

dancing in the dark with a titled nobleman or a rock musician or the world's greatest living Shakespearean actor or the world's greatest living revolutionary or an international playboy and sex symbol?

But no matter how bad the initial crisis (or crises) are, throughout the story they must worsen all the way to the Supreme Black Moment, which is the reverse of but the introduction to the Climax. In "Single Wasn't So Swell," the pangs of unmarried insecurity, loneliness, and temporary love affairs that brought "15 minutes of perfect rapture and 15 weeks of perfect misery" were far more agonizing than any problems of marriage and motherhood.

Whether you are writing comedy or tragedy, or for juvenile or adult markets, your plot will be only as successful and suspenseful as its progression of crises.

This "Must" is summed up in Kenneth Rexroth's tribute to Racine's classic play, *Phèdre*:

> Succeeding generations have never ceased to marvel at the construction of *Phèdre*. Racine has built it with the precision of one of those mathematical machines with which the *philosophes* amused the great courtesans of the French court. Each scene is a trap and they are all wired in series, each one setting off the next. The action clicks like the clicking jaws of some omnivorous and omnipotent cacodemon . . .

Every writer would do well to commit these words to memory or paste them above his or her typewriter, for they contain a valuable, rarely revealed secret of strong plotting: the necessity of traps that are "wired in series, each setting off the next." You simply do *not* have a plot unless the hero is opposed by a formidable villain who sets these traps, whether the villain is Fate, Nature, Society, His Own Character Traits and Flaws, Situation, or a Personal Villain.

Give your well-characterized protagonist a specific goal or destination that he is desperately trying to attain, only to be frustrated by the villain-set traps, each of which must be worse than the preceding one. The Super-Trap that threatens to be his nadir—his worst dilemma, predicament, quandary, or strait—somehow contains the seeds of the solution.

Of course the clever writer plants these magic seeds in the crisis beforehand, just as the clever magician conceals the rabbit before the performance, so that pulling it out of the hat will be easy. What is made to appear miraculous to the untrained observer is a simple fact of showmanship to the professional. In fact, this paradox applies to all fields: the *worst* thing that could happen turns out to be the *best!*

Historians agree with Arnold Toynbee who insists that civilizations rise to greatness only when faced with a crucial challenge that threatens their existence. British abuses against the American colonies led to our national independence, just as even worse French and Spanish tyranny spurred revolutions that liberated subject peoples. Thomas Paine chose the title *The American Crisis* for his vital pamphlet in which he wrote, "These are the times that try men's souls."

Be sure to give your hero tribulations and times that try his soul. How else can he prove he's a hero? In 1914, *Fortnightly Review* defined man as one "who in every serious crisis is invariably wrong." Fiction gives him the chance to be *right*, to convert adversity into advantage, or, as Shakespeare put it, "out of this nettle, danger, we pluck this flower, safety."

When your reader gives his time and attention to fiction, he wants the chance to identify with someone who has one big crisis (or more) that promises to *break* him, but that turns out to *make* him better, happier, more loved, or successful. Let the reader, if only vicariously, do something *right* instead of *wrong*. Better still, let something that promises to be wrong turn out to be right.

In Shultz' *Peanuts*, Lucy shouts: "I don't want any downs. I just want ups and ups and ups!" But if Lucy ever bounced a ball she had to realize that the harder *down* she threw it, the higher *up* it rebounded. This is the magic secret of plotting: the down bounces propel the upthrusts, and it takes strong "downs" of crises to produce the elated "ups" of solutions.

For example, in Michael Avalone's *The Incident*, the psychopathically sadistic bullies Ferrone and Connors terrify and tyrannize a subway-full of helpless passengers. After they've tormented each person without interference, Ferrone touches and threatens a sleeping little girl, whose parents are frantic. Teflinger, a GI whose broken arm is in a cast, tells Ferrone, "Hey you! You leave those people alone, do you hear?" *Crisis*: The thugs beat and knife him, taking advantage of his incapacitated arm. But this crisis infuriates Teflinger into beating his assailant into unconsciousness with his plaster-encased arm.

Since crisis is the most important and least taught aspect of plotting, why not plan it before writing your story? Begin right now by writing down a situation suggested by each of the following synonyms for crisis: emergency, exigency, conjuncture, crux, trial, turning point, decisive turn, contingency, pinch, rub, extremity, entanglement, stress, pickle, perplexity, kettle of fish, hot water, stew, deadlock, quandary, dilemma, predicament, scrape, imbroglio, fix, plight, hole, corner, impasse, difficulty, Gordian knot, maze, coil, mess, muddle, botch, hitch, and stumbling block.

This will be an excellent beginning for your invaluable Crisis File. As long as you keep adding situations and ideas to the categories, you'll have the makings for exciting (and therefore salable) plots. Each major crisis, however, must have these qualities:

1. It must be a two-pronged turning point forcing a decision.
2. It must be the antithesis of what the character wants.
3. It must be emotionally saturated and significant.
4. It must affect characterization.
5. It must lead to the premise.
6. The major crisis must be the culmination-explosion of a series of crescendoing crises.

1. *The crisis must be a two-pronged turning point forcing a decision*

We speak of the "crisis" in illness as the turning point at which the patient will either recover or die. In your fiction, the crisis should not be that passive but must hit the hero with a dilemma he must conquer, be conquered by, or run away from. The reader is held in great *suspense* as to which will happen. *Your fiction crisis should never be entirely out of the character's control* but should force him to make a decision or impel him to action.

In case you do use an illness crisis, be sure to have a decision impinging on it. In the case of Sinclair Lewis' *Cass Timberlane*, Jinny has left her older husband Judge Cass Timberlane whom she wants to divorce in order to marry her lover, Bradd Criley. The Judge refuses to free her, so she stays with Bradd's sister in New York, hoping that he'll change his mind. A diabetic, Jinny fails to follow her diet and becomes desperately ill. Suspense turning-point crisis: Will she recover or die? If she lives, will she still prefer Bradd to Cass? Will either or both men still want her? She finally awakens from her coma long enough to tell Cass to take her home, and eventually she realizes (because of his behavior during the crisis) that he is her real man while Bradd is a flighty, charming philanderer.

2. *It must be the antithesis of what the character wants*

If the character's goal is love, each crisis is a form of rejection and repulsion; if he wants wealth, each crisis is one of poverty or loss; if health, sickness; if power, emasculation; if beauty, ugliness; and so on. Each character's goal must be clearly worked out so that you can plan the various crises to be its opposite. Avoid monotony and lack of suspense by pre-planning a variety of unidentical crises.

3. *The crisis must be emotionally saturated and significant*

Fiction's primary purpose is emotion-involvement for the reader who can only *care* as much as the characters do.

Prescott Lecky claims emotion's main task is *reinforcement*. There is only one emotion—*excitement*—which manifests itself as fear, anger, hate, love, bravery, and other so-called "emotions," according to a person's goals. A desperate crisis compounded by emotion releases miraculous strength as in the case of the petite mother who lifted a car to save her son pinned beneath it; the man who saved another man's life in a fiery collision by raising a heavy truck off the victim, ripping out the brake pedal that trapped his foot, and beating out the flames with his bare hands—because he *hated* fire, which had killed his child; the non-flying wife who landed a plane when her husband had a heart attack at the controls; or the cripple whom an emotional crisis renders capable of walking, running, fighting, or some activity impossible before.

Plan a triple-play of: (1) crisis, (2) emotion, and (3) action. Strong emotion is the best spur to action; or in the words of Norman Vincent Peale: "Adversity can be the abrasive that puts the edge on courage. It can be the trumpet that calls forth the latent nobility in man."

How many fiction examples can you think of and plan? In William Chamberlain's "Conscientious Objector," Willy, a pacifist-soldier, promised his Ma he'd "never kill no one." He sticks to his vow in the midst of war until his unarmed Red Cross buddy is shot by the enemy. Willy's fury makes him drive a tractor over the foe's machine-gun nests in vengeance.

4. *The crisis must affect characterization*

When spoiled, seasick fifteen-year-old Harvey Cheyne is washed overboard from a swift ocean liner, picked up by a fishing schooner, and exposed to hardships and ribbing by the "toughs," he regenerates from an adolescent snob to a self-reliant young man who can make a living and judge people for what they are rather than what they have (Kipling's *Captains Courageous*). An alcoholic wife's biggest crisis is the disappearance of her little boy when she's in a drunken stupor. Her fears for his safety plus her daughter's angry reprimands and the neighbors' gossip compound her guilt to make her admit her need for help and confess her alcoholism for which she has previously blamed others ("Pariah" by Joan Williams in *McCall's*).

These are only two examples of this important principle.

5. *The crisis must lead to the premise*

The cliché about a drowning man seeing his life pass before him can have plot value if his reminiscences and self-examination show him his faults and lead to a worthwhile philosophy. In the *Argosy* story "Survival," Harry Forbes, alone in the ocean where he has been sighted by a school of sharks, reassesses his lonely life and realizes that the reason he has had no friends was because of his own unfriendliness; he also learns to value life now that he is about to lose it. Many life-and-death emergencies prove similar premises.

All the crises showing the violence, wastefulness, and frustrations of our materialistic society prove Emerson's century-old prophecy about our Thing-Is-King culture: "Things are in the saddle and ride mankind."

6. *The major crisis must be the culmination-explosion of a series of crescendoing crises*

In Bruce Jay Friedman's *Esquire* story, "The Punch," henpecked Mr. Harris is ridiculed by his wife who says he's not a man because in all the twenty years of their marriage he has never socked anybody. As in all well-constructed plots, each character begins with a goal to which each crisis is a *minus* trap that he springs with a *plus* effort, only to meet a new obstacle that he must overcome; the resulting structure is minus, plus, minus, plus . . . up to a major crisis that makes possible the climax.

Mr. Harris' goal is to prove to his wife that he's a man. His wife says that he's a cowardly sissy who can't deliver a punch. Each opportunity for him to sock someone is a plus, each failure a minus:

+   Before the war, a fresh guy raised a ruckus asking Mrs. Harris to dance.

—   A sick feeling made Harris retreat from a fight with him.

+   On their honeymoon, Harris hears a prowler. Here's a chance!

—   Instead of meeting the prowler with his bare

fists, he picks up a bottle and his wife laughs at him.

+   During his wife's pregnancy, the superintendent of their apartment building refuses to turn on the heat during a cold spell. His wife goads him into giving the super hell.

—   Harris tries but backs down when the super tells him to go fly a kite. His wife calls him a coward.

+   The janitor refuses to take away the garbage. Mrs. Harris tells her husband to punch the guy in the nose.

—   Harris speaks politely to the janitor, but he is disobeyed.

+   Harris disagrees with a critic at an art exhibit. The critic rushes at Harris with a beer bottle in her hand.

—   Harris makes a flippant remark and flees.

+   A group of kids in a car make insulting remarks to the Harrises as they cross the street. They'll be easy to subdue.

—   All Harris can manage to do is give the driver's nose a little tweak.

(A series of flashbacks occurs with the same + and — format.)

+   Waiting for a taxi after going to a nightclub, Mrs. Harris stays inside the lobby while her husband goes outside. When the taxi arrives, a Johnny-come-lately grabs it before Mr. Harris can, but our hero tells him *he* called the cab and it's his. When the man makes a nasty remark, Harris starts to walk away, then comes back and smacks the man almost cold. His victim finally gets up and runs away. This is Harris' Super-Plus! He finally did it! This'll prove to his wife that he's a man!

Super — Although he's trembling with excitement, she refuses to believe his story. If he had had a fight with anyone, there would have been some sort of crowd gathered on the street. She would have heard some noise. She tells him to stop acting stupid!

Without even reading the story you know what will happen! The Super-Minus or Super-Crisis sets up the inevitable climax: in order to stop his wife's nagging once and for all, she must *personally* receive the incontrovertible proof that he *can* throw a punch!

As in all good plotting, the worst thing turns out to be the best! The worst thing that could happen to Mr. Harris after all his wife's ribbing is for him to prove his manhood and *not* have her believe it, and for her to add insult to injury by saying he's not only a coward but stupid! But it will be his best thing, as it will stop her nagging in the future.

Plan some "worst" things that could happen to your protagonist, then make a list of "best" results that might be the outcome. Plotting will come easily after that.

If you're writing a girl's viewpoint story for one of the easy-to-crack teen magazines, you could preplan a crisis according to the character and sensitivities of your heroine. Being stood up is one of the worst things that can happen to a girl, especially a not-too-popular plain Jane. What are some of the ways in which this "bad" thing can lead to something "good"? Add your own ideas to the following:

A. When he doesn't show up for their date, she buries herself in her studies, which she wouldn't have all this time for otherwise. She writes such a brilliant paper that it attracts a better guy in her class (or an award or a scholarship).

B. She uses the evening to do something else that brings her reward later, perhaps busying herself to avoid her younger brother or sister's teasing. The heartbreak poem she writes wins a prize.

C. The party he was going to take her to, or he and his friends, get into trouble. Perhaps there are drugs and a narcotics arrest.

D. A boy who would ask a girl for a date and then stand her up without any explanation is an unreliable jerk anyway and has a serious accident, which she is spared.

E. Crushed and crying, she sobs out her humiliation and disappointment to a parent or relative or friend, bridging a gap that was widening before and seemed irreparable. She finds a valuable solace and friend.

F. To increase her embarrassment, she has mentioned the date perhaps to the "boy next door" who watches for the snazzy car to drive up. This, of course, compounds your heroine's crisis. Later, when the b.n.d. says, "I thought you had a date with _____," and she's wishing she could drop through the floor, he adds: "I thought you were an immature kid—falling for that phony's good looks. But I was wrong. You've got some sense after all, turning him down!" Then he reveals what a fast reputation the other guy has or something bad that convinces the girl that materialization of the date would have been much worse than being stood up. Then b.n.d., who's been watching her grow up, now takes an interest in her and proves to be a marvelous friend and date.

G. You could entirely switch the type of character of the boy who stands the heroine up, making him a fine person who's been in some personal or family crisis. It has been impossible for him to call or show up, but the fact that she doesn't go out with anyone else and waits for him makes him appreciate her reliability.

H. Perhaps you could use the balance-of-payments gimmick used in Ruth and Augustus Goetz' *The Heiress*, which they borrowed from Henry James's novel *Washington Square*. Rich but unattractive Catherine Sloper is flattered by the attentions and proposal of Morris Townsend and plans to elope with him to escape her father's sardonic, bullying attitude toward her (he hates her for not being as charming as her mother who died having her). On the night of their planned elopement, she waits for him in vain, for he's learned that her father would disinherit her, and, of course, money is his principal goal. Later, after Dr. Sloper dies, Catherine inherits his fortune and Morris manages to reinstate himself with her, handing her a fancy line and suggesting a sudden marriage. She agrees, but when he comes for her, he finds the door locked.

Catherine's crisis of being stood up had a triple advantage. It revealed Morris Townsend's true character, saved her from miserable years married to someone who wanted only her money, and gave her a chance for revenge, reinforcing her weak ego. Dominated by her father all her life, this is the first time she has been in command of a situation.

To paraphrase an old cliché, "Every crisis can have a silver lining." For example, a shipwreck can provide a marvelous action-drama crisis that produces fortunate results. It can lead the survivors to discover a new area or unknown flora or fauna. It can get rid of the white elephant boat the wife has always hated, and the insurance money can enable the couple to buy a house or something else that will draw them together. It can bring a clandestine affair out in the open to the relief of all, as in the play *The Hut*. It can reveal true character and ability as in the case of James Barrie's play *The Admirable Crichton*, in which butler William Crichton proves his superiority over his aristocratic masters. Back in England, he's happy to return to servant status, having shown leadership and built up his ego.

A big fight is often the crisis to clear the air and lead to understanding between people previously unable to communicate. In many plots like John McCracken's television play "Trouble Train," divorced parents shuttle a child back and forth until he hates taking the trouble train full of other children of divorce and runs away. In fighting and blaming each other, the parents voice grievances and accusations they both kept buried and festering too long. Facing exposed facts, they come to an understanding that leads to finding the boy in their old home where they had been a real family expressing thoughts and feelings freely.

The worst thing that could happen to a child who wants to keep a cat in a house that "is too full of people who don't like cats" is for the feline to be a nuisance. That's what happens in Neva Clarke's *Redbook* short-short "The Cat Who Cleaned House." Chances are slim for keeping Joseph, the mischievous cat. He is hated by Aunt Ellie who cherishes her antique furniture, particularly a love seat, chiffonier, and whatnot that he might sharpen his claws on; by Uncle Ned who is "not a cat person" and who swings viciously at Joseph with his golf clubs; by Grandma Jones who paints atrocious pictures and rages when Joseph sits on her papers and painting; and by Father who doesn't want a cat messing up his garden.

In less than 1,500 words there are multiple crises as Joseph does everything to lose friends and alienate everyone. Each gets worse until the cat's increasing girth proves Joseph is a "she" and pregnant. When Uncle Ned finds the feline washing itself on his bed, he chases and almost kills the pet, causing a fight with Father that results in Ned's leaving. His mother, Grandma Jones, goes with him, pleasing Aunt Ellie until the biggest crisis occurs. The cat has kittens on her super-precious love seat. This gives her such conniptions that she, too, leaves. Father is so glad to be rid of all the parasitical relatives that he lets the kids keep not just Joseph but all four kittens. The story's last words are: "As Father said, it seemed like a kind of insurance."

What's the worst thing that could happen to the proud, strong Hebrew warrior Samson, whose people are enslaved by the Philistines? To be captured by the enemy and lose his strength and independence. A well-plotted teeter-totter of ups and downs occurs as the beautiful Philistine spy Delilah asks him the secret of his strength, and he tells her several fibs, which the enemy use in vain to overpower him. Big crisis: When he tells her the truth, she tells the enemy, who shave, weaken, and capture him. *Worse crisis*: They blind him, bind him, and force him to do the work of oxen, grinding grain in the prison house. But this rebuilds his strength and self-discipline for the next crisis. He is called to entertain all the lords of the Philistines so they can laugh at him, but, he is now strong enough to pull down the pillars supporting the building and kill 3,000 of the enemy (more than he had in all his life as a soldier!).

The old melodramas used this technique of intensifying the crisis so that the worse it got for the hero, the better it turned out to be in the end. Binding, gagging, and tying the protagonist to the railroad tracks with rope wasn't bad enough, so the dastardly villain used wire, which was more painful and impossible to untie. But . . . the brightness gleaming in the moonlight could be seen by the engineer in time to stop. ("Curses, foiled again!")

In Alistair MacLean's *The Guns of Navarone*, the brave little band of Allies who are trying to rescue 2,000 British troops stranded on the Island of Kheros suffer many crises, which they overcome through courage and ingenuity. The worst crisis occurs when they finally reach the big guns they must dismantle, only to find that all their timers and fuses have been sabotaged. This proves that all their troubles and harassments have not been the outer enemy's fault alone but that there is a traitor among them. After much suspense and accusation, they learn it is the girl guerilla, Anna, who told them she had been tortured by the Nazis. When they strip her to see the Nazi-inflicted scars she had described, there are none. She is executed by the Greek partisan woman and they are free of sabotage to complete their mission successfully.

Since crisis is essential to plotting and a series of crescendoing traps are necessary to keep your writing out of the trap of rejection, start saving crises and peeves. They can not only strengthen the action and suspense of your short stories, but may be the stimulus and raison d'être of your greatest works.

8

Plotting from Values

The truly great author can and must juggle the professional careers of entertainer, preacher, and teacher in ways that can make writing a joy for him and life purposeful for his readers and viewers.

Irving Stone says there are only two kinds of writers:

> ... the natural and the unnatural. If a person takes up writing because it looks easy, simple, a surefire route to fame and fortune, that person is unnatural, and the writing process is slow and painful. But if he has great stories to tell or important values to communicate, that person is a natural and the writing process flows easily ...

It is vitally important for you to honestly evaluate your moral values and correlate them with your life goals and writing goals. Stone expresses his this way:

> I hope to leave behind me a testimonial that the human mind can grow and accomplish fantastic ends. That if you have the stamina and the courage, you can survive hardships, defeats, miseries, illnesses, poverty, crushing blows. Researching the lives of the people I've written about, I'm convinced it's possible to carry on, clinging by one's fingernails, and still accomplish a big, beautiful, gorgeous job of work. And I hope to continue to share that discovery with others.

107

Although one could debate the issue of positive versus negative moral values in literature, it is not the purpose of this book to entangle the reader in questions of philosophy. You will find, no matter which side of the debate you choose to champion, that moral values are a rich source of plot material.

What values will you write about? Preplan them thoughtfully before beginning to build your plot. Since your story is only as valuable as the values with which it deals, you can build a plot from moral basics that are timely and timeless. The trick is to start with integrity, individuality, loyalty, or some other quality, set it up in a dramatic conflict with its opposite value, then work out the struggle into a premise. This is the fundamental structure of every story that survives, from the Bible and folklore to television writing. Each tale dramatizes Amiel's description: "Every life is a profession of faith. Every man's conduct is an unspoken sermon that is forever preaching to others."

Make Your Characters Represent Values

One way to make sure that your story will have basic values common to all readers is to *personify* the plus and minus qualities into actual characters, even naming your hero and villain those qualities in your first draft! Ancient morality plays like *Everyman* named the dramatis personae Death, Good Fellowship, Kindred, and Goods (the antagonists); whereas Everyman's truer friend is Knowledge, his fickle friends are Strength, Discretion, and Five Wits, and his only reliable friend is Good Deeds. Ben Johnson named characters Old Morose, Tribulation, Wholesome, Mirth, Curiosity, Expectation, and Lovewit.

As old as this method of clarifying values is, it's making a magnificent comeback in Isaac Bashevis Singer's charming tale of Good Luck and Bad Luck, which appeared written for adults in *Redbook* as "A Match for a Princess," later appearing as a successful children's book titled *Mazel and Shlimazel or The Milk of a Lioness*. When Mazel (Good Luck) rejoices that everyone loves and wants him, Shlimazel

(Bad Luck) boasts that he is stronger and can destroy all Good Luck's work in one second. If Bad Luck wins, he will be given the precious wine of forgetfulness; if he loses, he must keep out of Good Luck's business for fifty years. In his one-year period Mazel picks Tam, the kingdom's poorest man, elevates him to the heights of success, winning for him the King's favor and the Princess' love. When the King falls ill and must have the milk of a lioness, Tam obtains it so luckily and quickly that there are doubts that it is from the ferocious beast. As Tam brings it to the king's sickbed, Mazel's year ends; Shlimazel takes over and makes poor Tam tell the king: "Your Majesty, I have brought what you sent me for—the milk of a dog." For this, he is condemned to hang. But when Shlimazel celebrates his victory by imbibing the wine of forgetfulness, Mazel helps Tam give the King a flattering explanation of his booboo. The lioness' milk cures the King, and Tam wins the princess.

One reason Mr. Singer is the most universally published fiction writer of our time is that, even though he doesn't usually make his characters such unmistakably recognizable values as Good Luck and Bad Luck, his work always concerns the essential basics that affect people everywhere and of every time. Although his story of Mazel and Shlimazel is a fanciful fairy tale, it presents a valuable format for structuring any story in which positive and negative values must clash.

Notice the similarities in Mary Jane Rolf's "The Loser" about thirtyish attractive "Poor Laura Hart" who is consistently unlucky in her relations with people. She has roommates who overdress, overact, teach her tricks about make-up, clothes, and little theater, but who skip, leaving her to pay their bills. Her male acquaintances are equally disappointing, including fancy-dressing opera-buff Harry Rockwell who turns out to be married with three kids in another town; Don, who's too poor to take her anyplace except to the museum, park, zoo, and art galleries; and her boss, Mr. Cunningham, who overworks her for years then goes out of business, leaving her jobless. But she keeps trying and learns enough from each to develop into an informed, cultured girl who attracts an artist-professor husband, Ben Millard. This very different modern story about very different modern characters shares Singer's premise: ". . . good luck follows those who are diligent, honest, sincere, and helpful to others. The man who has these qualities is indeed lucky forever."

The Active Conflict of Clashing Values Leads to the Premise

The vying basics in your story must lead to a moral truth you believe. Consider the conflicting values of innocence versus guilt. Franz Kafka's consistently pessimistic premise was that innocence is doomed and evil brutality will crush innocent virtue. His unappreciated works predated and predicted the Nazi moral holocaust and its destruction of goodness, all the way from his terrifying short story "Metamorphosis," which symbolized the dehumanization of the individual, to the innocence-exterminating police state in *The Penal Colony* and *The Trial*. In the latter totally innocent Joseph K is arrested and cold-bloodedly murdered, after being told by the priest: "It is not necessary to accept everything as true, one must only accept it as necessary." This morbid "you cannot escape your fate" premise has resounded throughout literature since Aesop's tale of the innocent lamb killed by the conniving wolf.

In direct contrast to Kafka's pessimism, innocence prevails, miraculously undefeated throughout violent corruption, revolution, and a symbolically world-blackening eclipse in Michel de Ghelderode's play *Pantagleize*. The author explains that his hero is:

> . . . that deep-secret goodness found in all men, goodness often deprecated, mutilated, buried forever, which doesn't come to the surface of mankind often enough. Most people are miserly with immortal things like goodness or love, but Pantagleize proves magnificently generous with heaven which he's full of. He gives his love to all humanity, humanity so cruel, so tender, so beautiful, so ugly, so disturbing, so reassuring, so good, so evil. Yet Pantagleize gives.

Innocence fares better in stories like "The Innocents" (by

Zena Collier) in which the naive young couple, Frank and Emma Baker, win a trip on which they are ridiculed and snubbed by their sophisticated, high-society co-travelers. But eventually the snobs come to realize that their money and false gaiety cannot make them as rich and happy as the truly-in-love innocents they try to scorn.

Still focusing on the contrasting abstract values, in the case of innocence versus guilt, you might choose to concentrate on the power of guilt, which Freud claimed was the strongest motivating force in human beings. You could plan a plot in which a character profits from another's guilt either through blackmail or by forcing him or her to do something against his or her will. In Francis Clifford's *The Naked Runner*, British agent Slattery is confident that he can convert easygoing "jolly-good-fellow" Sam Laker into a killer by preying on his guilt, and he does! He forces Laker into a tough situation in East Berlin by pressing his guilt at having deserted a German girl who saved his life during World War II, then forces him to commit murder to save his little boy whom he left unguarded.

Guilt for a murder he thinks he committed is the activating force that haunts such anti-heroes as Martin (in Clarice Lispector's *The Apple in the Dark*) who thinks he has murdered his wife and runs away, and in Susan Sontag's *Death Kit*, in which Dalton "Diddy" Harron, in a furious argument, kills a train trackman. After making love to and living with a blind girl, he manages to expiate his personal guilt by comparing it to the more horrendous guilt of All Mankind. To the guilt-versus-innocence factors, Miss Sontag adds the paradoxical values that appear also in Frederick Knott's *Wait until Dark*: the confusion and blurred insight of the sighted versus the clear inner vision of the blind.

Guilt cannot be expiated by conscience-ridden characters like Anna Karenina in Tolstoy's novel; Raskolnikov in *Crime and Punishment*; Mr. Thompson in Katherine Anne Porter's *Noon Wine*; and Eleanor in Katherine Tompkins's *All the Tea in China*. After Thompson kills the bounty hunter who tries to take his hard-working farmhand away, his lawyer trumps up a case of self-defense and he is acquitted. But he cannot acquit himself, and, after failing to gain forgiveness by repeating claims of innocence to everyone, he seeks atonement in suicide, proving the premise: "By the verdict of his own breast no guilty man is ever acquitted" (Juvenal: *Satires*). Likewise, Ellie, who has been acquitted of murdering her sadistic husband Mike, jumps overboard to her death in line with the English proverb: "A guilty conscience needs no accuser."

Guilt is also the underlying value and the stimulus to all plot action in Leon Uris's *QB VII*.

The author-protagonist, Abe Cady, is motivated by guilt to write *The Holocaust* to expose the atrocities of the concentration camps and the annihilation of twelve million innocent people by the Germans. His guilt is multiple: he has denied his Jewishness (although his aristocratic English Gentile wife accepts and admires it); he has consistently criticized his father for his "old world" Jewish ways and speech; and he so neglected his father after the latter moved to Israel that he was totally unknown to the old man's friends when he went there at his father's death. He has led an immoral, hedonistic, meaningless life. Added to those guilts was that stirred by the Memorial Museum, which aroused the conscience of a man who was smug and safe while his fellowmen suffered such horrors.

Dr. Adam Kelno's guilt for the inhuman medical experiments he performed in concentration camp motivated him to go to Kuwait after the war and doctor the backward natives there. Later (after being honored, knighted, and practicing successfully in London) he sues the author of *The Holocaust* for naming him, thereby calling attention to himself and his crimes, subconsciously trying to expiate his guilt. The fact that he wins the case and is awarded the lowest coin in the realm prevents his guilt-expiation and is a masterful touch.

Guilt, in one form or another, surfaces in much of the rest of the action. The guilt of the fathers is also visited upon their sons. Cady's only son, who has joined the Israeli Air Force, is killed. Dr. Kelno's son is so repelled by the exposure of his father's past that he rejects him and leaves his parents. A minor character, a Roman Catholic woman-psychiatrist, has spent her talent and energy working in an Israeli hospital to try to atone for the guilt of what her fellow "Christians" had done to their brothers and sisters. In Francis Ford Coppola's film, *The Conversation*, Harry Caul's guilt over the murders his wiretapping causes destroys his pride in his work. Culpability is also the subject of Maximilian Schell's *The Pedestrian*, which treats the guilt of an ex-Nazi soldier in the massacre of a Greek village.

After deciding on a value that you feel strongly about, use it as a basic platform or emotional reference to which each of your main characters relates. This will bring out their differentiating traits, spur their human behavior in actions and reactions, and will dramatize all-important premises.

Study how professional authors use this method to achieve structural consistency. Terence Rattigan's *Separate Tables* shows how loneliness affects all characters, and Iris Murdoch's *The Nice and the Good* dramatizes all types of love: self-love, religious love, love without commitment or forgiveness, jealous love, and so on. Specific values are dramatized in many of Shakespeare's plays: ambition in *Macbeth*, jealousy in *Othello*, gullibility in *King Lear*, love in *Romeo and Juliet*, and so on.

Animality versus spirituality

A favorite dichotomy is man's evil versus his good nature, often emphasized as animality versus spirituality. Man's carnal instincts conquer his humaneness in several works from Dostoevsky to Edward Albee's *The Zoo Story*, in which the man who describes the vicious dog's attack actually surpasses the animal's viciousness by killing without cause; Jean Genet's *Mademoiselle* in which a schoolteacher can't suppress her sexuality, and also *The Balcony*, in which characters act out their animality; in Eugene Ionesco's *Rhinoceros*, in which the insensitivity of human beings turns them into unthinking, thick-skinned rhinoceroses; and in Philip Barry's *The Animal Kingdom*, in which the women control Tom Collier through his animal instincts. In fact feminine bestiality is the target of several works like Joseph Kramm's Pulitzer Prize-winning play *The Shrike*, in which Ann crushes and destroys her husband like the shrill-voiced bird that impales its victim with its sharp beak, and Robert Ruark's *The Honey Badger*, in which the hero, Alec Barr, says:

> There is a bloody, brave little animal called the honey badger in Africa. It may be the meanest animal in the world. It kills for malice and for sport, and it does not go for the jugular—it goes straight for the groin. It has a hell of a lot in common with the modern American woman.

There is bound to be more and more emphasis on human bestiality and proof that we operate on what Yeats called a "bestial floor" since the publication of Desmond Morris' *The Naked Ape* and *The Human Zoo*, which examine people in zoological terms and come up with the premise that man's problems stem from his delusions of spiritual grandeur, while forgetting that:

> . . . his old impulses have been with him for millions of years, his new ones only a few thousand at the most—and there is no hope of shrugging off the accumulated genetic legacy of his whole evolutionary past.

If you think the Morris thesis is depressing, *Planet of the Apes* is even worse! Not only are human beings considered animalistic, but the civilized apes have evolved from a lower species: man. Thus ethological premises are spiraling downhill from the animal symbolism in Rostand's *Chantecler* and Orwell's *Animal Farm*.

Of course, no sex has the monopoly on animality, which always comes out when people are confined, as in James Clavell's *King Rat*, or in competition, as indicated in all the civilization-based stories with "Jungle" in the title. John Steinbeck often counters man's bestiality versus his spirituality. Critic Edmund Wilson points out that in "The Snake," the laboratory where Steinbeck's scientist feeds white rats to rattlesnakes and fertilizes starfish ova is the symbol of his method of dramatizing life in animal terms, of his consistent philosophy of group man as an animal. Man's exploitation of his kind permeates *Grapes of Wrath, Tortilla Flat, Cannery Row*, and his other social reform novels; even in *Travels with Charley* there's a hint of the author's preference for animals over more-brutalized human beings.

Individuality versus conformity

Another writer who used the same contrasting values in all his works was Henrik Ibsen, whose plays dramatize society's pressures on the individual. His greatest works stress, in addition to the war between honesty and hypocrisy, a values-clash that is popular today: nonconformity versus conformity. Each author who chooses this set of opposing values works out the action to a philosophy he believes. Ayn Rand's nonconformist hero in *The Fountainhead* is Howard Ruorke, the Frank-Lloyd-Wright-like architect who triumphs over stuffy, traditional conformism through his perseverance and originality. The message confirms Emerson's belief that "Whoso would be a man must be a non-conformist." Stick to your principles and you will win! Hooray for nonconformity! A slight variation appears in Gerald Green's *The Last Angry Man*, in which equally individualistic Dr. Sam Abelman learns a deeper lesson: Even though you should march to your inner music (as Thoreau put it), you must respect the individuality of others and not be a self-righteous prude who forces your standards on others.

Opposite premises that conclude the same battle of values show the dangers and impracticality of nonconformity. The rebellious hero of James Allerdice's *The Man Who Thought for Himself* learns that stubborn nonconformity can be an uncomfortable trap. Objecting to neighborhood restrictions and conventional advice, Andy Fletcher decides to paint his house himself, on Sunday, and not just red, a color the man next door objects to, but red, white, and blue with stars on the roof! He fights for his inalienable American rights so eloquently that he is stuck with the monstrosity! This agrees with the theme of Morris Freedman's *Confessions of a Con-*

formist: "Nonconformism for its own sake eventually becomes as stupid and restrictive as unthinking conformity." Another character who is trapped by obstinate nonconformity is Roberta Winters, the college girl in Jack Luria's *Harper's* story "The Hugger and the Hugged." Roberta goes to great lengths to alienate herself from her fellow students and the professors and even breaks strict rules in order to be expelled, so that, as a martyr, she will be noticed and pitied rather than scorned! Her need for approbation is so strong that she destroys her campus career in order to achieve it, as so many young rebels use nonconformistic acts as a reverse means of conforming!

A still different opinion of the conformism problem is that, no matter how ridiculous conventional patterns are, the individual cannot possibly win in his battle to be himself if he's a dissenter. Eugene Ionesco's play *Soif et Faim* (*Thirst and Hunger*) shows hero Jean's losing battle to withdraw from conformistic society. He merely experiences greater frustrations, finally returning to the group he left, which is portrayed as a prison-like "establishment" where "clowns in cages mimic man's indecisions." He joins the caged clowns voluntarily as Murray Burns does in Herb Gardner's more comic play *A Thousand Clowns,* which breaks down in the following way:

X-Plus Factor & Style	Comedy satire on television shows, Madison Avenue, New York
Characterizations	*Murray Burns:* Peter-Pan-young, nonconformistic, irresponsible, carefree, clever-with-words adult.
	Nick: Sophisticated, brilliant, adultish twelve-year-old nephew of Murray and full contrast character.
	Sandra Markewitz: Romantic, idealistic social worker whose heart rules her head (even though it's a good head).

Other characters are stock, stuffy con-
formists all.

Premise To win the game, you must play by the rules of
the game. Freedom has many meanings and
when compounded with unselfishness, responsibility, and concern for others is greater than
selfish, immature freedom.

Protagonist's Murray Burns, ex-television comedy writer
Goal who has quit the rat race, wants to live a
carefree, unfettered life with his twelve-year-
old nephew, Nick, who lives with him.

— Their Bohemian, beatnik life together has
aroused concern at Nick's school, and
social workers are going to investigate
Murray to see if he's a responsible (working)
citizen and a fit guardian.

+ Nick tries to talk Murray into getting a job
so they can stay together. Murray agrees
to look at classified columns only if they're
three days old.

— Two snooping social workers come to
investigate their apartment, etc. They ask
embarrassing questions . . . may take
Nick away.

+ Murray charms the girl social worker, Sandy,
so much that she breaks her engagement to
the man-worker, and moves in with Murray.

— She tries to domesticate him and feminizes
his apartment so much that he cries: "I've
been attacked by *The Ladies' Home*

Journal!" She talks him into dressing up and going out job hunting.

+ Although he's offered several jobs in television writing, he walks out on them. Maintains his nonconformistic integrity and freedom.

— Sandy walks out on him. The Board meets Thursday to decide Nick's fate.

+ Since Murray wants to keep Nick, it's a plus when Chuckles Chipmunk, the children's comedian for whom he used to write, offers him his old job back. (Murray is in charge, doesn't have to crawl.)

— After a word-battle between Chuckles and Murray and Nick, the boy doesn't want Murray to work for moronic Chuckles.

+ As Nick acts like a child and cries, Murray acts like an adult and develops responsibility and decides to go back to work.

Naturally you should work out such a blueprint for each character in the play or story. You can do it with Nick and Sandra just from reading this.

Be Sure to Work Out the Conflicting Values First

Decide on a value you'd like to write about, choose its opposite, decide which you are for and which against, and write your philosophical conclusion in one sentence. Also, before writing your story, blueprint the plot action that will lead to the premise you firmly believe, and see how other publications treat the same values-conflict so that you can contribute a fresh approach and not repeat what has been frequently done.

Imagination is favored as a refuge from harsh reality to make life endurable in many works like James Thurber's

"The Secret Life of Walter Mitty," *The Diary of Anne Frank,*
George Feifer's *The Girl from Petrovka, The World of Suzy
Wong,* and Jean Muir's *The Dragon in the Clock-Box* (which,
like the Isaac Singer story of values, appeared first in a
woman's slick magazine and then as a children's book). In
Bryan Forbes' *The Whisperers,* the same kind of fantasizing
and living in an inner dreamworld rescues Mrs. Ross from the
desolate loneliness of old age. The popularity of J. R. R.
Tolkien's trilogy *The Lord of the Rings* proves that many
people prefer fantasy to factual history.

An opposite stand is taken in many stories in which an
overactive imagination leads to superstitious fears of death, as
in Dori White's "Under Sentence of Death," Alice Glenday's
"Unhappy Returns," and Michael Shaara's "Premonition."
In the first, the heroine fears her own death; in the second,
the superstitious wife believes her husband is going to die on
her thirty-second birthday (because her father and grandfather each expired when their wives were thrity-two); and in
the third, the man suffers his own death-premonition. In
these yarns emphasis on the negative powers does not neces-
sarily lead to a morbid premise, rather it leads the reader to
conclude that it takes awareness of death to appreciate living
and that, as the sage said, we start dying the minute we are
born. It's inevitable, it's natural, so *carpe diem*, or seize the
day, and enjoy the moment, as Horace wrote.

Condemnation of too much imagination appears in several works like Tennessee Williams' *Streetcar Named Desire,*
in which Blanche Du Bois' exaggerated imagination is her
crutch that prevents her realistic maturity and eventually
leads to insanity. Or John O'Hara's *Appointment in Samarra,*
which symbolically suggests that negative imagination can be
a magnet to attract the negative, similar to Arthur Penn's
Mickey One, which shows the agonies of a young nightclub
comic who imagines he is pursued by the Mafia.

Imagination's good and evil aspects are stressed in *The
Prime of Miss Jean Brodie* (Muriel Spark's novel made into a
play by Jay Allen). The heroine's compensation for the
frustrations of spinsterhood consists of unbridled imaginative

outbursts that prove to be disasterous and self-defeating, but which also ignite the imaginations of the girls she teaches. Her ecstatic communion with romantic fantasies embellish her teaching and make her love it, gushing, "Give me a girl at an impressionable age and she is mine for life." Imagination does have this power; that's why the happy-medium premises that balance vision with logic and fantasy with fact are valuable. In *Put Your Mother on the Ceiling*, Dr. Richard de Mille writes: "Distinctions between reality and imagination are necessary and it is important that they be learned. But it is also important to teach the distinctions in a way which does not turn off the imagination." Or, as Thoreau said: "If you have built castles in the air, your work need not be lost. That is where they should be. Now put the foundations under them."

How many different ways can you work out this ideological conflict between imagination and reality? How many professional works can you think of that express their writers' philosophical conclusion? Some always favor reality, agreeing with Conrad who wrote, "Truth alone is the justification of any fiction which makes the least claim to the quality of art."

In *The Iceman Cometh*, Eugene O'Neill sets up his counter-characters to represent these specific values: Larry, the self-hating, aging, alcoholic anarchist argues for the necessity of illusions, whereas Hickey represents the curative powers of truth. Their intense battle affects other characters tragically and eventually arrives at the premise: Although weaklings need to be restored to their illusions, it is a fools' paradise regained and therefore meaningless.

O'Neill's theme is the opposite of that of many Tennessee Williams plays that show weak people clinging to illusions in order to survive. Nobel Prize-winning playwright Luigi Pirandello's dramas enact a still different message: Why worry about which is right and which is wrong. There isn't any difference at all (see *Right You Are If You Think You Are*). Darek Walcott's play *The Charlatan* proves that every phony has his truth and every truth is partly a lie.

If you choose to write a story based on a conflict of

values, your story will be strongest if you take a stand. Any professional script that doesn't come to a firm conclusion has a reason not to. In the movie *The Man on a Swing*, clairvoyant Franklin Wills (representing illusion or the supernatural) offers clues to a murder to the realistic sheriff who wonders whether he is implicated. Has he hypnotized the murderer? Is he really psychic? The author couldn't tell for legal reasons since the story is based on a true case.

Boredom versus enthusiasm

John Cheever writes of apathetic boredom versus activity and experimentation in his first-prize O. Henry story "The Embarkment for Cythera." Jessica Coliver is affected and infected by the ennervating *ennui* that enshrouds their suburb, Proxmire Manor ("the pretty place"), and seems to contaminate everyone with it. The town's only spurt of excitement was the brief arrest of Mrs. Lemuel Jameson—the result of the boredom of a police department with nothing to do. Her boredom causes her to fight the trivial charge with hysteria, screaming, and martyrdom, even calling a mayor's committee for the purpose of firing the policemen who entered her bedroom and hauled her off to the station house where she was forced to pay a $1 fine.

Mrs. Jameson typifies the Proxmire Manor wife: "Her children were away at school, her housework was done by a maid, and though she played cards and lunched with friends, she was often made ill-tempered by abrasive boredom."

Similar boredom of the rich makes Laura Hilliston turn to gossip and lead the crusade to ostracize and evict from the community Grace Lockhart, whose boredom causes her to be "intimate with just about everybody: . . . the milkman, . . . the man who reads the gas meter, . . . that nice fresh-faced boy who used to deliver the laundry, . . . and the grocery delivery boy." Instead of shocking and disgusting Jessica, Grace's amorous flights from boredom make Jessica feel she's missing something, and after trying to escape the ennui of her smug, rich, dull life in social activities and dances, illness and hospitalization, and playing with her baby, she eventually enters into an affair with much-younger Emile, Mr. Narobi's good-looking grocery boy who agrees to become her lover to escape from the boredom of his humdrum life and the loose and easy girls his own age.

In the various individual characters Cheever uses to represent the conflicting values of boredom versus experimentation (in order to escape *ennui* and seek excitement), boredom always wins out. The citizens of Proxmire Manor, so long conditioned to apathy and humdrummery, give up after feeble flickers of effort. The police, Mrs. Jameson, Grace Lockhart, Jessica, and Emile share a mutual inability to rise above boredom.

Cheever's "The Embarkment for Cythera" makes no distinction between Good and Evil, nor is Jessica's infidelity punished either by her conscience or by discovery. The author confines his message to the inescapable bonds of boredom, but this is a rare, sophisticated quality story that is specific *New Yorker* caliber, and *The New Yorker* is an unlikely market for nonprofessional writers. For less sophisticated publications, the plus and minus of the values would be brought out. In fact, a moralist can read these into Cheever's yarn: If the characters tried to escape from boredom in worthwhile, altruistic activity, they would have succeeded, or at least been too busy for self-pity and lassitude.

Because boredom is the antithesis of activity and excitement, and contrast is the essence of suspenseful drama, ennui is often the springboard for plot action. In juvenile literature, boring reality is fled from in books like Maurice Sendak's *Higglety-Pigglety Pop: Or, There Must Be More to Life* and Norton Juster's *The Phantom Tollbooth*, in which little Milo, out of sheer boredom, drives through a phantom turnpike tollbooth into a fantasy world of adventures.

As the chronology and sophistication of the characters increase, adults' boredom can motivate more morbid experimentation, such as we find in movies like Fellini's *La Dolce Vita*, Lars Gorling's *Guilt*, and Conrad Rooks' *Chappaqua*, which autobiographically emphasizes his psychedelic attempts to get "kicks" in what reviewer Charles Champlin calls "less a tale of terror than a schizoid Scheherazade."

In the naive pre-drug days, solutions to boredom and bores were found in such simple methods as the perfect squelch, such as Douglas Jerrold's line to a very thin man who had been boring him: "Sir, you are like a pin, but without either its head or its point."

Work Out Different Possibilities

If you choose boredom as a value in your story, the counter-value that will symbolize your character's escape from boredom should be either good or evil, affecting all action throughout.

(1) A morally *evil* escape from boredom could be experimentation with crime, as in the case of the bored kids Bonnie and Clyde who turned to robbery and murder for "kicks," or an apathetic, rebellious teen-ager who tries drugs "to turn on" or who joins destructive gang activity in vandalizing schools or indulging in other harmful mischief.

(2) A morally *good* escape would benefit humanity, as musician Albert Schweitzer changed his profession to medicine to administer to neglected underprivileged people rather than pleasing the ears of the privileged. Your character could join the Peace Corps or become a medical missionary to escape from a life of *ennui*.

One of mankind's most boring conditions is imprisonment. An individual's dominant character traits will determine whether his endeavors are evil and harmful—masterminding future crimes; teaching hatred and evil habits to younger, more innocent prisoners; or writing destructive books like *Mein Kampf*—or whether his outlets are constructive and creative—a John Bunyan writing *Pilgrim's Progress*; an O. Henry writing great short stories; a Charles Goodyear inventing vulcanized rubber; or an inmate applying himself to learning a new trade like television repair or electronics, or working hard to become a great artist (as in *Convicts Four*).

Boredom can lead to meddling with tragic results as in Françoise Sagan's *Bonjour Tristesse* or Ibsen's *The Wild Duck*, in which the gossipy meddler causes suicide, or to happy results as in *Bells Are Ringing*. In this play Ella, the good-hearted switchboard girl at Sue's Answering Service, is frequently torn between two concepts: "Love Thy Neighbor" and "Mind Thy Own Business." Since all action must be generated by character, and since she is a people-loving do-gooder who loves to be beneficially "involved," she chooses the first. Her personal concern for her clients leads to her own happy romance, and the conflict of values resolves into a comedy. Tragedies occur when the do-gooder tries to protect someone or prevent a crime and is forced to suffer for his efforts, as in *Witness to Murder*.

Honesty versus deception

Usually the good and bad of an abstract value is crystal-clear, but the more profound quality story may reflect an ambiguity that is often true to life. On the question of Honesty versus Deception, individual doctors have different ways of answering such questions as "Should a patient be told the truth about a hopeless condition? Should the family?" One might answer in the affirmative, the other favor the negative, believing that "while there's life, there's hope" and that it is the physician's duty to prolong life. Although euthanasia is illegal in the U.S., it is permitted and even recommended in certain cases in England.

You must work the vying values Honesty versus Dishonesty to a premise you firmly believe. Deception proves to be wrong in Ved Mehta's *Atlantic* story "Sunset," in which the old woman's favorite son is killed in the war. The family elders vote on a white lie: If they tell her he was captured by the enemy, she can adjust to his absence and be ready for the truth when the war is over. Her young grandson is opposed to fibbing to her and he proves to be right. When she learns that they have deceived her she loses interest in living, thinking that they consider her senile.

On the other hand, a classic story about a stubborn old man who wants a grandson to carry on the family name favors deception to the tune of an effective lie. The old man is sick and attended by the same doctor retained by his pregnant daughter-in-law who already has four girls. Knowing the old man will die happy if he has a grandson, the doctor tells him the new baby is another girl. This makes him angry enough to fight and conquer death, also it gives him a new incentive to keep on living, with something to look forward to in the future. The doctor has told a lie—the baby is a boy—to save his patient's life; therefore the negative value of deception is justified because it permits a greater positive value, life, to win out over a negative power, death. Here one of the morals is "the end justifies the means."

Well-motivated deception can be a plus value in stories like Vera and Bill Cleaver's *Where the Lilies Bloom* (screenplay by Earl Hamner) in which four orphaned children pretend that their dead father, Roy Luther, is still alive so that they won't be separated and put in a foundling home. They do not do this for gain—as other characters in similar situations might pretend that a deceased person is alive in order to collect his or her Social Security, unemployment, or other payments—so their lie is not reprehensible. Instead, they keep their promise to their father to "take no charity and keep the family together." The children support themselves by collecting, processing, and selling herbs from the curative mountain plants. The values-conflict between deception and honesty is colored by the plus values of self-reliance, backbone, family love, and togetherness in contrast to the minus values of dependence on others, acceptance of charity, and the separation of devoted children.

Be sure that your motivation is equally strong in order to convince your reader that normally "wrong" behavior is justifiably "right" in a particular case. One of my students, Harry J. Santon, wrote and sold a convincing first-person story of this kind. Titled "I Cheated without Scruples," it was about a blind fellow-patient in the Veterans' Hospital who had a hunch he was going to win the big bingo game. The narrator cheated to give him the first prize, adding a "lucky" silver dollar to bolster the blind vet's confidence in his luck since he was scheduled to undergo a serious operation the next

day. This "white lie" is better than the truth because it
enables hope and confidence to triumph over fear and
despair.

In your pre-story planning, work out conflicting values
that you will build your plot around, and work them out in
different ways. Take, for instance, living in the present versus
living in the past. How many stories do you know in which the
character(s) miss out on life's opportunities because they
retreat into the past, perhaps grieving over the death of a
loved one or torturing themselves over lost opportunities or
wrong decisions?

The heroine of *Summer Wishes, Winter Dreams* tells her
husband "We are like junkies trying to get a fix from the
past." L. P. Hartley writes in his novel *The Go-Between*,
"The past is a foreign country: they do things differently
there." Since each author is a unique individual with his or
her own philosophy or message to impart, each story will
stress different values.

In a period in which nostalgia is "in," the past may be
idealized or vilified. On the contrary, how many fiction
characters or real-life people do you know who pluck valuable
lessons from the past to solve contemporary problems? General Patton in World War II studying and applying battle
strategem from the ancient Roman conquerors. Lawyers using
past cases as precedents to prosecute or defend cases. Scientists applying long-ago discoveries to modern crises, as they
studied windmills, solar power, and other ancient sources for
our energy crisis.

Think through different ways you can develop the conflict of specific values to a philosophical conclusion that
proves your own beliefs.

Take inertia versus working or wishful thinking versus
realistic doing. In Robert Altman's *Thieves Like Us* (based on
Edward Anderson's novel that Nick Ray used for his earlier
movie *They Live By Night*), we see the lazy wishful-thinking
nature of the Depression bank robber Bowie in his lines: "I
should have robbed people with my brain instead of a gun. I
should have been a doctor or a lawyer."

Laziness and lack of ambition-in-action help him to rationalize his criminal life; these same factors are also evil in many other works like Erskine Caldwell's *Tobacco Road.* Ambition combined with ruthlessness are evil in stories about characters who ride roughshod over other people in their rush to success in many books including *The Hucksters, The Partners, The Philadelphians, Poor No More*, and Richard Haley's *Saxby for God* whose ambitous, unscrupulous protagonist is very much like the anti-hero of *Room at the Top.*

Make a list of contrasting values you are interested in and conclusive premises that express your moral feelings about them. Compare with professional scripts and study how their themes work out the same values. Choose published and original plots developed from some of these:

Hope versus Despair
Brotherly Love versus Bigotry
Responsibility versus Irresponsibility
Courage versus Cowardice
Tenderness versus Violence
Forgiveness versus Revenge
Activity versus Passivity (Apathy)
Unselfishness versus Selfishness
Sincerity versus Hypocrisy
Discipline versus Indulgence (Permissiveness)
Intelligence versus Stupidity
Sensitivity versus Insensitivity
Maturity versus Immaturity
Approbation or Appreciation versus Rejection
Idealism versus Materialism
Patience versus Temper and Impatience
Resilience versus Rigidity
Optimism versus Pessimism
Patriotism versus Betrayal

Better still, write down your own selection, making sure that you choose ones pertinent to your personal philosophy and to your characters, plot action, and market. The fiction you develop in this way will have the substance and significance readers hunger for. The concretes of your story—characters, action, dialogue, and atmosphere—are to your yarn what color and taste are to food: undeniable attractions. But your abstract values and moral basics are the nutritional ingredients.

9

Bible Stories as Sources of Plots

The best seller of all times has provided plots, characters, and premises for thousands of successive best sellers because every Bible story presents plus and minus values developed into a well-plotted parable on a timeless philosophy (moral). Each has well-defined characters with specific traits and problems, and each presents dramatic conflicts between virtue and vice that are resolved in such a way as to convey meaning to all people of all times and climes.

In the clash between Obedience and Disobedience, Abraham and Job represent the former and are rewarded; whereas Eve, Adam, Lot's wife, Jacob, and Cain disobey the Good Law and are punished. Such action dramatizes the premise: "Obey the Lord and win. Disobey Him and lose."

There are several ways the Bible has served as inspiration for later works:

1. Faithful dramatization of biblical stories.
2. Musical productions· based on the Old and New Testaments.
3. Characters of the Bible embellished into more intricately plotted stories than their brief appearance in the Bible.
4. Fiction novels and stories in which biblical characters affect the imagineered ones.

129

5. Original fiction of post-Bible times, the present or the future, but with plot structures obviously taken from the Old or New Testament.

For many reasons, most professional fiction writers (including television and screen scripters, short story crafters, and novelists) eventually write something in one of the above categories—if not directly about a recognized Bible character or event, at least a work with some similarity.

First of all, stories in the Scriptures deal with every human emotion: love, hate, ambition, jealousy, greed, lust, treachery, self-sacrifice, vengeance, forgiveness, etc. Second, the values are always clearly defined, with the positive ones eventually triumphing over the negative ones—as they often do not in our daily lives. Third, the plots are suspenseful and intriguing, always evolving from clashing goals, but miraculously offering a rich variety of conflicts. Fourth, there's something for everyone: every kind of love for tender hearts and plenty of violence from personal confrontations to massive battles and world-shaking cataclysms for thicker-skinned readers and viewers. Plus, of course, many instances of sex.

Birth, love, hate, quest for life's meaning, death, resurrection, the hereafter—these are the universal basics that will always concern people, and the Bible examines each of them. Individual authors can select and/or graft onto scriptural explanations their own interpretations and philosophies. Bruce Jay Friedman's drama *Steambath* is a metaphor for the purgatory for weirdos in which neurotics must make peace with their souls before going on into the unknown. This stopover between life and death is supervised by a Puerto Rican God- or Christ-figure called "Morty" from the Spanish *morte* meaning "death."

In Arthur Miller's *The Creation of the World and Other Business*, Adam is a:

bug-eyed Brooklyn nebbish; Eve a sexless ninny until she takes a bite of the inevitable big red apple proffered her by the inevitably sly Lucifer; and God a groaner and ranter like the senior Portnoy, straining titanically over the failed expectations of his egomania [from Brendan Gill's *New Yorker* review].

The Bible has always represented the supreme authorial challenge. As Milton adapted Genesis in *Paradise Lost*, English fantasist John Collier adapted Milton in his *Milton's Paradise Lost: Screenplay for Cinema of the Mind*. Collier adds updated meanings and transfers the cosmic epic to the realm of subjective psychology and dreams that have as little substance as the motion picture screen. This does not mean that characterization is unsubstantial. God is a powerful, kind personality who has an optimistic plan for man and who experiences love and regret. Adam and Eve are a pair of gullible yokels. The author's favorite character is Satan who hangs in darkness "like a surfer awaiting the wave" while teasing both the sunset and the sunrise. Satan ". . . is the rebel against the Establishment, the defeated, the exile, the endungeoned, the resurgent and the guerrilla . . . We watch in vain for some example of his wickedness . . . He inflicts no tortures."

Masterfully and relevantly written, the oldest most often-told tales are never shopworn, never stale or outdated.

One of the greatest advantages of plotting from the Bible is a legal one. Many plagiarism and libel suits have been avoided when authors claimed they based their works on Scriptures and proved the parallels. One of many cases is the movie *The Babymaker*, which Jim Bridges wrote about a childless couple who wants a baby who is at least half theirs since they cannot have one who is 100 percent their own flesh and blood. When a sexy teen-aged hitchhiker comes into their lives and is willing to be the host mother, everyone is happy—except a screenwriter who sued, claiming they stole his plot. The plaintiff lost, of course, when the Bible was cited with barren Sarah offering her handmaiden Hagar to her husband Abraham to produce the son Ishmael.

In addition to the works cited in the lists that follow, see how many examples you can think of for the ways the Bible has served as a plot basis or inspiration for later works. Also, after rereading the Bible, try to sketch out your own ideas for fiction you would like to write in each category. What changes would you make from the original stories or characters to dramatize your own original style, thoughts, and feelings?

1. Faithful Dramatization of Biblical Stories

Except for a few changes like having Judas Iscariot jump into flames instead of hanging himself, *The Greatest Story Ever Told* (Fulton Oursler) recounts the birth, life, death, and resurrection of Christ as it appears in Scriptures.

There is also no attempt to change the original in other productions like *The King of Kings, The Sign of the Cross, The Ten Commandments, Samson and Delilah* and such television offerings as Anthony Burgess and Vittorio Bonicelli's "Moses" and the television special "The Story of Jacob and Joseph."

As in all Bible plots, this one integrates moral values with plot action and premise. At his mother's insistence, Jacob (her favorite son) cheats his older brother Esau out of his birthright. Later, he is cheated by Laban, the father of beautiful Rachel, whom Jacob loves and must work for seven years to acquire in marriage. After the elaborate wedding, he realizes that his heavily veiled bride is Rachel's older sister Leah, and poor Jacob must work an additional seven years in order to add Rachel as a wife to his household. He is further punished for having cheated his blind old father and his brother by Rachel's barrenness, although his other wives bear him many sons and daughters. When Rachel finally has a son, Joseph, Jacob repeats his own mother's sin of favoritism and so loves this youngest that he arouses the other brothers' jealousy and hatred. They sell him into slavery and tell their father that he has been killed. After years of anguish, old Jacob and his family are reconciled to Joseph who is now powerful in Egypt. Evil is punished, Joseph is vindicated.

2. Musical Productions Based on the Old and New Testaments

Perhaps the old spirituals first made us aware of the effectiveness of music power combined with Bible power. Recent box office successes include: *Jesus Christ Superstar*, the rock version of the last seven days of Christ's life, by Andrew Lloyd-Weber and Tim Rice; *Godspell*, by Stephen Schwartz and John Michael Tebelak, which retells the Gospel according to St. Matthew in such current backgrounds as Coney Island and Central Park; and Johnny and June Carter Cash's *The Gospel Road*. There are also many choral dramas like Katharine Kester's *Gloria* and the opera *Amahl and the Night Visitors* by Gian-Carlo Menotti.

Menotti created not just beautiful music but an inspiring story to add to the literature of the Nativity. Amahl is a crippled shepherd boy who lives with his impoverished mother. Their flock has dwindled to nothing when one night the Three Magi stop in their hut to rest on their journey. When Amahl asks about their journey and their gifts, they reveal their rich treasures. While they sleep, the desperate mother tries to steal some of their gold and is caught. But Balthazar (one of the Wise Men) gives her gold in the name of the Holy Child. She realizes the power of the Babe, a belief strengthened when Amahl, no longer lame, is able to walk and go with them.

Based on the Old Testament are such famous operas as *Samson and Delilah*, as well as the musicals *Green Pastures* and *Joseph and His Technicolored Dream Coat* by Tim Rice and Andrew Lloyd-Weber.

3. Characters of the Bible Embellished into More Intricately Plotted Stories than Their Appearance in the Bible

In the motion picture *Solomon and Sheba* a complex drama is built from the Bible's brief reference of the Queen of Sheba's visit to Solomon's kingdom. Conflict spikes the action as Solomon's warlike brother wants his throne and conspires with the Queen and the Pharaoh of Egypt to destroy the wise king. Sheba goes to Israel to seduce and weaken the king for defeat by the Egyptian ruler who will give her a rich port on the Red Sea in exchange. He falls in love with her to the extent of letting her practice pagan religious rites on the soil of Jerusalem, thereby angering Jehovah who destroys part of Solomon's temple and the woman who really loves him. Meanwhile Sheba has also fallen in love with him and prays to his One God, promising to forsake her pagan ones and spread His word if He'll save her lover who's in the grip of defeat. Her prayers are answered and she returns to her own land, pregnant with Solomon's child, establishing a basis for Ethiopia's claim to be the "Lion of Judah."

The same wise, romantic, poet-king is the hero of many other works including *Love and Wisdom: A Novel about Solomon*, by Richard G. Hubler who says:

> . . . what gives Solomon body in all ages is that he is eternally modern. His piety and his sins, his flauntings and his flourishings, his transgressions and triumphs, all have a taste that stays savory. His follies fit the flesh.

In our troubled times the Bible story of Job is pertinent. Archibald MacLeish uses the basic biblical plot structure and message in his play *J.B.*, which takes place in the present in a worn and tattered circus that symbolizes the world. His characters are J.B., the contemporary Job who is a highly successful businessman, and two circus vendors, Zuss and Nickles, who represent God and Satan struggling for possession of Job's soul. Following the line of the biblical test, Job loses everything in an atomic disaster. His children are dead, his fortune is lost, and his wife leaves him, advising him to renounce God and die.

When J.B. asks God for a reason and insists on knowing his own guilt that brought on the tragedies, he receives no answer. Nor is he helped by three would-be comforters: a psychiatrist, a Marxist, and a dogmatic clergyman. Desperate, he again questions God who answers from offstage with biblical quotations to the effect that mortals are not meant to know God's reasons, but are given love as compensation. When he finally accepts this fact, he regains everything he has lost.

The echoes of the Job plot reverberate throughout literature, often with tragic rather than happy endings. In Bernard Malamud's NBA and Pulitzer Prize-winning novel *The Fixer*, Yakov Bok suffers fatal indignities and tortures although he is innocent of any crimes. Fresh realistic touches are added to the novel *Mr. Theodore Mundstock* by Ladislav Fuks, with its X-plus factor of Prague, Czechoslovakia, in 1942. The protagonist is a sensitive, kindly Jew who witnesses the tragedies of all his friends who are driven either to suicide or to concentration camps. He tries to cheer some by reading them false fortunes in playing cards and attempts to prepare for his inevitable future by rehearsing for it. He sleeps on an ironing board, practices sleeplessness and starvation, taunts bullies into roughing him up, but there is no preparation for such agonizing nightmares as he must suffer before being killed.

For happier, truer-to the-Bible endings we must turn to older classics like Oliver Goldsmith's *The Vicar of Wakefield*, which follows the biblical plot pattern with an Old English setting. Here Job is the guileless, unworldly, righteous vicar, Dr. Primrose, whose wife is ambitious for her two daughters, Olivia and Sophia, and for her four sons. Financial reverses force the family to move to humble quarters near the estate of lecherous Squire Thornhill who seduces Olivia after a mock wedding. The vicar's cottage burns down, he is imprisoned for debts, Sophia is abducted, and George is thrown into prison for trying to avenge his sisters. Dr. Primrose bears all misfortunes bravely, and the vicar is rewarded in a happy ending with both daughters happily married and the villain punished.

There can always be a new emphasis or version of any familiar story. Take the Nativity story, for instance. In Frances Blazer O'Brien's *The Guardian*, the spotlight is on its protagonist, Joseph, so often all but overlooked in many treatments of the story. Joseph is a hard-working, religious youth engaged to Mary but shocked and hurt when she comes home pregnant from a visit to her cousin. He still loves her too much to expose her, but he decides to break their engagement. In a dream, an Angel of the Lord explains all to him and he is proud to become Mary's earthly husband and guardian.

So many different works have been written about Jesus—each with a different angle—that it is impossible to mention them individually. If you wish to make comparisons that stress each author's individuality, don't forget to study Richard Bach's *Jonathan Livingston Seagull* and his use of the Christ figure. For other investigation, read *The Fictional Transfigurations of Jesus* in which Theodore Ziolkowski analyzes some twenty modern novels that pattern the theme of their contemporary action on the life of Christ, including John Barth's *Giles Goat Boy* and Thomas Mann's *Magic Mountain*.

Basing a work on a biblical character or event seems to stimulate originality rather than limit it. Practically nothing is actually known about Barabbas, the thief the crowd chose to free instead of Jesus. Yet many interesting novels and plays have been written about him, including excellent ones by P. Lagerkvist and Michel de Ghelderode.

Wolf Mankowitz wrote a hilarious comedy about Jonah's quarrels with God, *It Should Happen to a Dog*, whereas the same character is treated more seriously in the novel *The Reluctant Missionary*. Several dramas about Noah portray him as a drunk and/or comic or henpecked character. Perhaps you can come up with a new angle, even updated, now that space photos reveal what look like the original Ark, and archeologists have finally obtained permission from the Turkish government to search for it on 16,916-foot Mt. Ararat!

Many authors have produced fine novels that dramatically reconstruct the lives of figures from the Bible, giving readers familiar stories with innovations in style and plot—old wine in sparkling new bottles! The list of such novels includes: Frank Slaughter's *The Song of Ruth, The Curse of Jezebel, The Galileans, The God's Warrior, The Road to Bithynia,* and *The Thorn of Arimathea*; Nora Lofts' *Esther* and *How Far to Bethlehem?*; Gladys Schmitt's *David and the King*; Lloyd Douglas' *The Big Fisherman*; and Thomas Costain's *The Silver Chalice*.

What biblical character fascinates you and embodies your philosophy so much that you would be willing to spend years of research and hard work reconstructing his or her life? Taylor Caldwell worked hard for forty-six years in writing *Dear and Glorious Physician* and reading a thousand books about the Greek doctor Lucanus who became the dedicated apostle St. Luke, even though he never met Christ and did not even come to Israel until a year after the Crucifixion. She was as intrigued by the life of Saul of Tarsus who became St. Paul, and she worked long and hard to produce her novel, *Great Lion of God.*

Shalom Asch gives his inspired, researched version of the same character in his *The Apostle.* Other of his fine novels based on biblical figures are: *Mary, Moses, The Nazarene,* and *The Prophet.*

No matter how many dedicated authors write of the same person, each work is uniquely original!

4. Fiction Novels and Stories in which Biblical Characters Affect the Imagineered Ones

We have already cited original stories in which fiction characters' lives are changed by personnages in the Bible, including *Amahl and the Night Visitors.* In addition, there have been many best-selling novels of this type, often stories of conversion and regeneration. The author's characters may be developed from his own imagination, but his research is authentic.

Lloyd C. Douglas' *The Robe* tells the story of Marcellus, a young Roman soldier who is out of favor with the official higher-ups and is sent to command Roman troops in Gaza. In a crowd in Jerusalem he is magnetized to the extraordinary man on a white donkey who has drawn the people to him and who gives the Roman an unforgettable look. Later, Marcellus leads a detachment to officiate at an execution and sees the same man dying on Golgotha. The Roman soldiers cast dice for His garments and Marcellus wins the brown robe, and with it the spiritual awareness that leads him to study Christ's teachings and miracles and to reject the Roman pagan gods for the New One.

Another conversion story that has been popular in book and motion picture form ever since Lew Wallace wrote it at the beginning of this century is *Ben Hur.* The fictionized conflicts between cruel, conquering Romans and the victims, the people of Judea, and the specific clashes between the ambitious Roman Messala and the peace-loving but strong-willed Judah Ben-Hur are all affected by the Mystical Figure who gives Ben-Hur water on his way to the galleys (plus the spirit to survive). Later when He is on the way to Calvary, Judah helps Him and gives Him water, thus causing the miracle of healing of his leprous mother and sister.

5. *Original Fiction of Post-Bible Times, the Present or the Future, but with Plot Structures Taken from the Old or New Testament*

Many authors proudly acknowledge their debt to the Bible in otherwise extremely original novels like Leon Uris's *Exodus*, about efforts to save some Jews from the Hitlerian holocaust and bring them to the Promised Land of Israel. A. R. Gurney, Jr.'s *The Gospel According to Joe* is the life of Christ in contemporary terms including Woman's Lib, Volkswagons, and today's politics; Joe's courtship and marriage to Mary and the birth of their son in a barn belonging to a commune are obvious borrowings from the New Testament story.

Judith recalls the beautiful ancient Jewish widow who saved her beseiged people by slaying Assyrian General Holofernes, without whose leadership his army was routed. In the modern version, the Jewish heroine achieves vengeance on her Nazi husband who had sent her to concentration camp and is now an adviser to Arab enemies threatening Israel.

John Steinbeck's novel *East of Eden* takes its title and theme from Genesis (as was cited in Chapter 5, "Quotations —Rich Source of Plots") but takes place in Steinbeck's Salinas lettuce-country at the outbreak of World War I. Adam Trask is the righteous father-God figure who constantly quotes Scriptures but obviously misses its lesson on favoritism. He has always preferred his goody-goody son Aaron (Abel) to Cal (Cain), whom he considers evil like his mother. No matter how much Cal tries to please his father, the latter thinks he's as bad as Kate (Eve), who succumbed to temptation and left Adam and the boys for a more exciting life, although idealistic Aaron thinks she died at his birth and is an angel in heaven. After Adam loses his lettuce crop, Cal determines to make something of himself and give his father the money he lost. With World War I in the offing, he sees a chance for big profit speculating in beans. He borrows $5,000 from his mother who now owns a brothel in Monterey and succeeds in making the money, which he gives to Adam on his birthday.

Like God refusing Cain's offerings "of the fruit of the ground" and preferring Abel's offerings "of the firstlings of his flock," Adam rejects Cal's money, cursing it as immoral "blood money"—the profit of war and human suffering. He again blesses his "good" son and his forthcoming marriage. In jealous anger Cal doesn't kill Aaron physically, but he tells him the truth about their mother and forces Aaron to face her in her degradation. Resulting crisis: The shock sends Aaron into drunkenness, a violent brawl, and enlistment to go off to war, all of which gives his adoring father, Adam, a paralytic stroke. After these crises, Aaron's fiancée, who by now loves Cal, convinces both father and son that good and evil are not two solid white and black absolutes, but that love is the factor that accounts for character and behavior. She says, "Being unloved is the worst thing in the world. It makes you mean and vicious." We know that Cal has been "bad" because he was rejected and unloved. With the love of his father and his own wife he will be a good man.

Each Christmas sees a number of publications using stories with a Nativity-based theme—perhaps concerning a couple who is evicted, then given a home; or concerning people divided by hate who learn the lesson of love. Characters, background, action, and style may differ to create originality.

In one *Redbook* story a teen-age mixed marriage is unblessed by the Catholic and Jewish parents. The baby is due and the young couple is broke, homeless, and desperate in a bus station. The restless, immature husband deserts his wife but later returns.

Entirely different is Lois Duncan's short short story "Heavenly Child," in which a Caucasian American couple has adopted a Korean child Kim but doesn't know how the little girl really feels about their racial differences and whether or not she really considers the three of them a whole family unit. When they go to the kindergarten for Christmas festivities, there are other minorities there, but Black, Oriental, and Chicano families at least "match" within their own units. The parents' apprehension is erased when Kim shows them her artwork: a Nativity scene in which a blond couple gaze adoringly down at their Holy Oriental Babe!

How many examples of modern fiction can you think of in which a character is restored to a normal, active life after being "buried" in prison, an institution, the wilderness, or in a state of blindness, deafness, lameness, drug addiction, alcoholism, prostitution or (?) ? In some cases the plot structure seems more like Paul's conversion or Mary Magdalene's regeneration, but the formula is definitely reminiscent of the Scriptures and the many stories of the Resurrection or of reviving the dead (see Mark 5:35-43; Luke 7:11-17; John 11:1-44).

In the television drama "The Hanged Man" by Ken Trevey, the "Lazarus" touch gives a new twist to a Western. A gunman is hanged, pronounced dead, and then miraculously lives. Several different people shoot at him yet he doesn't die. Instead, he turns "good guy" and goes around helping people, especially a defenseless widow whose mine the villains are trying to get. Throughout the action, his character reminds you of Lazarus, the Lone Ranger, and Jesus, until the end in which there's a fire and he's surrounded in reds, suggesting that he might be the Devil! You might call this an "open end" plot!

Other parallels to biblical characters can be found throughout modern fiction, but these few examples simply demonstrate the debt many authors owe to the Bible.

Do not use the pros' trick of plotting from the Bible out of laziness, thinking "I won't have to work as hard if I use characters, plots, or other elements that are already there." On the contrary, you must work very hard in order to improve upon the Best Seller of all time. But you *can* renovate and reslant many of Scriptures' timeless tales to markets that were undreamed of in Biblical times.

Whether you start with your own ideas that are crying for

a substantial plot structure or whether you begin with a character or story from Scriptures, analyze its five major ingredients and seriously plan which you will change and how:

Character traits
Plot action from problem to solution
Premise(s)
Setting or X-plus factor
Style

Then evaluate your material from every possible angle as a photographer or artist studies a landscape from every view before representing it to the best advantage to express his meaning.

One of the most popular formats is that of David and Goliath. Everyone can identify with the "little guy" facing a formidable enemy because at some time or other everybody is an underdog who must joust with giants to survive, certainly in the success jungle. Here are a few examples: an individual of a minority group fighting for a place in a majority society; a child in opposition to the restraints of an adult establishment; a woman in a man's world (yesterday's suffragette or today's woman in politics, medicine, law, the military, sports, or any male bastion); a divorcee or parolee who is discriminated against; an inventor or explorer whose ideas are ahead of his time; a reformer, crusader or any far-sighted individualist— these are just a few of the dramatic possibilities for your David. The giant could even be impersonal like a corrupt government or society, or an abstract antagonist like drug, alcohol, or gambling addiction. Choose subject matter you know well and graft your original ideas onto the perennial David and Goliath drama.

No protagonist is dearer to the reader's heart than the virtuous underdog who pits his feeble forces against an overpowering vice just as the brave shepherd boy of Bethlehem used only his sling and five smooth stones to attack Goliath of Goth.

One of the most obvious applications of this ancient formula to a modern novel is Ann Fairbairn's *Five Smooth*

Stones, an impassioned attack on racism. Her David is a young Negro who leaves New Orleans to go North to college and to Harvard Law School, then on to Oxford in England. Having conquered many Goliaths of. prejudice, he finally turns down a State Department post in Africa to fight for civil rights. This brave, Black David's five smooth stones are wisdom, skill, dedication, nonviolence, and love, and his battle is as unevenly matched and suspenseful as the ancient one fought in the Bible story.

Some writers stick exclusively to this formula. Franz Werfel used it frequently with strikingly different backgrounds. In his play, *Juarez and Maximilian*, the underdog Mexican-Indian fights to free his people from the all-powerful conquerors; in *The 40 Days of Musa Dogh*, an Armenian David fights the Turks; and his heroine of *The Song of Bernadette*, like Joan of Arc, is pitted against The Establishment *and* disbelief.

You can plot the David and Goliath formula four different ways, the decision depending upon your material, market, purpose, and mood (tragedy or comedy):
1. David conquers Goliath.
2. David is conquered by Goliath.
3. David conquers Goliath but eventually becomes a Goliath who threatens a new David.
4. David is physically conquered by Goliath, but is undefeated morally and spiritually.

1. *David conquers Goliath*

This is, of course, the most frequent version, since the happy ending shows the virtuous "little guy" defeating gigantic villainy. You could pattern fiction characters after individualists in every field of interest, for instance: Picasso, Van Gogh, and Modigliani in art; Wagner, Shostakovich, and Stravinsky in music; Frank Lloyd Wright in architecture; Jackie Robinson in baseball; Disraeli or Ghandi in politics; Louis Pasteur, Pierre and Marie Curie, Jonas Salk, and Paul Ehrlich in medicine; and numberless others. Eva Gladney's fight against society's prejudice against illegitimacy was beautifully dramatized in *Blossoms in the Dust*. You can think of thousands of other fiction and real-life stories in which the brave, good hero is seemingly overpowered by opposition but eventually triumphs. In the old days of "children should be seen and not heard" and the Dickens era of "children should be exploited," the child was often the innocent David pitting pitiable forces against adult authority, teachers, or cruel society itself, as in the case of *Oliver Twist, David Copperfield*, and Charlotte Bronte's *Jane Eyre*. In recent literature the teacher is more likely to play the David role in opposition to a Goliath-like, incorrigible group of toughs, as in E. R. Braithwaite's *To Sir with Love*, Bel Kaufman's *Up the Down Staircase*, Evan Hunter's *The Blackboard Jungle*, or John Shaner's *Halls of Anger*.

Make a list of all the courageous little Davids you can think of, real or imaginary, who have fought or are fighting Goliaths in any field. Concentrate on characterizing your favorite underdog-hero who may be fighting taxation, cartels, air or water pollution, unhealthy or unfair conditions in hospitals, schools, or prisons, or who is in some phase of social or welfare work—whatever field is familiar to you.

Your hero could be fighting an affliction. Recently in my own community, three blind men have conquered gigantic difficulties to become, respectively, a high school teacher, a priest, and a college newspaper editor. The latter was blinded in a shotgun accident when he was eight and was given only three chances in 10,000 of surviving. Although permanently blinded, he concentrated on obtaining a good education, specializing in the visual field of journalism, and excelling. At his college, degrees were recently won by lady-Davids: a deaf-and-dumb mother and a senior citizen grandmother.

In *Death Wish* (novel by Brian Garfield, screenplay by Wendell Mayes) the hero fights the gigantic situation of crime and muggers in New York City.

2. *David is conquered by Goliath*

The majority of these stories are about victims of totalitarianism, like the selfless Swedish diplomat, Roul Wallenberg, who saved many Hungarian Jews from Nazi extermination, only to be imprisoned by Communists, his fate still unknown, though Soviets claim he died "of a heart attack" in a Russian jail. Kafka's famous novel *The Trial* predated and prophesied the many Goliath-conquers-innocent-David dramas, both true and fictionized that were to appear all over Europe after the author's death.

But long before Kafka or John Hersey's *The Wall* appeared, one finds Herman Melville's *Billy Budd*, the story of a good man who was forced to succumb to the pressures of a sadistic system. Winston Smith and Julia are eventually destroyed by Big Brother's totalitarian government in George Orwell's *1984*; the courageous deaf-mute, John Singer, is defeated in Carson McCullers' *The Heart is a Lonely Hunter*, producing the depressing effect you find in most tragedies; and Montag is conquered by a cruel dictatorship in Bradbury's *Farenheit 451*.

3. *David conquers Goliath but eventually becomes a Goliath who threatens a new David*

There are elements of this in the Bible story in which the humble shepherd boy becomes a tyrant, as well as in more contemporary political or labor stories in which the "little guy" becomes a bully in his bigness. In Robert Penn Warren's *All the King's Men*, Willie Stark was originally a brave David defying a corrupt building contractor and graft. After he triumphs and becomes governor, he is as corrupt or perhaps more so than the evils that he originally opposed.

How many examples come to your mind of the persecuted becoming the persecutor? A rookie on a team may have to fight many Goliaths: management, his experienced teammates, the opposition, the press, etc. Then he can become a bigshot and be even tougher with a new David. This format could work in a story with a college, teen gang, or POW background, or many other situations. Peter Ustinov's hero in *The Loneliness of Bolliwonga* is a former concentration camp inmate who later becomes a Goliath to an ex-Nazi living in Australia.

4. *David is physically conquered by Goliath, but is undefeated morally and spiritually*

Ibsen's *An Enemy of the People* has an excellent David and Goliath plot foundation for you to build upon, adding, of course, your own variations. The outnumbered, overpowered individual who fights for what he knows is right, refusing to compromise his integrity for gain or approbation can be the hero of hundreds of timely as well as timeless situations.

In the original play, Dr. Stockman, a brilliant but naive scientist, has been a town hero, for he discovered that the local water had healthy mineral properties and now its health baths have made it a prosperous tourist center. Now he learns that the wastes from a nearby tannery are polluting the baths. He plans to make his findings public and demands that the condition be corrected, expecting the community to be delighted with his honesty. But the town turns against him for threatening its prosperity. Even his friends who know he's right turn against him because their businesses are threatened by irate, mercenary citizens.

Dr. Stockman makes a desperate appeal in a public meeting but the mob opposes him violently. Unable to understand its fear and anger or to compromise his ideals, he is completely isolated and deserted by all but his family. By the end of the play, his daughter has lost her fiancé, and his younger children have been driven from school. But he courageously plans to start his own school for sidewalk urchins, his own Head Start and War on Poverty. He concludes the play with: "The strongest man in the world is the man who stands alone." David has conquered Goliath spiritually, if not physically.

All of Ibsen's Davids who are not spiritually defeated by Goliaths are not men. Nora Helmer, in *A Doll's House*, fights the formidable man-dominated society that keeps woman a pretty, mindless toy for man's amusement. When Nora closes the door to her doll's house, leaving Torvald and her children in order to seek a life where she can be more than a doll, she strikes a David-versus-Goliath blow as significant as the battles of Susan B. Anthony, Elizabeth Cady Stanton, and the other suffragettes, perhaps more, since Swedish women were given the vote long before those in America.

Any one of a number of contemporary situations can be a Goliath for your David to oppose—the newer, the better. Editors prefer an old formula in new dress, particularly an up-to-date controversy, well researched and authentically presented so that the reader feels he's peeking "behind the scenes" and learning something special while being entertained.

Your David could be fighting the building of a nuclear power plant that will bring such prosperity and prestige to a community that the brainwashed public is strongly in favor of it. The Goliaths have used mass media—television, newspapers, radio, billboards, etc.—and special giveaways and gala parties to win the community to their side. Perhaps your fictional David could be patterned after a real man like Cal Tech engineer J. E. McKee, professor of environmental health, who warns of the dangers of building nuclear power plants on Bolsa Island in California and on the Great Lakes. You can get fiction ideas from his own words:

> Rivers have a fortunate facility for flushing themselves, but the replacement of water in many lakes may take an almost interminable time. The Great Lakes are especially vulnerable.
> At the present time, 10 large nuclear power plants are being built or planned on the shores of Lake Michigan.
> If any one of them should ever have an accident and release millions of curies of mixed, long-lived fission products into Lake Michigan, the impact on this water resource would be catastrophic.

Your hero could add other dangers that can be set off by an earthquake, tidal wave, tornado, instrument failure, human error, or sabotage, or from a break in the pumps or pipelines.

You should write about a field that you know thoroughly.

This is just one example of the many current situations that are "naturals" as Goliaths who jeopardize a community that a courageous but lonely David could be trying, against odds, to defend.

Many Bible stories could be adapted for children. Elijah appeals to youth because it's easy to think of him as the first astronaut. You could develop a fantasy, science fiction, or time-travel yarn, such as Ray Russell's short-short story, "Ripples," in which ancient earth is visited by spacemen who decide not to land because the quarreling people of biblical times are not yet spiritual enough for contact with them.

A more down-to-earth fantasy about Elijah is Uri Shule-vitz' effective juvenile book *The Magician*, which tells the Peretz tale of an impoverished Jewish ghetto family who do not have the proper food for the Passover seder. But their kindness in inviting a stranger to share the little they do have is rewarded when the visitor turns out to be Elijah who performs the miracle of supplying bountiful provisions.

Whether your Bible-related script is beamed toward children or adults, you will find those important ingredients mentioned in the last chapter—values—implicit in all your plots.

10

The Cinderella Plot

Sexism in plot concept?

Yes, before Woman's Lib! Several authors used to agree with F. Scott Fitzgerald who said there are only two basic stories: the passive, female Cinderella plot and the active, masterful, male Jack-the-Giant-Killer format.

Novelist Paul Wellman classified all plots as either Male or Female, insisting that: "The story of the Doer is the Male plot. In Jack the Giant-Killer, the fictional male conquers every crisis that occurs. The Female plot is that of the Endurer, so-called because women are gifted with the ability to take it. They outlive men and are tough beneath their soft exteriors."

Today we realize that the Movement has freed Cinderella possibly more than the rest of her sisters because, even though readers will always love the "miracle" touch and the "rags to riches" formula with its happy ending, now she must be *active* in bringing it about.

Contrary to the fairy-tale heroine, today's Cindy must do more than household chores to make her dreams come true, working and training in her chosen field, which is not just marriage.

After many years of hard work practicing and singing

with minor opera companies, forty-five-year-old Brooklyn-
born soprano Klara Barlow scored success starring in *Tristan
and Isolde* at the Met.

With fidelity to the legend, *Time* opened its feature,
"Tristan and Cinderella" with:

> The obscure opera singer is kneeling on the floor of a small
> apartment in Munich. Before her lie cloth and scissors. She is making
> her own costume for another night's work in another small town.
> Suddenly, word arrives that in Manhattan the fabled Metropolitan
> Opera desperately needs a soprano in Wagner's *Tristan and Isolde*.
> Off goes our heroine in her Lufthansa pumpkin and lands the job.
> The audiences love her. So do the critics. The *New York Times*
> announces on page one: "A Triumph at the Met."

Crisis, of course, is a necessary ingredient in any story. In
this one, instead of a curfew that separates Cindy from the
Prince and reverses finery into rags, the Met almost closed
when tenor Jon Vickers bowed out of singing the first two per-
formances, conductor Erich Leinsdorf threatened to resign,
and other troubles occurred. But such obstacles make the
happy ending even sweeter.

Cinderella Liberty, by Darryl Ponicsan, offers a double
reminder of the famous fairy tale:

(1) The title is navy slang for a shore leave that ends at
midnight. In this story, Johnny's records are lost and he is let
loose in Seattle on Shore Patrol duty (without pay) until they
are found.

(2) Johnny, the hero, has a "Cinderella" personality:
kind, gentle, compassionate, obedient, (today known as
"square"). He befriends Maggie, a pregnant prostitute, and
her eleven-year-old mulatto son and even tries to marry her in
order to help her financially. Red tape creates a snafu and,
after other complications, Maggie, like Cinderella, flees (in
this case to New Orleans). By the time Johnny's papers are
found and he gets his back pay ($5,000), he realizes he wants
to go after Maggie instead of returning to naval duty. His
wishes are granted not by a fairy godmother but by another
ex-navy man who is eager to go back to sea and returns to

Johnny's ship with his papers as his replacement. There is a *Porgy and Bess*-like ending with Johnny going to New Orleans to find his Princess, taking her son along.

"Cinderella" has become a byword in our language. Even a man who catapults from unknown to well-known can be referred to as a "Cinderella." The world was as thrilled when commoner Captain Mark Phillips married Britain's Princess Anne as when, years before, Grace Kelly married Prince Rainier.

Inanimate objects are also sometimes classified as "Cinderellas." Here is an example of an article titled "The Cinderellas Have Aged but the Wooing Goes On and On." It opens with:

> Some men can't resist a Cinderella, especially one not so young anymore and one which has developed lots of character. Airmen are the worst. Show some flyers a middle-aged Aeronca with battered wings and holes in her head and right away they'll come on like the prince with the glass slipper. Planes are simply sweethearts to some guys and they have a love affair with them.

No matter what, who, where, or when the situation or circumstances, the Cinderella idea is bound to crop up in some frame of reference. Knowing this, you might consider this perennially popular formula as a substantial basis upon which you can graft your own original thoughts. Then, hopefully, you can produce a script that will answer a specific editor's, publisher's, or producer's question: "What will our new Cinderella story be?"

Each national literature has its own version of the sweet girl who is abused and overworked by her jealous stepsisters and stepmother who sadistically taunt her, glorify their ugly selves, and try to land the handsome, wife-seeking Prince. Whether the slipper Cinderella leaves behind when finery turns to rags is glass, fur, feathers, or vinyl-plastic, or whatever, there are similar characterizations of virtue oppressed by villainy and premises and plot lines that progress through several frustrations to a happy ending.

Cinderella in American Indian Literature

Long before any Europeans came to our continent there was a legend among eastern Canadian Indians in which a Prince uses the character trait of truth to choose his Princess—rather than using the standard material gimmick. As in many Indian legends, Nature plays a prominent role.

The beautiful Indian Cinderella is cruelly treated by her jealous older sisters who dress her in rags, cut off her long, black hair and burn her face with coals to make her ugly. They tell their father that she has done these things to herself and is demented. But she patiently and cheerfully goes about her work.

Strong-Wind-the-Invisible, the Prince equivalent, lives with his sister in a tent near the sea. He announces that he will marry the girl who can see him as he comes home from work. He makes himself invisible to everyone but his sister, and when each of a series of girls tells her she has seen him, the sister asks "With what does he draw his sled?" Each lies, saying such things as: "with the hide of a moose," "with a pole," and "with a great cord." Other questions produce equal fibs that disqualify many girls, including the cruel sisters.

Everyone laughs at Cinderella's burnt face and tattered rags as she walks miles to try her luck. When Strong-Wind's sister asks her if she sees him, she replies "No." Later, when the question is repeated, she says, "Yes, and he is very wonderful!" When asked "With what does he draw his sled?" she says, "With the rainbow." When questioned "Of what is his bowstring?" she replies, "His bowstring is the Milky Way."

Her honesty and patience are rewarded when Strong-Wind's sister heals her scars, dresses her in finery, and presents her to Strong-Wind who promptly marries the Truthful One. He also turns her sadistic sisters into aspen trees who thereafter tremble whenever Strong-Wind approaches.

Cinderella in Oriental Literature

Since family devotion is a strong theme in most Oriental literature, vengeance rarely occurs no matter how badly the stepsisters treat the heroine. After the abused Japanese Cinderella marries the Prince, she usually brings her cruel sisters to court and helps them find wealthy, noble husbands!

The Chinese Peking opera *Phoenix Returns* has a less ecstatic but happy "togetherness" ending. Sweet, lovely, intelligent Phoenix (Cindy) has only one half-sister who is ugly and mischievous enough for two. When the Prince comes to woo and become engaged to the famously beautiful Phoenix whom he has not yet seen, the ugly girl obnoxiously breaks into his room and tells him she is Phoenix, hoping he'll marry her. Instead, he runs away to the war in which the girls' father is a general. Meanwhile Phoenix is courted by a conniving clown who convinces her that he is the Prince to whom she is betrothed. She flees to her father's camp. On the wedding day, the imposter marries a heavily-veiled bride whom he thinks is Phoenix—but who is really the ugly sister who thinks she is marrying the Prince. After the ceremony and discovery, they are furious but must agree that they deserve each other. Meanwhile Phoenix and the Prince have met and fallen in love and ask the general to marry them. A happy family reunion ends the opera.

Another Chinese Cinderella is *Lady Precious Stream* who is dominated by two cruel older sisters and their ambitious husbands. Instead of a Prince, lovely Precious Stream loves a simple gardener who performs great feats to marry her, but who continues to be snubbed by her snobbish family. When he is sent away on a military expedition and is gone for eighteen years and believed dead, she remains faithful and hopeful. She searches for him far away and her virtue is finally rewarded when she finds him and they are reunited.

From Ancient to Modern Cinderellas

It's a long way from centuries-old legends to Hollywood Academy Award winners, but the universal appeal of the Cinderella plot never seems to diminish. It forms the basic structure of many hits like *My Fair Lady, Born Yesterday, Bells Are Ringing* and one of the world's greatest film successes, *The Sound of Music*. All are variations of the Cinderella plot.

Eliza Doolittle, the lowly Cockney flower girl who charms

high society at the ball and gets her Prince (in fact, two!) is a definite Cinderella, even though you can trace the roots of *My Fair Lady* also to G. B. Shaw's *Pygmalion* whose roots go back to the ancient Greek myth about the sculptor who carved a beautiful ivory statue. The original Greek Pygmalion fell in love with his work of art, Galatea, just as Henry Higgins eventually does with his perfected creation, Eliza.

In *My Fair Lady*, the roles of the Fairy Godmother and the Prince are telescoped into one character, Higgins, who is not only the means to the end but the end itself. He not only helps Eliza achieve culture and status but also turns out to be the love interest she wants.

This is true, also, of another mental Cinderella story, Garson Kanin's *Born Yesterday*. Billie Dawn is educationally, not materially, impoverished, and Paul Verrall, the tutor hired to help her gain knowledge, also becomes the object of her love.

Like the classic Cinderella and *My Fair Lady*, *Bells Are Ringing* also builds up to "The Ball." Mrs. Grimaldi is the Fairy Godmother who gives Ella such a gorgeous red dress that she is transformed into a real beauty who meets, attracts, but runs away from her "Prince," playwright Jeffrey Moss, whom she has fallen in love with on the phone. (She works at an answering service and becomes vicariously involved with her clients' problems.)

All these and many other Cinderella variations end happily after the heroine runs away from the Prince (always with good reason) and he finds her again.

Variations are always added to the classic fairy tale. For a juvenile story you don't need a Prince or romance. You could write about a poor child (ethnic minority perhaps) who, through perseverance and patience, achieves a goal. One example is *Lillie of Watts: A Birthday Discovery* by Mildred Pitts Walter. You could develop a story about a poor, hard-working child who is elected to an office at school, honored for bravery, honesty, or for some special talent or skill.

For a teen market the boy-girl angle is preferable. Your heroine could be unable to go to the Prom because of illness or duties at home, lack of proper clothes or other motivation, but she eventually attracts her Prince because of her conscientiousness. In one of my 'Teen magazine stories, the high school boy is taunted by the "In" crowd as a kook because of his way-out inventions and ridiculed as a "square" when he refuses money for them, preferring to donate them to worthy causes. But the very qualities that make him the butt of their jokes eventually win him recognition and the Princess.

Your protagonist—adult, child, or pet—could work hard, but have someone else take the credit or glory while he or she is forced to stay in the background. A different type of character could represent the Fairy Godmother who helps your protagonist obtain the deserved recognition and goal. Use whatever X-plus factor (background) you know well: farming, social work, teaching, real estate, acting, dancing, nursing, flying, engineering, sports, bookkeeping, politics, office politics, police work, medicine, or whatever you can use authentically.

Build strong characters who are capable of performing on the Cinderella trapeze. Your own story can soar and sparkle in many ways without being an exact duplicate. There is no Prince or Fairy Godmother in Paul Gallico's popular Mrs. 'Arris novels about the poor London charwoman whose travel dreams come true so that she escalates from her lowly status to ladylike heights. For a market interested in careers or Women's Lib, the strived-for and attained "Prince" may be a position, political office, honor, or trip instead of a person. For the confession magazines, Cinderella would be rewarded with a kind, hard-working, considerate man, realistic for the low-income readers.

Of course Cinderella doesn't have to be a girl or woman. Every Horatio Alger success yarn follows this format. So do other male Cinderella plots that have been popular since Fielding's Tom Jones or such Dickens stories as Oliver Twist in which the long-suffering, abused boy eventually achieves wealth and position. The motion picture Cinderfella presents a Fairy Godfather as well as a male hero and clever updating and satirical humor, but it follows the fairy tale's plot line faithfully.

Many Cinderella plots are so switched around that you may not recognize them at first. Others are amazingly identical, but readers will always love the miracle, rags-to-riches idea.

A recent novel is similar to the first English novel ever written. Catherine Cookson's *Katie Mulholland* is an English Cinderella who suffers multiple tribulations. As a scullery maid in the kitchen of a rich, rapacious mine owner, she bears an illegitimate child, but eventually finds her loving Prince, Andrew, who helps her become one of the richest, most powerful women in Newcastle. Katie's climb from poverty to wealth, from degradation to respectability, from misery to happiness, and from weakness to power is reminiscent of Richardson's *Pamela*, which is also about a long-suffering, exploited domestic who finally marries her Prince.

Necessary Changes in Modern Cinderella Fiction

The most important change is replacing the original Cinderella's *passivity* with *active* efforts to solve her problem. This is a must today! Readers do not admire or wish to identify with a crybaby, doormat character who waits for someone else or some supernatural power to solve her or his problem. Analyze new versions of the Cinderella plot to see how actively responsible for their own success modern Cinderellas are—and how much more interesting they are for it.

In *The Sound of Music*, Maria is the sweet, good postulant who wants to serve the Lord at Nonnberry Abbey, Austria, in 1938. But she is so exuberant, music- and nature-loving that she often breaks the strict rules against singing in the Abbey. If she had been as meek and sad-sack as the fairy-tale prototype, she would have fit in better at the convent where she would have stayed forever, never meeting the Prince.

Because she is so childlike and happy, the Mother Abbess, playing the role of the Fairy Godmother, sends Maria to the home of widower Captain Georg von Trapp to care for his seven children. She does this so brilliantly that she regenerates them from rebels into happy, well-adjusted youngsters.

The rival roles of the wicked stepsisters trying to capture

the Prince are telescoped into a more serious competitor in the
person of Trapp's beautiful fiancée, Elsa Schraeder, who is as
conniving as the original wicked stepsisters in trying to
eliminate Cinderella from the contest. But this villainess cannot triumph against such virtue, especially with Fairy Godmother Abbess on our heroine's side. Not only does she send
Maria back to the Prince after the girl leaves because of her
"earthly" love for him and the children, but she also explains
that God can be served through many different kinds of love,
not just spiritual. The oft-repeated Cinderella formula is
freshened and made more exciting by subplots in which the
Nazi takeover of Austria represents a threat to the family
from which the Mother Abbess and her Sisters save them. Such
extra embellishments plus the delightful musical score en-
thrall millions in spite of the antiquity of the roots of this
rainbow.

How many other examples of embellished Cinderella
plots can you find in addition to: Margery Sharp's *Cluny
Brown*, the British servant who doesn't stay in "her place"
and helps the author satirize social stratification and High
Society; Truman Capote's Holly Golightly, who rises from
Poor White Trash to glamorous comfort in *Breakfast at Tif-
fany's;* and Theodora, the prostitute who becomes the world's
most powerful empress, not by being passively patient but by
using shrewd cleverness and ingenuity to overcome tremen-
dous obstacles (in Paul Wellman's *The Female*)?

Make your Cinderella as exciting as *The Unsinkable
Molly Brown*—another modern Cindy!

You must give your Cinderella dimensional traits so that
she's not too goody-goody and therefore hard for the average
reader to identify with. In addition to having some character
flaw(s), she must *change* throughout the story, developing a
philosophy that will form the premise or raison d'être of your
yarn. For instance, the heroine of Rona Jaffe's *The Best of
Everything* is gullible and foolish enough to fall in love with a
deceitful cad who gets her pregnant and deludes her into
thinking he's taking her to be married when, in truth, he's
driving her to an abortionist. When she learns the truth, she

tries to jump out of the moving car and is seriously injured, losing the baby. Throughout the tragic crisis, she meets, falls in love with, and is loved by the good doctor who, of course, represents the Prince.

The versatility of the basic format is unlimited and the more surprises and fresh twists and reversals you add, the better.

In Warner Law's *Playboy* yarn, "The Thousand-Dollar Cup of Crazy German Coffee," Cinderella is a seemingly minor character and the emphasis is placed on the men: Faubus R. Broffman, a retired California millionaire and struggling Dr. Roberto Cajiao-Cigliuti of Cali, Colombia. Through a Person-to-Person Magazine Exchange Committee, the American sends the Colombian doctor magazines and confesses his love for good coffee, which he grinds, roasts, and blends as a hobby.

Roberto is impressed by the wealth of Broffman, whom *Time* calls "a financial genius." A friendly correspondence ensues. The doctor sends his nineteen-year-old movie-struck fiancée, Maria, to visit Broffman in Hollywood where she ecstatically wallows in wealth and hobnobs with stars and other VIPs. Roberto writes Broffman of a superior aphrodisiac "Crazy German Coffee" that grows high in the Andes and gets $1,000 from him to finance an expedition to get it. Maria is such a hit at the prolonged "Ball" that she marries Broffman who gives her $25,000 as a wedding gift. At first Roberto sends angry telegrams and letters, but he recovers from the loss of Maria and writes Broffman that the expedition's helicopter crashed and the only survivor has a small amount of the precious coffee, which he sends to the older American.

Maria then telegraphs Roberto that her husband died of a heart attack after drinking the coffee and that she is his sole heir and will marry her handsome chauffeur. Roberto sends her many angry, unanswered letters demanding his 50-50 cut and reminding her that he masterminded the whole plot that made her rich. Finally she sends him $12,500 (half of her wedding money) but refuses to send him any more of her millions. She tells him he can't intimidate her because she has kept all his letters about the phony coffee and even has some of the poisoned grounds in a bottle as evidence against him.

In revenge, he writes to the L.A. Chief of Police, informing him of Maria's guilt in Broffman's murder, which he explains was caused by digitoxin in the coffee. Gloatingly, he flies to California to reap rich rewards, but he is arrested at the airport and told there was no murder. Maria had warned her husband of the poisoned coffee and her subsequent correspondence was planned to spur Roberto's confession.

All the while the reader thought Maria was a conniving gold digger, she was really an innocent Cinderella manipulated by the mercenary Roberto. Cleverly, she not only stays happily married to her Prince, but also wreaks vengeance on her exploiter, who is a stronger villain than the original stepmother and stepsisters combined.

The more changes, reversals, and surprises you can add to any basic formula, the more it will become *your own story!*

11

The Faust Plot

"I'd give anything for . . . ." "I'd sell my soul for . . . ." "I'd give ten years of my life just to . . . ." These are such familiar phrases when someone desperately wants something beyond his reach that there's a perennial appeal to the Faust plot.

The real plot action of George Abbott's play and movie *Damn Yankees* (based on the book, *The Day the Yankees Lost the Pennant*) begins when Joe, a middle-aged baseball fan, watches his favorite team dip lower in its losing streak and wails, "I'd sell my soul for one long-ball hitter!" This conjures up Mr. Applegate, who is really Satan offering to fulfill his wish—at an exorbitant price, of course. Years before this, unlucky Jabez Stone, impoverished and about to lose his farm, says "It's enough to make a man sell his soul to the Devil and for two cents I would!" There appears Scratch (Satan) who offers him seven years of prosperity if he'll sign a contract relinquishing his soul, which the desperate farmer does (Stephen Vincent Benét's *The Devil and Daniel Webster*).

Temptation has been a problem ever since the Garden of Eden when Eve, the forerunner of Faust, succumbed to Satan's representative. The ancient formula is popular today when there's so much interest in the occult and so much corruption in high places. There is a general wave of suspicion of people in power and a tendency for the average man to ask "How did _____ get in that high position which I can never attain? To what Devil did he sell his soul?" There have been so many retellings of the Faust legend that you should study the details and development of as many as you can find and try to come up with something fresh and timely, adding your own original accoutrements. As you analyze each, isolate its individual:

> Characterization
> Plot
> Premise
> Setting or X-plus factor
> Style

Characterization

The Faust and Devil roles are reversed in Irwin Shaw's *Two Weeks in Another Town* and in John Collier's short story "The Right Side," in which Mephistopheles is a good influence who regenerates and saves Faust.

There is a clever detail in *Damn Yankees* that makes the happy ending possible. The old baseball fan, Joe (the Faust), is a real estate man, and when Devil Applegate makes his proposition Joe won't consider a contract that doesn't have an "escape clause," so there's an agreement that he can back out of the deal if he wants to at midnight on December 24!

Ira Levin's *Rosemary's Baby* adds freshness to characterization by a different viewpoint approach. We are in the feelings of the innocent wife who at first doesn't know what her Faust-like husband is up to, which intensifies the suspense. Her husband, Guy Woodhouse, wants success in the theater as much as the medieval Faust wanted youth, love, and knowledge. He makes a Faustian pact with Roman and Minnie Castevets who are modern witch-equivalents of the Devil. In exchange for star status, he delivers up his innocent wife Rosemary for impregnation by Satan to produce a devil-child. Supernaturally removed obstacles to his goal are the sudden blinding of rival actor Donald Baumgart, the suicide of Terry before she can warn Rosemary, and the death of Edward Hutchins before he can help free her from the spell. In the teleplay "The Devil's Daughter," the viewpoint of an innocent victim is also used for added suspense. A terrified young woman learns her soul was sold to the Devil by her deceased mother and she must wed a demon of Satan. She can't escape.

Plot

In Pushkin's "The Queen of Spades" the Faustian anti-hero tells the successfully gambling countess, "If only you'd allow me to know your secret!" In desperation he resorts to extortion, which causes her death and his own destruction.

Television frequently dramatizes many variations of the Faust plot. In one occult drama, a psychic rescues a young girl from her weird young fiancé who is the grandson of an old-time Hollywood actor who once played Faust in a movie that was so horrible that it was censored, after which he was rumored to have caused the death of the actress who played Marguerite. Through ESP, the psychic saves the girl in a violent fight, which reveals the fiancé to be the old actor who had sold his soul to the Devil in exchange for eternal youth.

In another television chiller a girl-artist is pursued and frightened at night by a hideous old man and delightfully wooed during the day by a handsome young man. They are, of course, one and the same. When the young man can't get an extension of his Satanic contract, the girl sells her soul to the Devil to be with him.

Premise

The plot and premises of James Cross' *Playboy* story "Pin Money" are different, although the goal of executive position in a big advertising agency is rather hackneyed. Two ambitious, competitive men in a Madison Avenue firm, Grafton and Fallstone, want the upcoming vice-presidency. Unknown to the other, each pays the devil-like Dr. Dee one thousand dollars for the fulfillment of his fondest wish, which will be obtained by sticking pins in a plastic voodoo doll-image of the other. The two men cancel each other out while a clever underling, Baker, moves into the enviable position—because he has had a similar but less negative negotiation with Dr. Dee. While Fallstone and Grafton each wished harm to his rival, Baker's wish was for the vice-presidency itself. The premises include: "Spite can be a two-way street." "The same devices you use to destroy another can be used by him to destroy you." "It's OK to do anything to get what you want as long as you don't hurt anyone else."

Other premises are reflected in the stories previously discussed. The hero of *Damn Yankees* learns: "There's something more important than being a hero." The theme of *Rosemary's Baby* is that although virtue can be overwhelmed by evil, in the final coexistence of goodness and malevolence, there can be a spark of hope.

A humorous television play featuring a popular teen-idol group was built on the fact that one of the boys admires a harp that he can't afford and can't play. When he says, "I'd give anything to have it," a Mr. Zero appears, representing the wish-fulfilling Devil. He not only gives the music-lover the harp but also enables him to play so magnificently that he becomes world famous.

At the showdown, the young harpist is scared and doesn't want to go to hell. His buddies try to help him in various ways (making exciting plot complications), but they are unsuccessful. A splendid climax occurs in a court scene, presided over by Judge Roy Bean and featuring as witnesses several historical villains who sold their souls to the devil for evil and selfish reasons: Blackbeard the Pirate, Billy the Kid, and Attila the Hun.[1]

One of the hero's friends testifies for him, claiming that he didn't want power, fame, or fortune but that he just loves

---

[1]This scene echoes the trial in *The Devil and Daniel Webster* in which the Judge is Witch-condemner Judge Hathorn and the jury all traitors whom Webster persuades to free Stone, saying,"Don't let the U.S. go to the Devil!" Acquitting Jabez Stone is their "second chance" to be Americans.

music. When Mr. Zero takes away the magic powers to prove the youth's indebtedness to him, the hero amazes everyone (including himself) by playing as beautifully as before. He is acquitted and saved from hell when his friend convinces the Judge that: "If you love music, you can play music. All it takes is love. In the final analysis, love is the greatest power." A charming premise for young viewers!

Setting

Let's examine the specific time, place, and special interests of some of the well-known Faust variations. In Peter Cook's and Dudley Moore's *Bedazzled*, a small Milquetoast-like fry cook in a modern London hash house sells his soul to the Devil to try to win the love of an unworthy waitress; whereas Oscar Wilde's *The Picture of Dorian Gray* occurs in Gay Nineties London. The play *Will Success Spoil Rock Hunter?* satirizes Madison Avenue, press agentry, and Hollywood. In John Hersey's *Too Far to Walk*, the scene is a modern college campus and John Fist is a sophomore who sells his soul via LSD. Stephen Vincent Benét's *The Devil and Daniel Webster* takes place in New Hampshire in the early nineteenth century, Ira Levin's *Rosemary's Baby* in contemporary New York, and *The Devil and Miss Jones* in Hell.

Style

Most Faust stories are serious, often melodramatic and tragic, so that humor is a fresh approach. *Bedazzled* is such a hilarious comedy that even the Devil is not a real villain, but a mischievous Mephistopheles described as "Peck's Bad Boy with logorrhea who crosses telephone wires and advances parking meters." There is gag-studded fun when each of the seven wishes the Devil grants the dazed hero backfires. When the protagonist asks to be articulate he becomes such a garrulous intellectual that he can't shut up enough to go into action. When he asks that his love swoon at his feet she does—with an embarrassing swarm of other people in a television studio where he is a pop singer.

George Abbott's *Damn Yankees* has an equally funny

and punny, if more malicious, Devil in the guise of Mr. Applegate.

The versatility of Ira Levin can be seen in the contrasting styles with which he treats his two entirely different developments of the Faust legend. No current novel or motion picture is more sinister than *Rosemary's Baby*, yet the author used a humorous approach to the Faust plot in his "The Devil, You Say." Nick Lucifer tries to win not an elderly man but a young housewife who bakes "hellishly" good devil's food cakes. He charms her and tempts her with wealth, fame, and other lures, but through it all she remains faithful to her husband —who turns out to be an angel who came down to earth to marry her when she won a cake-bake contest for her "heavenly" angel food cake!

What ideas do you have for original variations on the Faust formula? Decide on your specific characters, plot variations, premises, setting, and style and compare them with those of previous classic works of this type.

Popular in the sixteenth century, Christopher Marlowe's *The Tragical History of Doctor Faustus* recounts the tragic fall of the man whose pride and curiosity caused him to turn a deaf ear to the Good Angel and sell his soul to Mephistopheles in exchange for twenty-four years of earthly power and delight. The tragic scenes from the opening to the end with the terrified Faustus trembling in fear of his doom are interspersed with plenty of black magic, pageantry, and psychological fireworks such as we find in *Rosemary's Baby*.

Goethe's nineteenth century *Faust, Part I* uses the same characters and situation but has an entirely different philosophical angle and a less gruesome ending, at least for its anti-hero. The prologue takes place in Heaven with God permitting Mephistopheles to tempt the soul-seeking, highly aspiring scholar Faust who conjures up spirits but cannot cope with them. Brilliantly witty, irresistibly charming Mephistopheles lures Faust to the vulgar drinking party in Auerbach's Cellar and into Hell's Kitchen in much the same way that his modern counterpart takes the college sophomore

(John Fist) to the psychedelic LSD parties in John Hersey's novel *Too Far to Walk*. Goethe's anti-hero is crueler to his innocent Marguerite whom he seduces, deserts, and drives to child-murder and madness; whereas our modern college boy merely drops his innocent girl friend out of boredom to be taken in hand by a much more worldly wench.

It's in line with the premise and purpose of each novel that Ira Levin patterned *Rosemary's Baby* after Marlowe who stressed psychology, while John Hersey's study of the college crowd is more philosophical like Goethe.

Will your Faustian fiction be philosophical or psychological? As tragic as Hans Christian Andersen's "The Little Mermaid" who fell in love with a human prince and made a pact with the Witch of the Sea to make her human, but lost love as well as comfort and self-respect? Or as comic as *Bedazzled*? Will you write it for a juvenile, man's, or woman's market?

For a children's story, the "three wishes" plot that gives the young hero supernatural help in solving a tough problem is popular. Usually the child depends on a magic prop at first, but eventually learns to become self-reliant and get along without it as in Charles Dickens' *The Magic Feather* and its many imitators.

The heroine of a teen girls' magazine could in some way "sell her soul" to get a prize, office, or membership into a snob sorority or gang. Or she could make some "deal" to get her guy or become Prom Queen. After intriguing plot developments and a strong crisis, she learns true values and teaches them to her peers (at least to her readers).

The usual Faustian negatives are converted into positives in Disney versions of stories in which supernatural characters help mortals. One example is *Charley and the Angel*, scripted by Roswell Rogers from Will Stanton's nostalgic novel *The Golden Evenings of Summer*. During the Depression, Charley, a hard-working hardware merchant, neglects his wife and children for business until an Angel appears to take him to Heaven. Aghast, he pleads for more time and is told that he hasn't used well the time he's already had. From then on, Charley mends his ways and is an attentive father and husband, earning the Angel's help when he and his family are threatened by a couple of hoods escaping from the police.

In a women's slick or confession magazine, a fat girl or woman could seek slimness the quick and easy way and sell her soul to diet pills with disastrous results. The middle-aged heroine of Jean-Claude Tramont's *Ash Wednesday* sells her soul to cosmetic surgery to restore her youth and beauty in order to win back her straying husband. She enjoys a Faustian fling in Cortina d'Ampezzo with a gigolo half her age while waiting for her spouse. But, as Faust had to pay his debt, she winds up husbandless, alone, and cursing men, with telltale stitches, strict diets, and beauty parlors.

Your hero could sell his soul to a Satanic force in order to be the world's greatest golfer, football or basketball star, bowler, tennis player, balloonist, sky diver, race driver, actor, singer, doctor, salesman, politician, or whatever field you know well enough to make your story action and terminology authentic and exciting. Whatever you choose to do, don't ever sell *your* soul by carbon-copying without incorporating your original characters, plot action, premise, setting, and style!

12

Start with Clashing Goals

A successful plot, like an admirable life, is one in which a character does not achieve his purpose too easily. There must be several seemingly insurmountable obstacles to be hurdled. These are assured in a story when the antagonistic force is working constantly to achieve a goal that clashes with that of the protagonist. Right in or near the beginning you should set up the opposing entities—each with clearly stated goals that clash with those of the other.

Many lawyers like Erle Stanley Gardner, Robert Traver, Balzac, and Michael Gilbert became successful fiction writers because they were trained to think in terms of clashing goals—prosecution versus defense, with all the accompanying conflict and suspense that make good plots. Their experience in legal cases taught them the importance of thoroughly developed arguments for *both* sides in a contest.

The tragic truth about many rejected stories that are near-misses is *incompleteness*. The author may do a good job of dramatizing the struggle of a protagonist hurdling obstacles in his attempts to achieve a goal, but it may be a one-man show, lacking the counter-plot of one or more characters who work as hard as the hero to block him.

Be sure to develop the counter-plot with goals that clash

with the hero's desire, so that oppositional forces are clearly antipodal. If the hero's goal is escape, the villain's is to trap him; if his goal is to catch a criminal, the latter's purpose is to elude or even kill him. Preplan your clashing goals, emphasizing the counter-plot action so that it is as strong as the main story line.

You can develop marvelous stories by starting with contrasting characters who have clashing goals. For instance, a man is a meat-lover (perhaps even a butcher) and his wife, an antivivisectionist and vegetarian. One spouse loves culture, the other, wrestling matches and rough sports; one character favors formal education, the other life-living; one is a devout churchgoer, the other anti-dogmatic religion or perhaps even atheistic. In a relationship in which harmony is necessary, the clashing goals can result from contrasting character traits or rivalry that must be worked out for mutual benefit. In a hero-villain conflict story, one tries to destroy the other.

In either case, if your story is to attain its goal of publication, it must start with your protagonist wanting *desperately* to achieve a specific goal. If possible, introduce a time limit for additional pressure and suspense, as the scientists in the Wildfire Project must solve the riddle of the microorganism called Andromeda Strain that has killed all but two citizens of Piedmont, Arizona, and thereby prevent a worldwide epidemic.

Perhaps a protagonist *must* rescue himself or a loved one from nuclear or germ warfare, earthquake, fire, flood, a human villain, or some other catastrophe. He *must* win the girl, game, contest, election, job, fight, or the confidence of a group. Or he *must* kick a bad habit: drugs, drink, gambling, kleptomania, gossip, lying, or some other compulsion that's causing tragedy. The condemned man or his lawyer, friend, or relative *must* prove his innocence before his sentence is carried out; or the parolee *must* prove the guilt of the real culprit who framed him before he is returned to prison. These are just a few ideas to which you should add others that coincide with your interests and ideas.

Choose a character and goal you care about so that you

can intensify the emotional power of the goal desire. Your protagonist must want his goal as deeply as Abel wants Rima (William Henry Hudson's *Green Mansions*), as Murray Burns wants to be a nonconformist and rebel against society's rat-race (Herb Gardner's *A Thousand Clowns*); as Yakov Bok wants to maintain his integrity (Bernard Malamud's *The Fixer*); as Maria wants to serve the Lord (*Sound of Music* by Howard Lindsay and Russel Crouse); as Eliza Doolittle wants to become a lady and Henry Higgins wants to prove his speech theories (*My Fair Lady*); and as Mattie Ross *must* avenge her father's murder (Charles Portis's *True Grit*).

When you preplan your story, try to open with a situation in which the hero's desire to *gain the goal* is thwarted by the *impossibility of achieving it*. Such a confrontation will probably snatch reader interest immediately so that you will not lose it forever. Watch customers in a bookstore. How many read a first page, then either put the book down and pick up another, or decide to buy it?

One of Hollywood's top story editors always warns writers: *"A story begins when the conflict begins. A story ends when the conflict ends. All else is wasted."*

Conflict means *clashing goals*, which must be quickly established between the opposing entities who or which will keep defying each other actively throughout the whole plot. They must teeter-totter dynamically up and down, with one triumphing over the other in one place, and then being defeated in another—up, down, up, down, constantly alternating until the ultimate victory or defeat of the main character.

The private eye, law enforcement officer, or private citizen-hero wants to solve a crime and/or catch a criminal, whereas the latter wants to "get away with it." The prisoner or slave wants freedom, whereas the authorities or master wants to keep him or her confined. (*Papillon, The Great Escape* or the BBC-TV series *Colditz*, which dramatizes the many escape attempts of Allied officers from the notorious "escape-proof" German castle-prison twenty-two miles southeast of Leipzig.) The kidnaper wants money or acquiescence to certain terms whereas the law wants to catch the criminal(s) and recover the victim unharmed.

Police Chief Martin Brody wants to close the beaches to protect swimmers from the great white killer-shark, whereas Mayor Larry Vaughan and news editor Harry Meadows want them "open for business" (Peter Benchley's *Jaws*).

Harvard law student Hart and his classmates want to graduate and become attorneys but tough Professor Kingsfield makes it extremely difficult, doing everything to overpower, overwork, insult, and discourage them (Jim Bridges' *The Paper Chase*).

The more clashing goals you have, the stronger and more suspenseful your plot will be, especially if your hero must battle many different opposing entities. Serpico must fight not only crime and criminals but corruption in his own police department as well. In John McGreevey's telefilm *A Man Whose Name Was John*, Archbishop Angelo Roncalli (later Pope John XXIII) wants to save 647 German Jewish children stranded aboard a steamer in Istanbul harbor. He locks horns with Turkish, German, and Portuguese authorities, whose goal is to send the children back to Germany and death. His own sister opposes him, begging him to forget the kids and go to their dying father in Italy instead. He keeps on course to his goal, which seems impossible to attain. As in all good plots, the crisis contains the seed of the solution. His last hope, the Portuguese ambassador, whose baby he has previously baptized, says he isn't interested in saving anyone who isn't Roman Catholic. This inspires the hero to issue the children baptismal papers, which will enable them to enter Portugal and survive.

Study the multiple opposition each protagonist is up against in professional plots. Be sure to have at least that many in your own—even more, if feasible.

In Pat Conroy's novel, *The Water is Wide* which became the movie, *Conrack* (scripted by Irving Ravetch and Harriet Frank, Jr.), the white Southerner goes to teach at an all-Black school on a remote island off the coast of South Carolina. The natives are impoverished fisherfolk with no hope, knowledge, or ambition. He wants to enlighten the illiterate kids and, of course, there must be clashing goals to transform a so-what situation into an engrossing plot. He has three strong obstacles:

1. The abysmal ignorance of the traditionally illiterate Black children.
2. The Black woman principal who feels that knowledge would be a dangerous thing, arousing unrealizable hopes. Her dogma of despair is as much an opponent to the hero as she is.
3. The racist superintendant who upholds the biased Black-inferiority tradition and who hates the hero for making school a place to discover what could be instead of what is.

After you have decided upon a protagonist with a strong goal (against which there are stronger opposing goals), consider carefully the six ways you can work out the plot action:

1. Protagonist wins goal
2. Protagonist loses goal
3. Both characters win
4. Both lose
5. Compromise ending
6. Pyrrhic victory (winning the original goal but at an incredible price—named for King Pyrrhus of Epirus who defeated the Romans but suffered such heavy casualties that he said: "One more such victory and I am lost.")

Study professional plots that end in each of the six ways, keeping a file that may start with fairy story classics and go on through the newest publications and productions.

1. Protagonist Wins Goal

This is the most frequent formula, exemplified by such Bible stories as little David slaying Goliath, Daniel surviving the lions, and Moses leading his people into the Promised Land;

fairy tales like Cinderella, Jack the Giant-Killer, and the Ugly
Duckling; and the usual Western and whodunit in which Good
conquers Evil. In this hurray-for-the-good-guy happy-ending
story you must create strong obstacles for the hero to conquer,
but triumph he does! As the Santa Vittorians outwit the
Germans and save their 1,320,000 bottles of vermouth from
the Germans in *The Secret of Santa Vittoria,* as Sam Varner
saves Sarah Carver from murderous Salvaje in *Stalking Moon*
and as Dr. Mark Hall and Project Wildfire avoid world
destruction from *The Andromeda Strain.*

2. *Protagonist Loses Goal*

Here, the "good guy" loses out and there is a tragic ending, all
the way from Hans Christian Andersen's "The Little
Mermaid" and Little Red Riding Hood to Anne Frank's lost
goal of survival in *The Diary of a Young Girl* and the slice-of-
life stories of frustration in many quality magazines. In
Frederick Pohl's *Playboy* yarn "Speed Trap," Dr. Chesley
Grew's goal is to work uninterrupted and to perfect his theory
of the Quantum of Debate, the irreducible minimum of
argument that each participant in a discussion can use to
make a point understood, accomplishing his goal in one-
fourth of the usual time and having the remaining three-
fourths of the time for doing other work. His goal is totally
defeated by pleasant and unpleasant interruptions, by
friends, enemies, his own weaknesses, and by supernatural as
well as natural influences, all of which conspire to prevent
human accomplishment. Likewise in Evan Hunter's "The
Sharers," successful Negro accountant Howard's goal is to
maintain his high position in White society. A psychologically
sadistic white co-commuter, Harry Pryor, carries on an
insidious campaign by quizzing him daily in a shared taxi-ride
to work. Howard's pride, self-confidence, and goal are
eventually lost, and even his desperate efforts to avoid his
inquisitor make him feel like a runaway slave.

3. *Characters with Different or Opposing Goals Both Win*

In George Kelly's play *The Show Off,* braggart Aubrey

Piper's goal is to impress everyone with his back-slapping personality and his overinflated delusions of grandeur. His girl's mother, Mrs. Fisher, wants her daughter Amy to marry a worthwhile husband instead of a windbag like Piper. Although he's a poorly paid shipping clerk when he marries Amy and moves into the Fisher home, he proves he's not all brag and braggage by helping her brother get twice as much money for an invention.

Both ex-GI buddies win contrasting goals in Garson Kanin's "Buddy." Ambitious, self-motivated Rod wants success, whereas Pete Rossi wants love. Rod seems on his way to fortune by courting the boss's daughter Jennie, but upon learning that a man should marry the boss's daughter but not *his own* boss's daughter, he ditches Jennie for a richer, more brilliant redhead whom he marries. Later, to keep her ignorant of his affair with an English model, Rod enlists Pete to cover up for his weekends with the model. Pete pities the wife, takes her flowers, and they develop true rapport and love, which culminates in a happy marriage after Rod divorces her and marries still-rich Jennie (who by now is twice-divorced with two bratty kids). Pete gains the love he has been seeking and Rod is able to conceal any disappointment behind a facade of wealth.

In Robert Louis Stevenson's *The Sire de Maletroit's Door*, everybody wins: the hero vindicates his honor, the old gentleman puts an end to scandal and restores his self-esteem, and the girl, who has suffered rejection, finds true requited love.

4. Both Lose

This method of plot resolution is most frequently found in stories of unfulfilled love. In "The Prison" by Harry Mark Petrakis, Alexandra, lonely forty-year-old librarian, finds companionship, rapport, and love with forty-five-year-old bachelor, Harry Kladis, whose father has died, leaving his mother to smother him. "They were delighted to find they both enjoyed concerts and chop suey with black pekoe tea and almond cookies." Their planned marriage is postponed by

Harry's devotion to his grieving, widowed mother and her hold on him. When his mother finally dies, he tries futilely to regain Alexandra's love, but gets a furious rebuff and slapped face in the "Hell hath no fury like a woman scorned" ending.

A classic example of lost goals for all characters appears in Edith Wharton's *Ethan Frome*. Ethan, unhappily married to hypochondriacal invalid Zenobia, loves Mattie Silver, Zenobia's lovely young cousin who is persecuted by the jealous, irascible wife, whose goal is to have both Ethan and Mattie wait on her as her slaves. When it is clear that Ethan and Mattie cannot live and love together, their goal is double suicide by sledding into an elm tree. But they lose even their suicide goal as both are hopelessly crippled so that Zenobia must hereafter take care of them.

5. *Compromise Ending*

In John Hersey's *A Bell for Adano*, Major Victor Jappolo's goal is to bring American democracy and friendship to the formerly German-occupied Sicilian town. The military's goal is to rule by might, regimentation, and red tape. The Major brings to the people American good will and the bell they want, but in bucking military brass, he is transferred to North Africa and forced to leave Adano and its people whom he loves.

Alexander Frater's *New Yorker* story "The Practitioner" opens with a tight stalemate of clashing goals between a Tonkinese husband and his wife. Matua is an ardent pearl-diver who wants to spend all his time pearl diving, whereas his wife wants more of his time and companionship. She precipitates a crisis by taking a B.O.A.C. flight bag full of her husband's most precious pearls to the crest of a steep cliff from which the men think she'll jump or throw the pearls. She increases their fears by talking about feeding imaginary dragons in the sea. "These Tonk ladies have very weak heads, you know," says the Ravu, the Medical Practitioner. He gives his diagnosis and prognosis: "She is perfectly well . . . But you, Matua, if you don't mind my saying so, could help by spending a little more of your time on dry land. I mean here at home with your . . . spouse." A happy, compromise ending is achieved when Matua rescues the flight bag of pearls and promises: "Listen, Mister. Tomorrow I'll take this woman and her kite up Mount Koro, and we'll fly it in the trade winds."

Compromise endings are popular because of their usual valuable premise: "You have to give in a little to gain a lot." Most relationships benefit from each member compromising to the other person's goals rather than insisting upon gaining his own. In Sophie Kerr's "Madame Learns about Americans," Madame Flanier, "French as the Eiffel Tower," dislikes her daughter's new country, America, and her in-laws, whom she considers uncouth. They, in turn, hate her hostility and snobbishness, and the two mothers-in-law, Madame Flanier and Mrs. Jenkins, continue a battle royal until young Arthur Jenkins tells a story about two bears who keep fighting to see which can put the highest scratch on a tree. All they accomplish is killing the tree and proving what destructive claws they have. This makes each woman call off hostilities and compliment each other's cooking. Complete family happiness results from compromise.

6. Pyrrhic Victory

By refusing to compromise, characters in certain works stubbornly strive to achieve a specific goal (usually a selfish one), do actually win it, but lose something greater. In short, they win the battle but lose the war. In George Kelly's *Craig's Wife*, Harriet wants a meticulously beautiful house, which she gets at the cost of losing her husband and any hope for marital happiness. In Guy de Maupassant's "The Necklace," Madame Loisel succeeds in winning her social-climbing goal of borrowing a rich woman's necklace to become "the belle of the ball," and eventually in earning money to repay her when the necklace is lost, but only after years of exhausting work that costs her youth, looks, and energy. The bitter irony is that the necklace was only paste!

In the movie *The Way We Were,* the radical, idealistic wife wants to combat the Establishment, whereas her conventional, materialistic husband wants to become successful within its framework. Each achieves the immediate goal but loses their marriage and family togetherness with their little girl (similar to the *Craig's Wife* structure). In Uris' *QB VII*, Dr. Kelno wins his lawsuit for libel against Abe Cady but loses his self-respect, son, and reputation.

An excellent way to preplan your story is to begin with opposing goals and tentatively work out the action to each of the six different types of endings. How many professional examples can you think of in which a sharp generation gap is caused by an adult's wanting to discipline a child or children whose goal is to be rebellious and untamed? The following illustrations demonstrate how each method of resolution has been used.

1. Adult protagonist wants to tame child (or children) and wins this goal. In Enid Bagnold's *Chalk Garden,* Miss Maitland civilizes wildly destructive Laurel; Annie Sullivan tames savage blind-deaf-and-dumb Helen Keller in William Gibson's *The Miracle Worker;* Maria wins over the hostile von Trapp children in the *Sound of Music;* Mary Poppins enchants her wild youngsters; and each teacher tames, disciplines, and teaches antagonistic pupils in James Clavell's *To Sir, with Love,* Bel Kaufman's *Up the Down Staircase,* and Evan Hunter's *The Blackboard Jungle.*

2. Adult protagonist loses goal of reforming a revolting child. *Bad Seed* (by William March) dramatizes the futile efforts of a mother to civilize her hopelessly delinquent daughter. She loses not only her goal but also her life. Less gruesome but as unsuccessful are Aunt Sally's and the Widow Douglas's goal to tame and educate the untamable Huckleberry Finn in Mark Twain's classics. Adults also are conquered by the will of youth in Alan Sillitoe's *The Loneliness of the Long Distance Runner,* when the teen-ager deliberately loses the race that his schoolmasters want him to win.

3. Both win. Study happy-ending generation-conflict

stories like Jean Webster's *Daddy Long Legs,* or any drama in which a creative child wants to be or expresses himself or herself; the adult tries to modify the child's exuberance and win respect and the youngster's successful expression of ingenuity brings rewards to both of them. Other successful uses of this ending can be found in the motion pictures *Popi* and *Me, Natalie.*

4. Both lose. In Lillian Hellman's *The Children's Hour,* the teachers, Karen Wright and Martha Dobie, want to run a successful girls' school. A neurotic troublemaker, Mary Tilford, defies their authority and seeks to destroy them by spreading a rumor that they are lesbians. The teachers lose all their goals: their desire to educate the girls and discipline Mary; their school, which is ruined by the scandal and ensuing lawsuit; also Karen loses her fiancé and Martha, her life through suicide. Although Mary appears to win her goal of defying and destroying her teachers, she loses her greater goal: power over her grandmother and her schoolmates who will never completely trust her again.

5. Compromise ending. In Lesley Conger's *Good Housekeeping* story "When You Give Your Heart," the mother wants her six-year-old son Ted to break off his friendship with a mentally retarded boy, Perry, whereas Ted wants to keep playing with Perry. A crisis scene in which Ted battles other boys in defense of the retarded child proves to the mother her son's maturity that cannot be held back, since he has true kindness, understanding, and compassion. She compromises by not breaking up the friendship, he, by going to school and making new friends but not giving up Perry completely.

6. Pyrrhic victory. Adult Riccardo Ghione wanted to capture childhood from one to three in a film. He succeeded with his unrehearsed, revealing movie, *Il Limbo,* but in capturing the spontaneous actions and expressions of the toddlers he lost his illusions about childish innocence. He learned that: "Every authentic child is a rebel and an anarchist; if one allowed him to develop following his instincts there would be

such a radical transformation of society, any adult who allowed him to develop following his revolution would be put to shame."

By now you probably realize how vital clashing goals and the correct resolution of them are to your story. *Conflict* is achieved when the goals of people who love each other clash, or when rivals fight for the same goal, which only one of them can attain. *Suspense* is achieved when the reader cannot guess who will win out and when there is an exciting teeter-tottering of triumphs and defeats. *Surprise* is achieved when unexpected events explode to generate unexpected (but credible) drama. *Satisfaction* is achieved by the ways in which the goals are won by deserving characters and lost by villains in a commercial story. In a quality yarn, however, the hero may not win and the villain may not lose, but *Insight* is achieved as the tragedy illuminates a great moral truth and adds significance in the form of a revealing premise. *Salability* is assured when your plot action dramatizes the attainment of goals that are emotionally valid, identifiable, and timely.

Before writing a story, novel, or play, list the goals of each character, why each wants what, the steps he will take in his goal-direction, and what obstacles he will meet. Remember that:

1. The plus or minus nature of the goal usually determines the type of character. A person who wants to destroy, expose, or harm an innocent victim for his own selfish advantage is a villain. A person who endangers himself to help others is a hero.

In Noah Gordon's *A World Apart* all the medical personnel share a general goal: to cure illness. Nurse Beth Sommers altruistically dedicates her life to helping humanity, which makes her a radiant heroine. Older Dr. Weintraub shares her love of people but has an added specific goal of wanting to make better doctors and is especially interested in softening the character of young Dr. Michael Cooper, whose original goal was to become rich through medicine. All the while he is calloused to human suffering and uses patients for selfish means, he is unsympathetic. But after his affirmative-goaled co-workers kindle his finer instincts and he becomes considerate, he regenerates into a hero. In all scripts, whether the character has a good or evil goal determines whether the reader likes or dislikes him.

2. All characters must have goals, even the minor actors. Usually the goals are revealed when each person steps into the story or shortly thereafter. But in certain cases the goal may take shape after a specific action, for instance a revenge or reward goal resulting from motivating incidents. In novels like *The $300 Man*, the boy's search for his replacement begins *after* he learns how his own father cheated to get him out of the draft. Changed goals often appear in stories like *Ben Hur*, whose original goal was peaceful coexistence with the Roman conquerors of his country, particularly Messala. Later, after his mother and his sister disappear, his goal is to find them. Throughout the rest of the plot action as Messala's sadistic villainies increase, Ben Hur's original plus goals of peace and love reverse to revenge and destruction. *The Guns of Navarone* travels in the opposite direction. The original revenge goal of the Greek colonel was to kill the English officer whom he blames for his wife's death. Later, when the two men are assigned to the same mission of destroying huge German cannon to save 2,500 British soldiers, his goal switches to cooperation to the point of risking his life to save the Briton. Then, after they've shared hardships and dangers and the Colonel has found love, he abandons his original hate-revenge goal for a new goal of building a new loving life.

3. The goal must be in line with basic human values that concern all people of all time and with which the reader can identify: life, liberty, happiness, approbation, security, retribution, fame, etc.

4. The goal must never be too easy to attain nor the means of attaining it transparent and guessable by the reader.

5. The goal must have emotional significance so that the reader shares the character's involvement.

6. Before starting to write be sure to ask: What does

each character want? Why? Why can't he have it? Who or what opposes him? What steps will he take to overcome each obstacle? Who or what will help him? Are there enough obstacles for a long script? Too many for a short one?

Don't be satisfied with a single-goaled situation, rather, plan an opening that presents an exciting stalemate caused by a clash of antipodal goals, something along the lines of the irresistible force meeting the immovable object. In *Wild River*, Chuck Glover's goal is to clear the land for flooding for the TVA project, which means removing Ella Garth from her home; her goal is to remain. In Roger O. Hirson's "The First Day," Nora's goal after release from the mental institution is to build a brand new self; her family's goal is to make her the same old Nora.

Like a football, hockey, soccer, or polo game, a story derives its suspenseful action from opponents competing and clashing to reach opposite goals. In any court trial the prosecutor tries to convict, the defense attorney to acquit. In any war, game, or in any relationship, opposing entities aim toward their respective objectives throughout a teeter-totter of failure-success, success-failure, and so on to the end.

For variety, try reversing the ordinary goal-clashing situations. It is usual for a girl to want marriage, a man just an affair. In Max Shulman's *How Now, Dow Jones?*, the heroine consents to the affair but refuses to marry the boy. Your hero could want home and kiddies and the domestic life, while the girl is a Women's Libber and wants to stay single and unfettered. Since most people want success, fame, or fortune, your protagonist could go to great lengths to be poor and unknown. Or, like Mr. Deeks in John Hess's *The Wicked Scheme of Jebel Deeks*, your character could sneak money into the bank instead of robbing it.

All the time you are working out the individual goals of your actors, you'll be speeding toward your overall goal of writing success. Christopher Isherwood is right when he says that if this is your goal and you work hard enough, you can't miss! He insists that "If a person wants to become a writer, he'll become one . . . *The desire is the vocation.*" He adds that no discouragement will stop the real writer, whereas no one has to discourage the others. They'll do it themselves.

What is your writing goal: success or failure? Being goal-conscious will make the difference.

13

Plotting from the Classics

Just as astronauts are guided through space by a successful combination of ancient and modern devices—the sextant plus electronic computers—many writers achieve prolific publication by combining elements of the old classics with modern techniques and relevance.

You'll find timeless values and gripping emotions like revenge, hate, lust, greed, love, grief, and hope powerfully dramatized in plots from the past, some of which may serve as appropriate vehicles for your own message and style.

Readers like the glint of recognition and often the snob appeal of the erudite touches. Add your own original ingredients with plenty of reader identification and timeliness and you'll have your own super-production.

C. C. Colton wrote: "If we steal thoughts from the moderns, it will be cried down as plagiarism; if from the ancients, it will be cried up as erudition."

An allusion to a classic often adds deeper meaning and symbolism, frequently appearing in titles like Arthur C. Clarke's *Playboy* story "A Meeting With Medusa" (and his novel and movie *2001: A Space Odyssey*) and Michael Crichton's *The Andromeda Strain*. Although the latter is space age up-to-date, its title reminds us of a prophetic legend that suggests a sinister warning of today's dangers.

As if war destruction wrought by nuclear science weren't deadly enough, Operation Scoop has been devised to discover stronger methods of germ warfare. It has orbited capsules into space to collect lethal interplanetary bacteria. Due to an error, one landed at Piedmont, Arizona, killing everyone in town except a crying baby and an old man with ulcers. The Wildfire team of scientists and doctors are assigned to solve the mystery and try to prevent a widespread epidemic caused by the deadly microorganism.

The title recalls the fable of Andromeda, warning us of the possible consequences of our pride in our scientific advances. In fact this is implied in the two premises before the novel began: "The survival value of the human intelligence has never been satisfactorily demonstrated"; and "Increasing vision is increasingly expensive."

In the original classical legend, Queen Cassiopia dared to compare her own beauty to the Nereids (the Sea Nymphs). Furious, they sent a horrible sea monster to ravage the coast. The Oracle proclaimed that the Queen and her husband, King Cepheus, must sacrifice their beautiful daughter, Andromeda, to the monster. But before she could be devoured she was saved by Perseus who heroically destroyed the monster as he had previously beheaded Medusa.

The modern novel is lifted above ordinary science fiction by the scientific research knowledge that saturates its pages and by the classical title and basic structure of salvation from destruction that threatens to result from boasting. As we are proud of science's ability to compete with and control Nature on so many levels, are we not arousing Nature's vengeance as Cassiopia did? Innocence that is victimized has a double implication here—not just the unknowing people who are killed and the millions more threatened by the fatal microbe, but that very Andromeda Strain itself torn from its home in outer space against its will or knowledge.

The hero of the ancient tale, Perseus, is represented by the Wildfire team, especially Dr. Mark Hall who achieves a split-second success in the exciting ending. But will there always be a happy ending if man continues to tamper with Nature and exploit it for destructive ends?

Basing your original work on a classic does not limit your creative imagination, as John Barth proved when he reversed and modernized ancient myths throughout his NBA-winning novel *Chimera.* In the "Bellerophoniad" section, as in the original legend, Bellerophon had his affair with the Amazon, Melanippe, "perky priestess of his passions," but then, years later, with a dusky damsel who looked just like her, but who really was her daughter—and his (a fact that never deters him).

Previously he has rejected the advances of older Queen Anteia while he was a guest in the castle of her husband King Proetus. In a plot paralleling Pharaoh's wife propositioning Joseph in the Old Testament, Anteia tells her husband that Bellerophon seduced her and must be drastically punished. In the Bible Joseph is sent to prison, whereas the mythical hero must fight warlike Solymians, Amazons and the Carian pirates. Fortunately he has the help of the winged horse, Pegasus, who rides him up in the sky from which he aerial-bombs enemies with boulders. His toughest assignment is to kill the deadly, fire-breathing she-monster, Chimera, who has the head of a lion, the body of a goat, and the tail of a serpent.

With ecological awareness, Philonoe, his teen-aged girl friend, begs Bellerophon not to kill the Chimera, but to bring her back alive for the University's Zoology Department. This girl who loves all creatures tells him, "We'll keep her in an asbestos cage and her breath can be used to heat the whole zoo free of charge, maybe the poorer sections of the polis as well."

You'd think he'd appreciate such a doll, but—another Barth reversal—eventually Bellerophon winds up with the Chimera!

You feel convinced that the Genie-of-the-Future in John Barth's *Chimera* is the author himself. He and Scheherazade agree that no one *invents* a plot, but only *recounts* the stories of all times that everyone always wants to hear. Acknowledging his debt to ancient, time-tried classics, he tells her:

> In all the years I've been writing stories, your book has never been off my worktable. I've made use of it a thousand times, if only by just seeing it there . . .

He explains his function as an author thusly:

> My project is to learn where to go by discovering where I am by reviewing where I've been—where we've *all* been . There's a kind of snail in the Maryland marshes . . . that makes his shell as he goes along out of whatever he comes across, cementing it with his own juices, and at the same time makes his path instinctively toward the best available material for his shell; he carries his history on his back, living in it, adding new and larger spirals to it from the present as he grows.

Does he not express the wish of all creative artists when he says he wants to add "some artful trinket or two, however small, to the general treasury of civilized delights"? If the world's treasury of art "could not redeem the barbarities of history or spare us the horrors of living and dying, at least [it has] sustained, refreshed, expanded, ennobled and enriched our spirits along the painful way."

ANCIENT CLASSICS IN MODERN DRESS

Charles Webb's *The Graduate* was considered the most original plot of the century. Perhaps the idea of a middle-aged woman loving a young boy was new to the teen-agers who flocked to the film, but it's been a popular perennial ever since Euripides wrote *Hippolytus* in 428 B.C.

In this drama, King Theseus' son Hippolytus scorns Aphrodite the Love Goddess and worships chaste Artemis instead. To punish him, Aphrodite inspires his stepmother Phaedra with overpowering lust for him. She vainly fights her impulses, goes on a starvation diet, and at the point of death confesses her love to her nurse who tells Hippolytus. His repudiation of Phaedra is so vicious that she hangs herself, leaving Theseus a note saying his son violated her. The King curses and exiles Hippolytus, who is killed before his father learns of his innocence.

Euripides' tragedy has been rewritten in thousands of "original" works, many of which use the same names for the characters, although the emphasis of importance varies. Racine starred the ill-fated Phaedra in his famous drama of

that title, as did Robinson Jeffers in his *The Cretan Woman*.
In the latter, Phaedra, incensed when the boy rejects her love,
tells the King that he seduced her. After Theseus kills his son,
she berates him for his stupidity, tells him the truth, and asks
him to kill her. When he ignores her, she hangs herself and
the grief-stricken King hurls himself on the body of his dead
son.

You can find many other adaptations of the Phaedra plot
in the works of yesterday, today, and tomorrow, each author
adding his own changes in characterization, plot action,
premise, setting, and/or style. Jules Dassin's *U.S.S. Phaedra*
updates the ancient tale with a jet-set cast: shipping magnate
Rafe, his much-younger wife Phaedra, their child, and his son
by a former marriage, Tony. Rafe is so involved with business
affairs that his neglected wife has an affair with Tony even
though they both try to fight their mutual attraction. After a
business crisis in which Rafe loses several ships and personnel, he learns of the affair, confronts and beats up Tony, who
speeds away to be killed in an auto accident. After learning of
Tony's death, Phaedra takes poison, leaving Rafe to bring up
their baby alone.

Sometimes there is a less tragic stepmother-stepson relationship as appears in Harold Robbins' *The Carpetbaggers*.
Often there are vast differences in backgrounds and characters so that the stories that derive from the same classic are
very different. Frederich Schiller's *Don Carlos* dramatizes the
love of Spanish Infante Don Carlos for his stepmother and his
tragic death by order of his father, King Philip II. In Eugene
O'Neill's *Desire Under the Elms*, Abbie Putnam, the third
wife of rich, tyrannical old Ephraim Cabot, seduces her step-
son Eban in order to have a baby she'll claim is old Ephraim's,
therefore insuring her property rights and a secure future.
When Abbie and Eban fall deeply in love, she smothers the
infant to prove her love for Eban who, repelled, reports her
crime to the sheriff. But he stands by her and admits his guilt.

You will recognize this plot in *A Most Happy Fellow* and
find the older-woman–young-man rapport in many more
scripts like *Forty Carats, Harold and Maude* and *O Lucky*

Man. In the modern treatments the characters *must be* responsible for their actions, whereas the ancient Greek and Roman stories show human beings as mere puppets manipulated by the gods. Charles Webb combines the two in his novel *Love, Roger,* in which the young hero is dominated by women, and in *The Graduate* where Benjamin is maneuvered by adults, but finally takes things in hand in the exuberant ending.

In many cases the attraction of a younger man for an older woman may be so strong that we realize why some primitive peoples enforce strong taboos against a man ever seeing or speaking to his mother-in-law. These tribes seem to realize that the sex appeal and wiles of the more mature female will lure a man away from his young wife, which of course could be fatal to the continuation of the race from the standpoint of reproduction if the woman is too old for child bearing. Even if not, fatal wars could occur between her husband and son-in-law.

Such worldwide primitive taboos may be the ancestors of our mother-in-law jokes in which the older woman is made the butt or ogre to mask the young husband's attraction to her.

If you want to argue with this concept, fine! The purpose of this book is to stimulate and nourish the growth of your plot muscles, so any conflicting or unusual ideas may lead to a worthwhile, productive payoff!

Peter De Vries seems to go along with this thesis, however, in his novel *Forever Panting,* in which protagonist Stew Smackenfelt is so attracted to his mother-in-law that he divorces his wife and marries the older woman.

When the older-woman–younger-man situation is empathetic but nonsexual, it is referred to as the Candide plot and usually ends with the wife going back to her husband after enjoying the attentions and friendship of the youth. G. B. Shaw used this format with different backgrounds. His *Candida* takes place in London and the wife of a parson is loved by a young poet, Eugene Marchbanks; whereas *The Devil's Disciple* has a 1777 American Revolutionary War setting, with the impetuous young rebel, Richard Dudgeon, attracting the wife of a Puritan minister. In Robert Anderson's *Tea and Sympathy,* the sympathetic coach's wife helps a sensitive college boy overcome his fear of actually being the homosexual he has been called. Humor and a hip Hollywood setting freshen the plot in Alan Levenstein's *Whose Little Boy Are You?* All are original and quite different although they are variations of the same Candide plot so popular today with so many relationships following this pattern.

Probably the classic formula most used in today's television, pulp and movie detective, spy, and war stories is the Greek classic chronicling the Labors of Hercules. Even satires like *The Third Eye* are based on the ancient legend. Here Etienne Leroux updates the heroic labors of Hercules to fit our unheroic times. He blasts the commercialism of our shopping-centers-and-movie-stars civilization while producing suspenseful plot action in which the Hercules role is played by a pop-art Dick Tracy named Demosthenes de Goede who performs anticrime feats that seem to leap from today's headlines.

We've already seen how the *Pygmalion* legend of the ancient Greek sculptor who carved a statue that became human is the basis of *My Fair Lady.* You can add to it many educational stories like *The Miracle Worker* in which one person improves another through loving teaching.

The legend of *Alcestis* (dramatized by Euripides in 438 B.C.) is brilliantly updated in T. S. Eliot's *The Cocktail Party.* In the original, King Admetus, ill, must die unless he finds someone willing to die in his place. No one volunteers except his wife Alcestis. In the later work, which is set in sophisticated London, the host's wife has disappeared, and it isn't until the end that we learn that she has been in a mental hospital taking the therapy he needed.

The love story of Orpheus and Eurydice is another Greek fable that has been rewritten in many different ways, usually stressing marital fidelity and eternal love. Newly-wed Eurydice, pursued by the shepherd Aristaeus, flees from him, stepping on a poisonous snake that bites and kills her. Her grief-stricken husband Orpheus, a brilliant musician, goes to the Underworld to beg Pluto and Persephone to give him back his bride. He plays such irresistible music that they consent, on condition that he not look back at her until they reach the upper world. Later when he forgets and turns to see if she is still following him, she vanishes. Unable to regain her, he stays so faithful to her memory that he's killed by the jealous Thracian maidens whom he has rejected. Death reunites the lovers.

Most stories based on this tragedy repeat the love-is eternal theme and sombre mood although in different settings. Jean Anouilh's *Eurydice: Legend of Lovers* takes place in Paris. Eurydice is an actress who falls in love with Orpheus, an itinerant musician. They are so in love that she leaves her acting company, and he his father with whom he lives, and they elope. After a blissful night in a third-rate hotel, she learns that her former lover, the company manager, is coming after her. She runs away and is killed in a bus collision. A supernatural character, Monsieur Henri, agrees to bring her back from the dead if Orpheus promises not to look at her before dawn. When he meets her he asks if she still loves the manager, and she says no. Doubting her, Orpheus looks into her eyes, losing her until "death do us join."

Jean Cocteau's *Orphée* has a grim, surrealistic tone and unique touches. A horse hoof-taps cryptic messages in the living room of the married couple, Orpheus and Eurydice, to the delight of the husband and the fury of the suburban housewife who dies trying to poison the horse. Death comes for her in the guise of a beautiful woman whom Orpheus falls in love with and follows through a mirror to the Underworld. After losing his wife a second time, he provokes the girls of the Bacchantes Club to lynch him (as the Thracian maidens killed the original Orpheus). There is a final shocker when the decapitated head rolls out, is put on a pedestal, and proclaims itself to be the author, Cocteau (symbolically beheaded by critics).

Thoroughly tragic is the musical *Black Orpheus*, with its weird, hypnotic carnival locale and its vivid emphasis on the triangle love story, with villainous Mira fighting to win back her ex-fiancé, guitar-playing Orpheus who is now in love with Eurydice. Death stalks and captures her at the colorful fiesta. Through his magic music Orpheus reclaims her but loses her again when he looks back at her. As he is carrying her body, Mira causes him to fall to his death, therefore being united with his beloved.

Contrastingly humorous is the ahead-of-its-time opera *Orpheus in the Underworld* by Jacques Offenbach. Back in 1858 he reversed the tender love story into a neurotic interaction marriage. Orpheus, a music teacher in Thebes, is married to a nagging Eurydice who can't stand his infernal practicing day and night. She elopes with a shepherd, Aristeus (who is Pluto in disguise) leaving her husband a note that has become world-famous:

Dear Orpheus:
        I love Aristeus and am eloping with him. Our marriage has been a failure. I hate you! I hate you! I hate you!

                                                        Love,
                                                        Eurydice

Orpheus is glad because he loves Chloe, a shepherdess, but unfortunately tradition demands that he try to reclaim his wife. He asks Zeus for help and the latter orders Pluto to surrender Eurydice to her husband, with the same conditions of the original fable: Orpheus must not look back at her until after they have crossed the River Styx. By now Zeus is in love with Eurydice and hurls a bolt of lightning, which causes Orpheus to look back and lose his wife. In a surprise ending that shocked purists of the day, Orpheus winds up with Chloe, and Eurydice and Zeus live happily ever after! Who said wife-swapping is new?

Other adaptations of the Orpheus and Eurydice legend keep appearing in fresh new guises. You may have recognized the format in the Swedish movie *Elvira Madigan*. Tennessee Williams updated it with a motorcyclist-hero in his *Orpheus Descending*, which became the film *The Fugitive Kind,* just as he used the Persephone legend of the woman who must go to the Underworld to live with Pluto in *The Milk Train Doesn't Stop Here Anymore,* which was the movie *Boom!*

The ancient legends are enjoying greater immortality than their gods hoped for because, as allegories, they have universal truths wrapped up in suspenseful stories. One sage said, "The allegory is literature's answer to sugar-coated cereal." As you reread classics in *The Golden Bough,* Bulfinch's *Mythology,* or other excellent collections by Edith Hamilton, Larousse, and others, look for ideas that apply to today's reader and his problems.

When delinquency and school vandalism hogged the headlines, John Updike updated the fable of Chiron, "noblest of all the Centaurs" who was accidentally but agonizingly wounded by a poisoned arrow in his heel during a wedding feast at which another Centaur tried to steal the bride. In the Updike novel, *The Centaur,* the innocent victim is the high school teacher George W. Caldwell, whose heel is similarly pierced in the first sentence and who also seeks and eventually finds death, learning "that in giving his life to others he entered a total freedom."

Mary Renault does not bother to modernize her mythological characters in her historical novels *The Bull from the Sea* (which gives still another version of the Phaedra story), *The Charioteer, The King Must Die, The Last of the Wine,* and *The Mask of Apollo.* Her powerful style and characterization add originality to the ancient stories.

As you rake through the time-tried classics for plots, you may be inspired to rewrite some basic situations that are relevant today. How many timely conflicts can you develop spurred by the jealousy, vanity, and hurt pride that led to the Trojan War? Modern aerospace and flying plots can be developed from many myths in which characters had the power of flight, including such mortals as Daedalus, who made wings by which he and his son Icarus escaped from the Labyrinth, and such flying animals as the winged horse Pegasus.

What fun you could have planning a modern, getting-away-from-it-all story on the structure of Aristophanes' *The*

Birds. As many people today want to escape smog, water pollution, the energy crisis, violence, and other evils on earth, Pisthetaurus and Euelpides are fed up with the pests that inhabit ancient Athens and fly up to the land of the birds. Once there, they persuade King Epops to set up the city of Cloud-Cuckooland in midair, and they make men and gods pay them tribute for letting prayer incense smoke pass through their territory. There is nothing new about con-men, and with your own variations you could develop a successful science fiction, fantasy, or realistic plot using similar or original characters and modern space details.

Aristophanes' *The Frogs* introduced a duplicate world that exists in outer space and that mirrors everyone and everything in ours. This idea was recently updated in a television drama in which an astronaut returns after having visited that other world, but when back on earth he sees that everything is reversed as though seen in a mirror.

Select a classic that fits your premises and characters. Outline the original plot and then pattern your own, with as many barriers and conquests. Yours may be different or as similar as Euripides' *Electra* and Eugene O'Neill's *Mourning Becomes Electra.*

Plot blueprint of Electra *by Euripides*

Protagonist and Purpose	Electra wants to kill her mother Clytemnaestra and replace her in her father's affections. Later her goal is to avenge her father's murder by her mother and her lover Aegisthus.
Barrier	She is a mere woman, powerless, further weakened because Aegisthus now rules the land and has married her off to a poor farmer (so that her sons will not be able to take revenge). He has also banished her brother Orestes who could, as a man, avenge their father's murder.

Conquest After many years Orestes returns. In him Electra has an ally. She can use his power for her revenge.

Barrier They make plans. He will kill Aegisthus while she calls Clytemnaestra to her house. Electra promises to kill herself if they fail.

Conquest Orestes kills Aegisthus.

Barrier He doesn't want to kill his mother whom he loves as much as Electra loved their father.

Crisis Electra persuades him. He kills Clytemnaestra (which is what Electra wanted most).

Climax The Erinyes (Furies) descend upon them, banishing Orestes for his crimes and Electra as an accomplice. She has achieved her revenge but it is a barren victory, for her father is dead and she cannot be with Orestes.

Euripides' Electra *from the viewpoint of Orestes*

Protagonist and Purpose Orestes wants to kill Aegisthus who has murdered his father and taken what he considers *his* rightful place in his mother's affections.

Barrier Aegisthus is now more powerful than Orestes (as was his father) and has banished him. He cannot take revenge.

Conquest After many years in exile, the Oracle tells him to return to Greece and Kill Aegisthus. His disguise, together with the fact that he has been gone so long, enables him to enter Greece unidentified. He finds his sister Electra and kills Aegisthus.

Barrier	Aegisthus' servants prepare to kill their master's murderer.
Conquest	When he reveals his identity as their former master, they welcome him. Triumphant, he returns to Electra bearing Aegisthus' head.
Barrier	When Electra insists that he kill their mother, he is so overcome with love that he cannot kill her.
Crisis	Electra fills him with her strength and hate and he is able to kill his mother, achieving the full revenge that befits a hero of the times.
Climax	After the act, however, he is paralyzed with grief. By killing his beloved mother he has destroyed that which he wanted. The Erinyes banish him and he will be pursued by the Furies (his own guilt) for years to come, perhaps forever!

Eugene O'Neill took full advantage of the popularity of Freudian psychology in his *Mourning Becomes Electra,* which he laid during the Civil War.

Plot blueprint of O'Neill's Mourning Becomes Electra *from Lavinia's viewpoint*

Protagonist and Purpose	Lavinia wants to kill her mother Christine, because of a life-long rivalry with her for her father's love. Later this goal is reinforced because Christine and her lover, Adam, have killed Lavinia's father.
Barrier	Lavinia, being alone and a mere woman, is helpless. Charming, charismatic Christine tells everyone that Lavinia's accusations are the result of a disturbed mind.

Conquest   Orin, her brother, comes home from the Civil War. She has always had great influence with him and now plans to persuade him to kill their mother.

Barrier   Orin did not love their father as Lavinia did. She cannot control him on this level. Furthermore, Christine temporarily convinces him that Lavinia is insane. Again Christine is winning control over a man, as she has over father and lover.

Conquest   Lavinia plays on Orin's intense jealousy regarding his mother. She makes him promise that, if confronted with proof of Christine's affair with Adam and the murder of their father, he will take revenge.

Barrier   When he is confronted with this proof, Orin panics and almost kills them both in a rage.

Conquest   Lavinia stops him. Later he kills Adam in his ship and they arrange the cabin so that it will look as if he has been killed by robbers.

Crisis   They return home. Orin (having enacted his life-long fantasy) now wants to live with his mother, persuade her to forget Adam, and make her love him alone. Christine, overcome by Adam's death, kills herself. Orin is tortured and broken by guilt.

Climax   Lavinia now has what she wants. The conflict brought about by her mother's death is resolved. She begins to exercise the power she sought as she is now full mistress of their mansion.

Plot blueprint of Mourning Becomes Electra *from Orin's viewpoint*

Protagonist and Purpose	Orin wants to be rid of his father and replace him in his mother's affections.
Barrier	He has been to war where his father totally controlled him as he has all his life. His mother isn't as affectionate as she used to be.
Conquest	He learns of his father's death. Now, at last, he will have his mother Christine all to himself.
Barrier	His sister Lavinia meets him at the station and tells him that their mother has a lover, Adam Brant, and that together they killed his father.
Conquest	When he sees Christine he is sure that this can't be true. She loves him and perhaps they will go away together. She convinces him that Lavinia is insane and lies.
Barrier	Lavinia takes him to the room where their father lies in state. Even in death the old man is powerful enough to upset and frighten him. He loses the elation he so recently gained by being with Christine. Lavinia shows him the poison with which Christine killed their father and makes him promise that if confronted with proof of Christine's affair with Adam, he will take revenge. Temporarily this becomes his goal.
Conquest	When they discover Christine and Adam together he is overcome with jealousy. Under Lavinia's direction, he kills Adam. Now that he has fulfilled his fantasy—killed his father, his rival for his mother's love—she will be his alone.

Crisis   Christine, overcome with grief at Adam's death, kills herself. Orin has lost her for all time to another man.

Climax   Orin is broken with grief at the loss of his mother and guilt for the murder of his father. (Throughout his life he has murdered his father in his dreams and his killing Adam was just an enactment of this dream.) It is obvious that he will be tortured and defeated for the rest of his life as Orestes was hounded by the Furies.

Many other works follow this structure, even so far as to the major divisions of the action. Aeschylus' trilogy, *Oresteia,* consists of: (1) *Agamemnon,* in which the conqueror of Troy is murdered by Clytemnaestra and Aegisthus; (2) *The Libation-Bearers,* in which the murderers are killed by Orestes; and (3) *The Eumenides*, in which Orestes is haunted forever.

How similar is O'Neill's division: (1) *Homecoming* establishes the mother-daughter hatred between Christine and Lavinia and General Ezra Mannon's murder by his wife and her lover; (2) in *The Hunted,* Lavinia persuades Orin to kill Adam, and Christine commits suicide; and (3) *The Haunted* proclaims the premise that the guilty cannot escape their fate in expiation for their crime.

A Hardy Perennial

One of the most imitated classic formulas is Homer's *Odyssey,* which has always been popular because it gives readers and viewers an opportunity to travel and have various adventures enriched by different backgrounds and cultures. The television and motion picture markets use it frequently because of the *action* which becomes more in demand as our lives become more sedentary.

The best-seller *Watership Down* by Richard Adams is advertised as "the odyssey of a band of rebels who risk everything in quest of a new home and a new life." Although this was written for children, it appeals to all ages. Readers seem to acquire their hunger for the Odyssey plot in childhood with such old classics as *Alice's Adventures in Wonderland* and the *Oz* books and more recent books like *The Phantom Tollbooth, The Incredible Journey,* and *Higglety, Pigglety Pop*—a hunger that keeps growing throughout adulthood and, at the other extreme, seeks fulfillment in criminal escape works like *The Getaway, Slither, White Lightning, Badlands, Sugarland Express, Dirty Mary, Crazy Larry, Thomasine and Bushrod* and others.

The Last Detail recounts the odyssey of two military Shore Patrolmen who take their prisoner from Norfolk, Virginia, to the Brig at Portsmouth, New Hampshire. As Ulysses sampled life through his many experiences, so do they by bus and train with stopovers in Washington, Camden, New York, and Boston, and on shabby streets lined with tattoo parlors and brothels where, like their ancient forbear, they are "seduced by sirens."

Henri Charrière's *Papillon* is an odyssey of escape from some of the world's worst prisons and work camps. Quite different but in the same plot category are immigration novels that follow their characters from lands of oppression to America the dreamland of opportunity, as in *The Migrants, The Emigrants,* and *America, America!*

A Counterculture version of the ancient classic appears in Gurney Norman's *Divine Right's Trip,* in which D(ivine) R(ight) (for David Ray) Davenport, stoned crazy, makes his way from California to his home territory of Appalachian Kentucky where he finds tranquility and purpose in soil reclamation via rabbit manure. His companions on the trip are his girl Estelle and his VW bus called "Urge."

The Poet Game by Anthony Terpiloff gives us a "free-wheeling Irish poet who drinks and brawls his way along the American lecture circuit. The tour becomes an odyssey of the soul as he attempts to redefine himself through his volatile relationships with his wife, mistress, father and manager."

Sometimes the odysseys are physiological (*Fantastic Voyage* through the human body), sometimes physical, sometimes psychological (*The Sightseer*), sometimes philosophical, and often a combination of all these elements. No matter which, they are always on the bookshelves, on television, and in the theater. Sometimes the journey is close to the area of Homer's original, as protagonist Grover Brand of Wirt Williams's *The Trojans* voyages through wine-dark seas from Piraeus to Piraeus by way of Delos, Baxos, Paros, and Syros. Sometimes it's far out into space as in Arthur C. Clarke's *2001: A Space Odyssey* and Gene Roddenberry's television series *Star Trek.* It can be anytime and any place, so use the backgrounds you know well to plan your original presentation. Perhaps yours will be as successful as James Joyce's psychological novel *Ulysses*, which is divided into episodes paralleling those of Homer's *Odyssey* and which Marjorie Barkertin dramatized in her play, *Ulysses in Nighttown.*

In how many modern works do you recognize plots from the Greek classics? Certainly in all of Claude Chabrol's prize-winning, Greek-tragedy-echoing movies. Perhaps this is because the ancient themes of violence and neurosis are so timely today. *La Rupture* begins when a father goes berserk and nearly kills his little boy so that the mother must beat him into submission with an iron skillet to protect the child. In *Just before Nightfall* a masochistic woman invites her lover to pretend to strangle her, which he really does. In *Leda*, a young man murders his father's mistress because of the unhappiness their affair causes his mother. In *La Femme Infidele,* a man tries to save his marriage by bludgeoning his wife's lover, but, ironically, he is jailed and deprived of the very relationship with his wife that he had sought to preserve.

Chabrol attributes his art and his success to the ancient classics. He often uses old biddies referred to as the *"Parcae"* who emphasize the tragic action in the manner of the Fates or Greek chorus. In *This Man Must Die* a man obsessively tracks down the hit-and-run killer of his son and then takes the blame when, apparently, the killer's own son murders his father instead. At the end, the protagonist says it is "like a Greek tragedy."

SEEK PLOTS IN MANY OTHER CLASSICS

Do not feel limited to the stories of any one period, place, or age. Any legend or tale that intrigues interest and has endured the test of time deserves to be called a classic, which Webster defines as "most representative of the excellence of its kind; having recognized worth."

The rich treasury of Greek mythology is only one of many. Your plot El Dorado may be found in foreign folklore, nursery rhymes, and literature of all times and climes.

There are several advantages to studying the favorite yarns of all history and choosing appropriate ones on which to graft your own values, characters, action, atmosphere, and other unique accessories.

Most of them have universal lessons that are dramatized by clever action and suspense. In most cases they offer readers a welcome familiarity to which you can add exciting surprises and originality. An extra bonus is that most classic stories are in the public domain, so that you will suffer no penalties for "borrowing." In fact, this protective umbrella may shield you from possible charges of plagiarism or libel when you cite your sources.

Fairy Tales and Folklore

In her book, *Tales from Eternity*, Rosemary Haughton writes: "Fairy tales can open our minds to the human and make us able to hear more sharply the demand for the transformation of the human into its own completeness." They are "the distillation of vintage human wisdom."

They also have intriguing, tersely presented plots, each of which has a clear-cut beginning that presents a problem, a middle that develops it, and an end that resolves it. That's why they have so often provided the structure for so many successful scripts.

Just as Erich Segal's novel *Love Story* borrows from *Romeo and Juliet*, his following novel, *Fairy Tale*, chronicles happenings in the life of the Kennedy family told in the guise of an updated "Jack and the Beanstalk."

When you add fresh ingredients you can develop an original story that glimmers with the glint of recognition, as the hit musical *Once upon a Mattress* (book and lyrics by Jay Thompson, Marshall Barer and Dean Fuller) is obviously a takeoff on the old "Princess and the Pea" fairy tale.

The Robin Hood format is becoming more and more popular now that criminals are delineated as heroes. Any thief, kidnaper, or murderer who helps "those in need" seems to win the reader's and viewer's sympathies. How many modern stories, novels, television plays, and motion pictures can you think of that are reminiscent of legends and fairy tales? Margaret Edwards' *Redbook* story "A Beautiful Pea-Green Boat" recalls the nursery rhyme "The owl and the pussy cat went out to sea in a beautiful pea-green boat. . ." which the hero recites.

"Rip Van Winkle" is the probable granddaddy of many stories in which a character (or more) wakes up many years later, as in Woody Allen's *Sleeper*, Pierre Bouelle's *Planet of the Apes*, or Gene Roddenberry's *Genesis II*.

Sometimes the story is more like "Sleeping Beauty," reappearing frequently in the works of many talented authors from Peter Ustinov to Joyce Carol Oates.

In Ustinov's *The Love of Four Colonels*, the American, the Englishman, the Frenchman, and the Russian stationed in Berlin after World War II vie for a sleeping beauty in a castle on the Rhine. She will awaken briefly as a fantasy-ideal for each, and will remain forever with the first one who succeeds in seducing her. Quite different is *Do With Me What You Will* (by Joyce Carol Oates), which takes place in Detroit during the recent past in which civil rights, pot, and radical politics were big news. The enchanted princess is Elena Howe, a frozen beauty who drifts through girlhood and a bad marriage while in a trance. The bad fairy is Elena's heartless, nagging mother, and her Prince is attorney Jack Morrissey who becomes the heroine's disenchanter and lover and who brings her shivering back to life.

The old fable of "The Boy Who Cried Wolf" is updated and terror-tinged in Bob Homel's horror movie *The Boy Who Cried Werewolf*. After a boy's father is bitten by a rampaging werewolf on a camping trip, the child tries to convince the sheriff that his dad is a werewolf and is disbelieved—with dire results.

There have been many imitators of "The Ugly Duckling" plot, all the way from Plain Jane stories in which the dull-

nonentity protagonist eventually becomes exquisite and
fascinating, to reversals like science fiction yarns in which a
person considered good-looking by our standards is rejected
as a freak by hideous denizens of another planet.
Try to work out a "different" twist. In your search for
relevant touches, read as many newspapers and current
publications as you can to make your work "trendy." For
instance, how could you develop an original fiction plot based
on Danny McCoy's founding of "Uglies Unlimited" for the
Ugly Ducklings of America who were previously unorganized?
Fighting to make the Equal Employment Opportunity Commission add "physical appearance" to the non-discrimination
code that lists race, creed, color, sex, religion, and national
origin, he insists:

> We open our door to secretaries with warts, stewardesses with
> pimples, policemen with freckles, hostesses with lumps, barbers
> without hair, and businessmen with hook noses, but most of all we
> embrace the ill-made masses wallowing in self-pity.

A popular fairy tale that keeps turning up in various
guises is *Snow White*, now the title of a sophisticated, satirical
novel by Donald Barthelme. In a modern commune, Snow
White lives with seven men, all of whom disappoint her so that
she is continually searching for her "Prince." When Jane, a
jealous witch-equivalent, tries to poison Snow White, she accidentally kills Paul (one of the seven men) instead. His death
makes the heroine realize that the "Prince" she has been
seeking is nothing more than Peace of Mind and that her
lifestyle and fantasizing are as insubstantial as a fairy tale.
Do not limit your reading and plot-searching to our
culture and language or you may miss some fabulous ideas
from exotic fables, which Leo Rosten calls "one of man's
oldest and most cherished forms of moral instruction."
One splendid modern novel, *The Barking Deer*, resulted
from Jonathan Rubin's experiences as a Green Beret and his
knowledge of the language and legends of the Montagnards of
Vietnam. One of their ancient fables seemed to prophesy their
tragic fate. It is about a barking deer coveted by Kra the tiger

and Bru the eagle. As they fight over which will give the deer the warmer home, their claws and talons turn him into "a red splotch on the ground." This tale becomes the metaphor for the Montagnard village of Buon Yun, which is fought over by Americans who want to save it from the V.C., who are equally as anxious to protect it from the Americans. Rubin was sensitive to these people who became casualties of insensitive modern war.

Folklore of many cultures offer intriguing stories with problems and solutions that appeal to men's magazines that feature "ribald classics." It's good practice to research and to prune legends down to brief wordage. The following are two examples.

"The Purple Grapes of Queen Julishka," retold by William Danch

Beautiful but cruel, vain Queen Julishka of Hungary wanted every man's love and adoration. When Lt. Bodie preferred her youngest lady-in-waiting, she was so furious that she subjected him to the Test of Bacchus —putting a white and purple grape in a silver chalice for him to choose one, blindfolded. If he took the white, he'd go free; if the purple, he'd be torn apart by a pack of wild dogs. Knowing that the conniving queen would trick him with two purples, he quickly swallowed one, then told the nobles present: "I can tell by the taste I drew the white grape. Look in the chalice and you'll find the purple one!"

"The Most Wicked Novel," retold by Robert Mahieu

Wang Shih-chang, Confucian scholar-author, wanted to avenge his father's murder by the father of treacherous, lascivious Yen Shih-fan. Solution: He wrote an obscene novel about Yen's sexcapades, rubbing poison into the corners of each page of thin rice paper. As Yen eagerly read of his own sexploits, he licked his fingers after turning the pages. The poison worked and, after enjoying 1,600 pages of his own sins, "Yen Shih-fan was found with his head bowed against the book, quite dead."

You can receive quick checks as I have done by examining exotic classics for intriguing plots and then retelling them succinctly for specific magazines. All reading is enriching, but reslanting and pruning old classics can be especially remunerative. Here is one I adapted from a long Chinese story by Chan-kuo Tseh (403-222 B.C.) for a men's magazine to which I sold many similar tales:

Cheng Pao was the Chief Favorite of the King of Ch'u, who was as proud of her fine character as her sultry beauty.

"She is the exception to all evil things that have been spoken of women," he would say whenever someone quoted a proverb like, "There is no such poison in the green snake's mouth or the hornet's sting as is in a woman's heart" and "Women are the demons that make us enter Hell through the door of Paradise" and "Woman's tongue is a sword which never rusts" and "Never trust a woman even though she has given you ten sons."

No such malice was true of Cheng Pao who was kind, loving—yea, faultless.

She showed no jealousy—that jaundice of the soul—even after the King of Wei gave her lord, the King of Ch'u, a new lady of exquisite beauty, Yung Ping-lin. Instead, she went to extremes to make her feel welcome and loved. She ordered the most elegant gowns made for her, gave her the finest suite in the palace and tried to please her even more than she tried to please the king, who told his courtiers "Cheng-Pao has no trace of the green-eyed monster."

Indeed, Cheng Pao was like a sister to Yung Ping-lin, who often sought her advice, especially on matters pertaining to pleasing the King, and Cheng Pao graciously and generously acquainted her with his particular likes and dislikes. Soon Yung Ping-lin was entirely dependent upon the more experienced woman.

One day when she asked Cheng Pao if she were fulfilling her duties to the King with satisfaction, the latter hesitated.

"Oh, please tell me," the new lady urged.

"Are you sure that you want the truth?"

"Of course. I want more than anything in the world to know what His Majesty truly thinks of me."

"Well, then," Cheng Pao said. "He admires your manners, your flute-like voice and your poetry . . . and your beauty . . . all except one feature."

"And what may that be?" Yung Ping-lin asked, trembling.

"He does not like your nose. You would do well to cover your nose whenever you are in the King's presence."

Eager to please, the new lady was careful to cover her nose every time she was with the King—day or night, in the gardens, in the High Hall, at mealtime and in his bedchamber.

The King of Ch'u was totally mystified and asked Cheng Pao about this strange behavior.

She cast her eyes downward and hesitated.

He demanded of her, "Do you know why she covers her nose in my presence—but at no other time?"

"Yes, Sire, I know the reason, but I dare not tell it to you."

"You must tell me, no matter what it is," he persisted.

Then Cheng Pao told him, "Your Majesty's breath offends her. That is why she covers her nose in your presence."

"So that is it!" the King of Ch'u roared. He was so furious that he ordered Yung Ping-lin's nose cut off immediately.

Cheng Pao then resumed her role as the Chief Favorite of the King of Ch'u.

Updating Shakespeare's Plays

The Bard of Avon who freely borrowed from other sources in all his works would be delighted with such modern adaptations as George Abbott's *Boys from Syracuse*, based on *Comedy of Errors*; *Shakespeare Wallah*, based on *Midsummer Night's Dream*; *Love and Let Love* based on *Twelfth Night*; and *Catch My Soul*, the Rock musical version of *Othello*. The new title of the last-named adaptation comes from Othello's lines, "Perdition, catch my soul, but I do love thee," and the plot lines match the original—but the mod music and the interracial angle are as Now as you can get.[2] Quite different but based on the same Shakespearean play was the motion picture *A Double Life* in which the actor playing the *Othello* play-within-a-play used his role as an opportunity to murder his wife who played Desdemona.

In *Rosencrantz and Guildenstern Are Dead*, Tom Stoppard reverses the importance of the characters in *Hamlet*. These heroes are seen as minor tools of Fate as well as of the main characters: Claudius, Hamlet, Horatio, Ophelia, Polonius, and Gertrude. The author focuses on the minor players, feeling that most of us are the helpless victims of bigwigs in the ruling class who direct our lives. Stoppard uses the same historical period, characters, and story line of the original, changing only the character emphasis. For example, Hamlet and Ophelia become unimportant, "crazy, mixed-up kids."

---

[2]There's also an echo of the Faust plot as Iago is the Devil incarnate who collects as many souls as he can get!

Philip Yordan transplants the ruthless ambition and bloody deeds of Lord and Lady Macbeth from ancient Scotland to Chicago's underworld at the height of racketeering violence in his story *Joe Macbeth*. Egged on by his mercenary wife Lily (the equivalent of Lady Macbeth) and her fortunetelling friend Rosey (who represents the witches who prophesied his success), Joe Macbeth kills the gang leader Duke (King Duncan) so he can take his place. As in the classic, murder begets more murder. One victim, Banky, appears to haunt the drunken Joe at a banquet scene that duplicates Banquo's ghost scene, with equally devastating effects. Lots of fast-paced action dramatizes the premises: "Blood will have blood" and "Not in horrid Hell can come a devil as bad as that within Macbeth."

Mary Stewart's novel *This Rough Magic* is so deliberately patterned after *The Tempest* that each chapter begins with a quote from the Shakespearean play.

In this modern book, Lucy Waring (Miranda) is a young actress who loves all creatures so much that she saves a dolphin's life when it is speared. She has always admired, as the finest actor on the London stage, Sir Julian Gale, who is now retired in grief over the tragic death of his wife and daughter in a car accident in which he was driving. He is now renting a seaside villa at Corfu, which Lucy's brother-in-law owns. She is shocked to learn that he is becoming an alcoholic, although he does have an attractive son, Max Gale, who is the Ferdinand-equivalent love interest for our heroine.

The conniving Calaban-like villain is a murderer who poses as a photographer and whom Lucy discovers to be a smuggler. He takes her out in the storm and tries to kill her by throwing her overboard. But her previous kindness to all creatures, especially the dolphin she rescued, works "This Rough Magic," and after she is totally exhausted from swimming, a dolphin nudges her to shore. She returns to the villa in time to expose the villain, who breaks away shooting. He runs down the cliff to a motorboat in which he plans to escape, but he is killed when a gas leak causes the boat to explode. Sir

Julian comes out of his alcoholic haze to bless Lucy's marriage to his son.

Variations of the *Romeo and Juliet* plot will always be with us, probably because it includes universally appealing elements: love; youth; conflict; contrast between different cultures, backgrounds, or viewpoints; ecstasy; suffering; and usually death, which is more tragic when it is untimely.

Do not think that because it has been done so often there isn't room for your own unique version. There is, if you concoct "different" ingredients. This theme has always provided a rich variety of different characterizations, plot developments, styles, and settings.

One of the closest locales to the Shakespearean play's Italian city, medieval Verona, is scenic Sicily during World War I as is used in the movie *The Voyage*, based on Pirandello's story "Adriana Takes a Trip." This Juliet is separated from her Romeo by her arranged marriage to his brother. After her husband is finally killed in a motor accident, she must (by custom) live as a "buried widow" with her only son and her mother. She contracts a mysterious ailment, and in the course of being taken to Palermo and Naples for treatment, she resumes her relationship with her Romeo who takes her to Venice for a passionate love affair before she dies.

In Robert Altman's film *Thieves Like Us*, Romeo is the criminal Bowie and Juliet is Keechie, and their romance is doomed not by parental interference but by their life of crime, which must lead to a dead end. During their first lovemaking, the radio is presenting a version of *Romeo and Juliet*, with the announcer's unctuous voice repeating his summary of the story of the ill-fated lovers each time they embrace.

Both lovers die in Altman's version of *Romeo and Juliet*, as well as in numerous other versions, including Maxwell Anderson's *Winterset* and the film *Thomasine and Bushrod*. However, Juliet is the only fatality in such versions as *The Voyage;* Erich Segal's *Love Story,* in which Jenny dies of cancer; and *Warm December*, the movie in which the Black Juliet dies of sickle cell anemia. In George Feifer's novel *The*

Girl from Petrovka, young Oktyabrina Matveyeva is separated from her American-journalist Romeo when she is sentenced to a Communist labor camp for setting a bad example "to the riffraff who hope to weaken the Socialist State"—a fate worse than death.

In some adaptations of the age-old plot, there is a happy ending. In Chuck Barris's *You and Me, Babe*, Romeo is poor but happy Tommy Christian, strongly disapproved of by the rich parents of Samantha Jane Wilkerson whom he loves, courts, and marries, expecting to become rich this way. Her parents, however, disinherit her and the couple live poorly but happily until he obtains a fortune and fame by inventing "The Cinderella Game" for television.

Other humorous versions include *The Fantastiks*, which offers delightful reversals of the original. The two fathers are fast friends instead of enemies like the Montagues and the Capulets. Realizing the perversity of youth, they do not push their offsprings' romance but pretend to hinder it, building a high wall between their adjoining properties. Since forbidden fruits are sweeter, the couple who disliked each other before become longing lovers. Peter Ustinov's *Romanoff and Juliet* is also a fun-play in which the Soviet hero and the American heroine are set in opposition by their contrasting ideologies, governments, and parents, but whose romance is encouraged by the president of a neutral country (who is being pressured by both blocs) as well as their own developing ingenuity and love.

Variety is possible in characterization, and the couple can be of any race or of different races—for love is universal (and so, unfortunately, is bigotry). Both are Black in *Warm December* and *Thomasine and Bushrod* and in many television series, but they could still represent different factions; that is, one could be rich, the other working-class, or one could be an American Negro, the other an African. Often the characters are racially different: Black and White in such stories as *Guess Who's Coming to Dinner?*; Oriental and Occidental in *Love Is a Many-Splendored Thing, A Majority of One,* and *The World of Suzy Wong*. In Harold Heifetz' play *Harry Kelly*, Juliet is a Nisei girl interned in a relocation camp in Arizona while Romeo is an Indian. The Juliet of Hugh Wheeler's play *Look, We've Come Through* is a well-educated, wealthy WASP, whereas Romeo is a poor Polish boy from New York's Lower East Side. Romeo and Juliet are Jewish and Gentile in many works like Noah Gordon's *Rabbi*, Leon Uris's *Exodus*, and Ernest K. Gann's *The Antagonists* in which a Roman soldier loves a beautiful Jewess.

The stronger the differences between the lovers, the more conflict your script can have: culturally, socially, racially, religiously, and internally. Be sure to write about people you know.

You can set your Romeo and Juliet plot in any period, preferably one you are thoroughly acquainted with and one that hasn't been overdone. In the few examples given above, the locales have been as varied as Italy, Sicily, New York, Massachusetts, Kentucky, Moscow, the South, Hollywood— and the stories have been set in the past as well as the present.

The more changes you make, the better. Don't hesitate to "borrow" the basic story. After all, Shakespeare took it from previous works dating back to 1303 and including Masuccio's best-seller of 1476, Luigi da Porto's novella (1530), Bandello's romance (1554), Girolamo dalla Corte's *L'Historia Di Verone* (1594) and Arthur Brooke's poem "Romeus and Juliet" (1562).

Compare different *Romeo and Juliet*-based plots and see how similar they are in structure.

Plot chart of Shakespeare's Romeo and Juliet *from Juliet's viewpoint*

A—I   Juliet Capulet of Verona wants love and happiness.

A—B   She falls in love with Romeo Montague of an enemy family.

B—C   Their love is so great that the Friar marries them secretly.

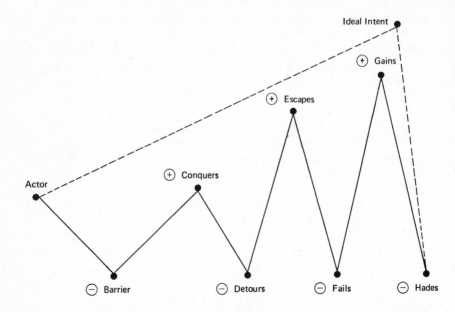

C—D Juliet's cousin Tybalt, kills Romeo's page and Romeo kills Tybalt. This intensifies the family feud; Romeo is exiled to Mantua; Juliet's parents plan her marriage to Paris.

D—E In desperation, Juliet seeks help from the Friar who concocts a plan to save her from marrying Paris and to reunite her with Romeo. She is to take a sleeping potion that will make everyone think she is dead. She will be buried in the family vault but will be rescued by the Friar who will have notified Romeo to be there when she awakens.

E—F Pestilence closes town gates, preventing the messenger from getting through to Romeo with the Friar's note explaining that Juliet's death is feigned.

F—G In spite of Juliet's worries about the sleeping potion, it works. At the anticipated hour of her awakening, she wakes up in the vault to which the Friar comes to rescue her.

G—H Romeo did *not* receive the message about the plot. He has already come to the vault to mourn her and believing her dead, he has taken poison. She joins him in death by stabbing herself.

Plot chart from Romeo's viewpoint

A—I Romeo Montague wants happiness.

A—B He loves Juliet Capulet although his family and hers are sworn enemies.

B—C Anticipating their parents' furious objections to their marriage, they are secretly wed by the Friar.

C—D When Juliet's cousin kills Romeo's page, Romeo kills him, increasing the family enmity. He faces death for his crime.

D—E Instead of the expected death sentence, he is exiled to Mantua. "Where there's life, there's hope," and he determines to get back to Verona to Juliet.

E—F When he does he finds her dead.

F—G At her burial place he runs into his bitter rival, Paris. They fight over Juliet. Even though Death now possesses her, Paris wants the right to be buried beside her. Romeo asserts his right as her husband and wins by killing his rival.

G—H   Wishing to join Juliet in death, Romeo poisons himself. The tragedy is underscored by her awakening to life, finding him dead, and her suicide.

In *West Side Story* (the musical based on the book by Arthur Laurents) New York replaces Verona and the gang-war between the Puerto Rican "Sharks" and the American "Jets" subs for the hate motif of the Montagues and Capulets. But the theme is the same: Hatred is a poison that destroys love.

Plot chart from the viewpoint of Maria (the Puerto Rican Juliet)

A—I   Maria wants love and happiness.

A—B   Her brother, Bernardo, brings her to the U.S. to marry Chino, but she's frustrated: all she's done in her first month here is sew all day in a dress shop and sleep all night.

B—C   Her first social outing is a dance at which she determines to have a good time. She meets an American boy, Tony, and they fall in love.

C—D   Bernardo breaks it up; asks Chino to take her home.

D—E   Tony loves her and they arrange secret meetings in spite of the growing gang hate. They have a mock wedding in the dress shop where she works, planning a church marriage later.

E—F   The hatred between the groups increases, exploding into a violent rumble (gang war) at which the leaders, Bernardo and Riff, die.

F—G   The love between Maria and Tony is greater than Hate, Vengeance, or loyalty to the dead. They plan to escape together to the country.

G—H   She is delayed meeting him at Doc's drugstore by the police lieutenant who comes to question her. She sends Anita to tell Tony to wait but the Jets mistreat Anita who, in revenge, tells them to tell Tony that Chino has killed Maria. Tony then wants to die and runs into the dark streets, calling to Chino to kill him. He finds Maria alive, but as they run to each other Chino jumps out of the shadows and shoots Tony who dies in Maria's arms.

Plot chart from the viewpoint of Tony (the American Romeo)

A—I   Tony wants happiness and fulfillment.

A—B   He is disappointed in his gang "The Jets" who hate Puerto Ricans.

B—C   He falls in love with Maria, sister of the Puerto Rican gang-leader, Bernardo.

C—D   Violent antagonism between their groups makes their relationship seem hopeless. Bernardo wants Maria to marry Chino; sends her home from dance to keep Tony from her.

D—E   Tony and Maria's love soars above the hate. They stage a mock wedding, swearing eternal love. She asks him to stop the planned rumble (big fight between the Jets and Sharks).

E—F   He not only fails to stop it but in trying to promote peace, he brands himself "chicken" and invites violent insults from Bernardo and the Puerto Ricans. When Riff, his own gang-leader, tries to protect him from Bernardo, the latter knifes Riff. Enraged, Tony kills Bernardo. A free-for-all follows, ended by cops' sirens. All escape except the dead gang-leaders, Riff and Bernardo.

F—G   Maria is heartbroken by her brother's death, but she still loves Tony. He hides out at Doc's drugstore where she will meet him and they will elope to the country.

G—H   Their plans misfire. When the police lieutenant comes to question her about Bernardo's death and what boy he fought with at the dance, she is delayed meeting Tony. She sends Anita with her message. Embittered by Riff's death, the Jets attack Anita who, in revenge screams out "Tell Tony Maria can't meet him because Chino found out about him and Maria and shot her!" When Tony thinks Maria's dead, he wants to die, too. He goes out of hiding into the dark streets, calling loudly to Chino to come and kill him, too. A small Plus, or Temporary Reversal, occurs when Maria appears and they run to each other. But this brief promise-of-happiness merely intensifies the irony of the tragic Crisis-Ending: Chino jumps from the shadows and shoots Tony, who dies in Maria's arms.

As in *Romeo and Juliet,* hatred has destroyed happiness for the lovers, yet out of the same hate and tragedy, new tolerance and understanding are born. In *Romeo and Juliet* the Montagues promise to build a golden statue of "true and faithful" Juliet. In *West Side Story* there are gestures of the first friendship between the Jets and the Sharks.

Plot chart of Romanoff and Juliet *from the viewpoint of Juliet* (*daughter of U.S. ambassador*)

A—I   Juliet wants love and happiness.

A—B   Although she's engaged to American Freddy (whom she doesn't love, just likes) she falls in love with Igor Romanoff, son of Russian ambassador . . . Friction between their antipodal ideologies, etc.

B—C Her only happiness is with Igor, but what happiness!

C—D Increased conflicts: parental opposition; his engagement to Party-appointed Communist girl; hers to American Freddy; both of whom are coming to claim their respective fiancés.

D—E Igor, who has been fighting their love affair because of strong anti-U.S. indoctrination, declares his love unconditionally; Freddy releases Juliet from their engagement.

E—F Overpowering conflicts between their parents, countries, duties, ideologies, etc. cause their first big fight. Both are miserable, Igor so much that he plans suicide (his fiancée is so Sovietly unfeminine that he cannot live without Juliet).

F—G The President-General of the European country where their fathers serve as ambassadors stops Igor's suicide; hatches a plot to marry Romanoff and Juliet in a traditional ceremony of his country.

G—H After the celebration, boths sets of parents fight more furiously than ever and declare the marriage invalid in the U.S. and U.S.S.R.

H—I Their objections are overruled and the power of true love and the serene charm of the peace-loving country triumph over hate. (Even American Freddy and the Russian girl fall in love.)

Plot chart of Romanoff and Juliet *from the viewpoint of Igor Romanoff (Romeo) son of the Russian ambassador*

A—I   Igor wants happiness and fulfillment.

A—B   Contrary to his Communistic, anti-U.S. training, he falls in love.

B—C   Strangely, he finds greater happiness in loving Juliet than in his political loyalties.

C—D   Parental and party objection; his sense of guilt and obligation to marry a certain Russian girl designated by the Moscow superiors.

D—E   Their mutual love conquers all minuses.

E—F   Their many differences plus parental and ideological conflicts cause them to quarrel bitterly. His Russian fiancée arrives, turning out to be his former ship captain. Ugh! Igor plans and starts to commit suicide.

F—G   His suicide is stopped by the President-General, who manipulates a trick marriage between Igor and Juliet.

G—H   The ceremony causes increased friction between their parents who swear it will never be recognized by the U.S. or U.S.S.R.

H—I   They are overruled and reconciled when the magic of love and peace conquer hate and war. Human likeness and liking blot out differences . . . even Igor's and Juliet's former fiancées find happiness together!

Instead of the classical premise that "Hatred destroys Love," Ustinov promulgates the idea that tragedy can be averted if and when people think and feel for themselves instead of letting their ideas and emotions be ruled by others. Also love and peace can triumph over hate and war . . . and *must* if we are to survive nuclear annihilation.

Additional Classics as Sources of Plots

Of course ancient legends and Shakespeare are not the only excellent germs for plot development. You should seek inspiration in all masterpieces of the past that have relevance for today's readers.

Our society is so materialistic that there have been numerous revivals of *The Miser*, which authorities mistakenly think was Molière's original idea. Molière would be amused to be credited with such innovation since he lifted the character and plot of *The Miser* from Plautus' *Pot of Gold*, which was produced in 194 b.c.! In the original (which may have been taken from an earlier source as all Roman drama was copied from the Greek), the miser Euclio is so greedy that he is almost out of his mind when his precious pot of gold is stolen by a slave. Eventually Lyconides, the slave's owner who loves Euclio's daughter, returns the pot of gold, which the miser finally gives to his daughter as a dowry, secretly glad to be freed from the strain of guarding it.

Molière changed Euclio's name to Harpagon but did not change his character. His miser is a widower who embarrasses his grown son and daughter with his avarice and his trying to force them to marry mates of his parsimonious choice. His cash box containing his beloved money is stolen, but this time by his own son who loves Marianne, also desired by the father. The son makes Harpagon choose between the money and the girl. Of course you've guessed the denouement!

All of Molière's plots were borrowed from previous works for his motto was *"Je reprends mon bien ou je le trouve"*—"I recover my property wherever I find it." He always improved the originals with increased plot complications and his sparkling, satirical wit.

Greed is also the subject of Ben Jonson's *Volpone, or the Fox,* in which avaricious Volpone feigns mortal illness to trick

Voltore, Corbaccio, and Corvino into giving him their wealth in order to become his beneficiaries. In the modern movie and play *The Honeypot,* seeing this play on stage gives the protagonist the idea of using a similar ploy to pretend to choose a wife from among his different girl friends.

"The Magi Hangup" by William Cox (*New Yorker*) introduces contemporary reversals and a fresh, realistic ending to the original O. Henry yarn. Instead of the wife cutting and selling her hair to buy her husband a watch chain while he sells his watch to buy her a comb, the modern husband, Clarence, is a long-haired hippy who has been expelled from the senior class until he chooses to return "looking like a recognizable, normal, well-trimmed American male." His wife, Clarissa, has a twelve-string, supersonic but non-electric guitar which she loves. He sells his golden hair to buy her an amplifier only to learn that she sold her guitar to pay for a tutor so that he can graduate with all his hair on!

Instead of the double sacrifice being appreciated as in the original, it adds disappointment and disillusionment that weaken their marriage. She accuses him of selling out to the Establishment, and he tells her he doesn't want a tutor. They spend a cold, white Christmas staring across the street at the snow-laden Psychedelicatessen sign, then at the wet pavement. Clarence says, "It's turning to slush. Everything's turning to slush!"

Cox changed O. Henry's old-fashioned romanticism to modern cynicism, which necessitates a reversal of the original premise. In one of his few moments of optimism, O. Henry has built a story from the premise that "the greatest gift is love" and that "he who sacrifices his most precious possession for another shall find a greater gift." Cox refutes this, implying that "no matter what sacrifice you make you can't win." Also that "when you try to be a hero you usually turn out to be a fool." Such reversals make for a fresh reading experience, although the plot line and the title "The Magi Hangup" proudly proclaim a debt to "The Gift of the Magi."

If you wish to write an ecological or environmental story of a modern project (nuclear power plant or freeway or whatever) that demands the sacrifice of beauty for progress, you should study Chekhov's *The Cherry Orchard*. Here the Ranevskayas must sell their beloved cherry orchard to meet expenses or else lose everything. Although it is financially necessary, no one can agree to do it because of its deep meanings. To Madame Ranevskaya, the orchard symbolizes a time when she was young and happy with her husband and son. To brother Gayess it is a reminder of a youth bright with billiards instead of banking. To Lopahin, the freed serf, it symbolizes a time when loyalty and love meant more security than material success. Each sees the foolishness of the others but not his own impracticality. Eventually they cling to their dreams of the past and lose their entire estate.

Mary Shelley's classic has been the springboard for a number of plots. In older versions of the Frankenstein plot, a specific doctor or scientist creates a monster he cannot control. With today's technology advancing frighteningly, the government, NASA, a scientific group, or society itself, produces much more terrifying threats to mankind. Dr. Michael Crichton updates the Frankenstein plot in his novels *The Andromeda Strain* and *The Terminal Man*. In the latter, doctors unintentionally create a homicidal maniac out of computer scientist Harry Benson by implanting forty electrodes attached to a minicomputer inside his brain in an attempt to control his psychomotor epilepsy.

This is certainly one of the most original and ingenious Frankenstein plots of all time and proves how greatly a carefully researched X-plus factor can disguise and enhance a familiar story structure. A plutonium power pack is implanted in Benson's shoulder to power the tiny computer. When activated, the electrodes prevent his seizures, but two of the electrodes are designed to produce a pleasant sensation when a seizure is about to begin, thus preventing it. This stimulation is so pleasant that Benson's brain goes into a new learning cycle and imitates seizures in order to experience pleasurable shocks. The sensations occur closer and closer together until his brain becomes overloaded and he has an ultra-violent seizure during which he commits murder.

There have been so many horror classics of the man-created monster that reversals are always welcome. In Mel Brooks's comedy *Young Frankenstein,* the protagonist, scientist-surgeon Frederick Fein, grandson of the original Baron Bennet von Frankenstein, tries to break away from his family's blood lines and live a normal life. After several of his attempts fail, he gives in and creates a new monster out of various dead tissues and other pieces of dead beings. In this movie, slapstick and *double entendre* replace terror and gore.

The television series "The Six Million Dollar Man" is also a benign reversal; government scientists have rebuilt an accident-destroyed astronaut, giving him bionic parts that make him a Superman capable of performing superfeats—all used to conquer villainy.

The current plethora of transplant stories run a wide gamut from saved lives and improved bodies to horror tales of "organlegging," which is much more gruesome than bootlegging in such movies as *Choice Cuts.*

If you're not a constant reader, become one, for "reading is to the mind what exercise is to the body" as Addison wrote. Even the Common Book of Prayer advises: "Read, mark, learn and inwardly digest." Successful writers spend much time reading, agreeing with Dr. Sam Johnson who said: "The greatest part of a writer's time is spent in reading in order to write. A man will turn over half a library to make a book." This won't reduce your originality but will increase it by making you aware of what has been written and how.

G. B. Shaw patterned most of his work on classics, insisting that no one could write a better tragedy than *King Lear* or a better comedy than *Peer Gynt.* It's a waste of time to try to concoct new plots.

14

Crisscross Your Plot and Hope to Sell

The majority of unsuccessful fiction fails to sell because the plot is fragmentary, dull, or not thoroughly developed with sufficient suspense complications. Just as a successful life is the result of a master plan, successful fiction is the product of masterfully planned plotting. This does not mean just working out the protagonist's action line from his initial problem at the beginning to a resolution at the end, but also developing a story line for each prominent character, with intricate interweaving of the different plot strands.

If you open with clashing goals, you already have two opposing entities in conflict with each other trying to reach antipodal targets, similar to football teams fighting to get to their opposite goalposts. Given this goal conflict, you'll be less likely to turn out a near-miss that doesn't have crisscrossing plot lines. However, if you wish to reach your destination of professional publication, you must still preplan your plot itinerary ahead of time for each important character. The best way to construct a full-bodied story is to crisscross different plot lines, preferably using several of the ten plot types:

1. Purpose Achieved
2. Biter-Bit or Villain Foiled
3. Decision

4. Purpose Abandoned
5. Come-to-Realize
6. Doesn't Come-to-Realize
7. Character Regenerates
8. Character Degenerates
9. Purpose Lost
10. Villain Triumphs

Throughout this book there have been examples of preplanning the ups and downs of a story so that you will be sure to include all the necessary ingredients:

Beginning: Each character is well-defined, with a specific problem and goal, as well as obstacles in his way.

Middle: Several incidents of progress and regress in the character's attempts to achieve the goal—all lead to a strong crisis, which is the direct opposite of the denouement or final resolution.

Ending: How it all turns out, plus the premise or moral theme for which all plot action has been a dramatized parable.

In various chapters there have been three different ways of structuring a plot: blueprinting; A—G plot charting; and A—I plot charting. Choose the specific method of preplanning you prefer and develop the habit of using it to outline published stories as well as your own *before you begin writing it.*

Blueprinting

In this system of outlining, you begin with the *Problem* (sharply delineated WHO wants WHAT), which is complicated by *Obstructions, Hurdles, Hindrances,* or other complications in an alternating pattern of plus (+) and minus (—), suspensefully leading up to the *Crisis* or *Turning Point,* which contains the seeds of the *Solution* or *Resolution.*

The following is an example of a blueprint of a professional short-short story. Longer yarns usually have many more pluses and minuses.

Title and Author	"The Good Doctor" by Allan Seagar (in *Playboy*)
X-Plus Factor and Style	Satire on medical profession; hypochondria and gullibility of U.S. public; Madison Avenue; and mass media.
Character's Traits	Dr. John Tenorio—ambitious, conniving research doctor. Dr. Ellis—dull, sycophantish research doctor.
Protagonist's Goal	Dr. John Tenorio wants recognition and fortune.

— He's an underpaid, obscure, unappreciated research medic.

+ He decides he can achieve fame and fortune by inventing a new disease, since Americans are suckers for anything "new."

— After pouring over drawings of the human figure, he fails to find a new disease. Mankind's pretty well "diseased up." Disgusted, he eats a dreadful carbohydrate lunch at St. Christopher's hospital and gets indigestion.

+ Stomach pains from the starchy cannelloni and the pasta casing remind him of the myelin sheath of the nervous system and he gets the idea for a new disease: myelinitis, the wasting away of the myelin sheath.

— Hurriedly, he slaps together a paper reporting it, in which he invents four phony cases. Will it be rejected, suspected, or accepted by the *Journal of the American Medical Association?*

Will the whole medical world expose him as the phony he is?

+ He succeeds in fooling them and the editors make his article its lead feature for the month. Within a week, Dr. Tenorio, as well as his disease and its symptoms, are world famous. He guest-appears on major television shows and receives plaudits from major publications.

— He's under a strain wondering if any cases will show up or whether he will be exposed.

+ Policeman's wife and several others in Los Angeles report the classic symptoms: tremor of hands, leg dragging, buzzing in ears. He's a success!

Crisis He awakes with symptoms of his invented disease. Must confess all to Dr. Ellis and threatens to cut his heart out if he tells anyone.

Climax Dr. Ellis cooperates. Now they'll set up a corporation and get funds from Ford Foundation to begin researching for a cure.

Premise "What fools these mortals be." He who digs a pit for others falls into it himself, but if he's clever enough can climb out of it one way or another. One man's meat is another's poison.

Below is a schema of the A—G plot chart that would be used to construct your story.

The A—G Plot Chart

A—G First, state Actor's Goal—something or someone he wants passionately, desperately, often immediately.

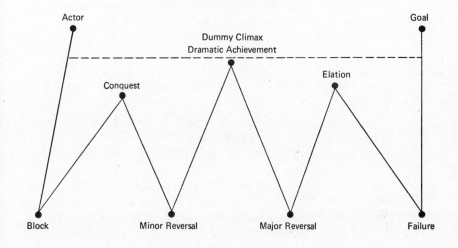

A—B	The first block or barrier that makes it impossible for the Actor to get what he *must* have (may be an external antagonist or block within himself).
B—C	What the Actor does to conquer this block.
C—Mi.R	Minor Reversal that sets back his preceding success or Conquest.
Mi.R—D	The Dramatic Achievement or Dummy Climax that promises full success.
D—Ma.R	Major Reversal that upsets the Dramatic Achievement to a disappointing, disastrous subcrisis.
Ma.R—E	Elation or Elevation, where Actor sights his goal and expects to achieve it.

E—F   Failure slaps him down to the most frustrating, ferocious crisis of the entire story.

F—G   Goal is gained through the magic paradox of the crisis giving birth to the climax. From the ashes of defeat arises the phoenix of success!

A sad-ending story or biter-bit (in which the Actor is villainous and is defeated) ends at F.

A happy-ending yarn always continues from the F crisis to G (Goal gained).

Remember to work out this plot chart for each Actor in the story.

The following analysis of "The Extravagant Heart" by Eleanor K. Woolvin (*Redbook*) will serve as an illustration of preplanning your plots using the A—G plot chart.

Story   Ken Walker, young salesman of modest means, envies his high-living neighbor, investment counselor Sherm Dixon, who drives a sportscar, goes to the races, and enjoys all the luxuries that Ken's budget-conscious wife Barbara has eliminated from their own life. Fed up with her penny pinching, Ken talks her into a gala night out, but when they go to the Dixons' to get the name of their favorite restaurant, they're shocked to find the Dixons moving away. Sherm has gone broke, tried to recoup his losses at the races and failed, bursting the huge credit bubble that the Dixons have been living on. When Ken takes out his wallet to offer them cash, Barbara stops him, *not* through stingy mean-heartedness as he first supposes, but because she has a much greater gift for the Dixons. The Walkers will take five-year old Midge Dixon away from the sad, squabble-scene of packing and give her a happy night to remember, instead of a night-

mare that would haunt her whole future and
shatter her father image and sense of security.
Ken reappreciates Barbara.

Plot chart from Ken's viewpoint

A—G   Ken wants to feel successful, to have the
things in life that mean status.

A—B   Sherm Dixon, his flashy-dressing, high-living
neighbor emphasizes his inadequacy as a pro-
vider (his own image).

B—C   Ken's wife Barbara loves him, saying, "I
wouldn't trade you *and* a million dollars for
the kind of chrome-plated class that Sherm
Dixon has."

C—Mi.R   But economical Barbara keeps such a tight
rein on their income that they never go out. He
complains of this.

Mi.R.—D   She agrees to "borrow" from their child's
education fund for a gala fun-date. She's
beautiful in a trousseau party-dress; they start
out, anticipatingly aglow.

D—Ma.R   First they stop by the Dixons to find out their
ritzy restaurant favorite, find house dark,
little Midge crying. Sherm's lost everything at
the races. Now broke, they're sneaking out
ahead of creditors. Will go to live with Maxine
Dixon's folks in Chicago. Their wealth's a
sham.

Ma.R.—E   Ken reaches for his wallet to offer financial
help.

E—F   Barbara stops him. Can she be so heartless
and stingy?

    F—G   She offers to take Midge out to spare her grief and Sherm humiliation. They do. Ken realizes Barbara's generosity.

Plot chart from Barbara's viewpoint

    A—G   Barbara Walker wants security—financial and emotional.

    A—B   They're not wealthy. Baby came two years ahead of schedule.

    B—C   She budgets carefully so that eventually Buddy (their baby) will go to college and their future will be secure.

    C—Mi.R   Ken's envy of the high-living Dixons and his dissatisfaction cause her to borrow from Buddy's education fund for the night out that Ken wants.

    Mi.R—D   Exposure of the phony, show-off prosperity of the Dixons proves she was right to budget and save.

    D—Ma.R   Ken starts to give Dixons some of their hard-saved cash.

    Ma.R—E   She prevents this with a look (doesn't humiliate him with words). He gets her silent message and stops.

    E—F   Ken may despise her for being "tight." Threat to their love.

    F—G   She offers something more helpful than money: to share their "night out" with Midge.

Plot chart from Sherm Dixon's viewpoint

    A—G   Sherm wants to show off, impress, get money without working.

A—B He's not exceptionally brilliant.

B—C He has an easy "soft-hours" job and lots of credit, which he uses to get the approbation he wants.

C—Mi.R He strains the credit until they're almost broke.

Mi.R—D Wins the Daily Double at the races. Surely luck will hold.

D—Ma.R It doesn't. He loses everything—is completely broke.

Ma.R—E He can take his family to in-laws' home in Chicago.

E—F In trying to gain respect fraudulently, he's lost everything, including self-respect and all status-symbols, which are no substitutes for real values of success.

Premises Giving isn't purely financial any more than happiness is based on materialistic values. The grass is always greener . . . Pride goeth before a fall. The credit balloon can be inflated only so far. (Barbara's: You must live today to make tomorrow worthwhile. There are many ways to skin a cat and convince a husband you're right.)

The Actor—Ideal Desire Plot Chart

In order to preplan your story, you might use the A—I (or Actor—Ideal Desire) plot charting method. The following outline is used for this method.

A. Characterize the Actor and state his Ideal Desire and why he wants it and cannot have it.

B. Major Barrier that sets off the major, to-be-continuing conflict.
C. Actor Conquers this barrier (usually cleverly or bravely).
D. Dangerous Detour sends the Actor off in the wrong direction.
E. Escape from the Detour by the Actor.
F. Failure or setback when the Actor thought he was on his way to achieving his Ideal Desire.
G. Greatest Gain so far is made by the Actor. He or she is sure that the Ideal Desire is within grasp.
H. Hopeless Hades, supercrisis, or reversal of the Ideal Desire. Whatever the Actor has been striving for is certainly impossible to attain at this nadir or lowest point of the story. Although failure seems unavoidable, the Hopeless Hades magically contains the means of accomplishing the Ideal Desire. (An unhappy story ends here.)
I. The Ideal Desire is achieved and "All's well that ends well."

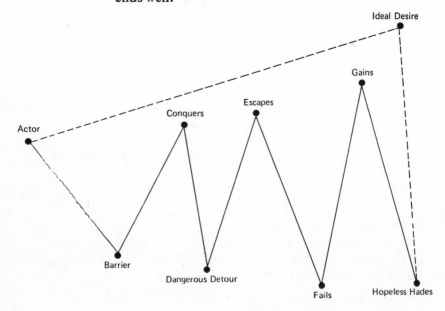

Using the A—I method, you could develop the following plot chart for *Bells Are Ringing* by Betty Comden and Adolph Green.

Ella's viewpoint

A—I   Ella, warm-hearted switchboard operator, wants love.

A—B   Stuck behind the switchboard of Sue's Answer-Phone, she has no opportunities to meet anyone.

B—C   Loving people, she helps the unseen customers; plays Santa to kids; brings lonely cat-lovers together; pretends to be sympathetic old lady, "Mom," to playwright Jeffrey Moss, with whom she falls in love.

C—D   Sue makes fun of her living vicariously, since she means nothing to these people, and they so much to her. Police inspector and his aid suspect Sue's Answer-Phone of being a "front."

D—E   When Producer Larry Hastings gives Jeffrey Moss a noon deadline to finish the outline of his play, *Midas Touch*, and Ella can't reach him, she goes to his apartment to wake him. Meeting for the first time, they like each other, even though he doesn't know who she is. She calls herself Melisande Scott and explains her knowledge of his play, etc. by saying she's psychic.

E—F   While police are suspecting Sue's Answer-Phone of crimes of which it is innocent, Sandor, a smooth-operating bookie, woos the old-maid owner Sue and becomes her partner.

He takes bets under the guise of Titanic Record Co., using a code in which Beethoven means Belmont Park; Humperdinck—Hollywood Park; Puccini—Pimlico; Handel—Hialeah.

F—G   Ella (still pretending to be Melisande Scott) and Jeff are in love. He takes her to a swanky party to meet his friends, to whom he raves about her and her psychic powers.

G—H   Because they want her to perform a séance and because she feels like a phony (since Jeff loves Melisande Scott who doesn't exist), Ella leaves the party and drops out of Jeff's life without leaving a trace. This crisis is strengthened as the bookie subplot comes to a head and thugs come to beat up Sandor because always-helpful Ella has changed all the record orders for Beethoven's Tenth Symphony to Beethoven's Ninth (which was his last). At this crisis the inspector and his man close in on Sue's Answer-Phone.

H—I   Ella avoids prison by proving her innocence and rounding up bookie mob and turning them over to the inspector. Jeff tracks her down and is not angry at her masquerade. In fact he's happy that "Mom" and pretty, young Melisande Scott are the same. Clincher.

Premises   Unselfish loving kindness to others leads to one's personal happiness.
No matter how small our role in life may seem, each of us has a widespread effect on others and we should make this influence a good one, not a bad one.
It's better to Love and Help Thy Neighbor than

to Mind Thy Own Business—or "a person
who's wrapped up in himself makes a mighty
small package."

Jeffrey Moss's viewpoint

A—I   Jeff wants happiness and success as a playwright.

A—B   He is a procrastinating playboy playwright;
doesn't accomplish anything work-wise, just
party-wise and is becoming "all play" "no
write."

B—C   The only friend in whom he can confide is the
sympathetic old lady at Sue's Answer-Phone
whom he calls "Mom."

C—D   Producer Larry Hastings gives him a deadline
to finish the outline of his play *Midas
Touch* or he'll lose his big chance. He *cannot*
write; struggles in vain; falls asleep.

D—E   Next morning he is awakened by his Hi-Fi
and a girl named Melisande Scott. She's zany
but understands his problem, gives him coffee
and confidence to finish his outline on time.

E—F   Although they have fun together, she won't
tell him much about herself or where she lives.
He doesn't know it, but a downpoint for him
is her decision NOT to keep their next date
because of her guilt in deceiving him. This
barrier is overcome when, via phone, she hears
the voice of a girl with him and jealousy sends
her to Jeff to chase Olga away from him.

F—G   His work improves as their love is mutual and
he shows her off to his friends.

G—H   Melisande disappears and he can't find any clues to her whereabouts, even though evidence keeps cropping up that she has brought together the principal characters who make his play a success.

H—I   He traces her to Sue's Answer-Phone, is delighted to learn that "Mom" and Melisande Scott are the same.

Premise   A man needs a wife and a mother. If he can find both in one woman, so much the better! Or: No matter how much talent you have, you cannot go it alone. Someone *must* have confidence in you and love you if you are to succeed.

Sue's viewpoint

A—I   She wants romance.

A—B   She's an unattractive old maid with no prospects.

B—C   She achieves some success through her answering service where her appearance doesn't matter.

C—D   Police suspect her Service of being a "front" and start snooping.

D—E   Sue attracts a boyfriend in Sandor, who becomes her partner.

E—F   She notices that Sandor becomes nervous, especially when followed by suspicious characters.

F—G   He asks her for money and when she offers her savings, he says they'll marry and travel together, happy ending, etc., etc.

G—H   She learns Sandor is a bookie using her Service for illegal purposes; hoodlums come for revenge; police close in, close Sue's Answer-Phone.

H—I   Sandor still loves her, asks her to wait for him. Love wins out over pride.

Premise   Many of the old chestnuts combine to give a comic-opera touch; "All is not gold that glitters." "You must take the bitter with the sweet." "Love is blind to deception and lasts longer." "No man is perfect, but an imperfect man is better than no man at all." etc. etc.

X-plus Factor   How an Answering-Service acts as a focal point to bring lonely lives together.

Universal Basic Factors and Spiritual Values   Love versus Loneliness. Sincere desire to help people versus prying into their affairs. Complete honesty versus well-meaning deception or "A white lie told with good intent beats telling damaging truths."

Once you have started preplanning your story using one of the methods described above, consider which of the ten basic plot types you will use and in what combinations you will use them.

1. Purpose Achieved

A sympathetic protagonist with a positive goal overcomes many obstacles that worsen to a strong crisis. Through his own efforts and ingenuity he does win his goal at the climax. This is an "All's Well That Ends Well" story.

Since fantasy writer Ray Bradbury is an optimist, several of his yarns have Purpose Achieved plots. He says that an author should be a medicine man, "a Doctor of the spirit . . . I depress people with my optimism."

But his goal-gained plots are not saccharine. Instead they treat serious subjects, sometimes rectifying life's tragedies.

Bradbury's "The Kilimanjaro Machine" lifted Hemingway from his ignoble suicide end to lofty heights and gave him a hero's burial. Ray insists, "I had to bury Papa in a proper grave." Another Purpose Achieved plot that honors Hemingway is "The Parrot Who Met Papa" in which El Cordoba, the parrot to whom Hemingway told his last novel is kidnaped from the Cuba Libre bar in Havana. The hero, Raimundo, tries to solve the mystery and rescue the valuable bird. Cleverly, he finds the kidnaper, a con man named Shelley Capon, who is holding it for the highest ransom fortune from publishers and the television media. Against great odds and dangerous enemies, the hero seizes the bird and threatens to wring its neck. They let him take it away after he promises to keep it alive and let them bid for it later. While El Cordoba keeps quoting Hemingway's precious prose, Raimundo carries him away—to the airport where he fears alerted guards and the Castro militia will prevent him from taking a national treasure out of the country. He uses ingenuity to solve the problem: He dyes the parrot with black shoe polish and teaches it to say over and over the word "Nevermore."

"The Life Work of Juan Diaz" (also by Bradbury) is a double Purpose Achieved plot. A poor widow in Guanaguato, Mexico, wants to save her husband's corpse from being dug up and displayed with other mummies as is the custom if you cannot pay the annual burial rental fee charged by the cemetery. Finally she and her young son succeed in purloining his mummy and setting it up in their *casa*, charging *turistas* to see it. Thus, even in death Juan Diaz achieves his life-goal of providing for his family.

Here's a schema of Stan Dryer's "The Conquest of the Washinton Monument" published in *Playboy*.

Hero and his goal   Technical monument-climber Stan wants to perform a feat never successfully accomplished: to scale the Washington Monument.

— It's illegal, the police are tough and one climber can't do it alone.

+ He selects for his co-climber Warrington Hull of the New York Skyscraper Club who's been in prison for climbing the west face of the U.N. building and who writes that he'd been "climbing the walls" of his prison cell for the past 3 months.

— Several enumerated technical difficulties, bright floodlights and risk of discovery and arrest.

+ They start at 2:30 A.M. and solve all problems. They cover the floodlights with blankets and take new explosive impact bolts and carbide-tipped spiked boots. Everything's A-O.K.

— At 5:30 A.M. police see them, call firemen who climb fire ladders and shout threats of jail.

+ The climbers can't be reached and keep on scaling the monument.

— A National Guard policeman is lowered on a rope to talk to them. Another reads a court order demanding that they desist from desecration of a national monument.

+ Hero insists they come not to desecrate, but to consecrate.

— A hose rigged to the top shoots water at them.

Hull weakens, slips and is bushed after all that time in jail. He admits that "climbing the walls of his cell" was a figurative for "up-tight."

+   Hero keeps climbing and is cheered by crowds below.

Sub-crisis   Hull totally deserts him, defecting to the police, whom he joins in urging Stan to give up. They may grab him at the top.

+   He swings his line of attack toward the edge of the face.

Crisis   Danger increases as he's running out of bolts and must space his reaches as far apart as possible. With only two precious bolts left, he drops one—is desperate. A cop awaits him at the top (by a trap door). He jams piton in a crack.

Climax   A news helicopter snatches him from the police and makes a deal. In exchange for exclusive rights they'll land him in Virginia. On way to fame and fortune he eyes the Capitol dome!

Premise   "A man's reach should exceed his grasp or what's Heaven for?" Achievement is not an end but a spur to a greater goal.

2. Biter-Bit

The Biter-Bit is the reverse of the Purpose Achieved plot. Instead of a sympathetic hero, this character is unsympathetic with a selfish goal. His crisis is a Plus instead of a Minus and is the point in the story where he and we think he will attain his purpose. The climax, however, reverses this and he loses out because of his own actions and/or characterization. The following analysis of "A Place to Avoid" by David Ely (*Playboy*) is an example of this plot.

Character and Goal	Bauer, big, burly, surly, brutish, hard-sweating resort developer wants to build a swanky resort on a beachfront in Italy that he liked when he was a Nazi soldier in that area during World War II. He now owns it.
—	His property doesn't seem too promising. Its only beauty lies in its pine-filled promontory that juts out high above the ocean.
+	He has hired Italian workers to develop it into a remunerative resort area with tennis courts, golf links, and a residential area with apartments, cottages, shops, and restaurants to remind the world that Germans again occupy Italy with an army of tourists instead of soldiers. He thinks, "If Kesselring had had such forces under his command . . . the Allies could have been swept out of Italy altogether!"
—	The work lags and the workmen are idle because the equipment keeps breaking down.
+	The Italian work manager, German-speaking surveyor Giachetti is efficient. He has sent a man to Grosseto to get a replacement part for the broken bulldozer. He promises Bauer he'll tell the men to work harder than they have been doing.
—	Bauer senses resentment and hostility from the workers. Giachetti explains their superstitious beliefs that the breakdowns are caused by evil spirits that don't want anyone to

tamper with the piney woods on top of the promontory. They fear it as a place to avoid—*un luogo da evitare.*

+ The German feels superior to the stupid peasants and is determined to build his project with or without them. He is elated by visions of his rich resort where Italians will be servants to the moneyed Germans.

— More frustrations. He orders a new bulldozer that won't come for two more weeks.

+ Disgusted with the laborers' apathy, he picks up a shovel and works furiously to show them how it should be done. Offers bonuses.

— Nothing seems to spur them and he faces the real reason: the Italians remember his regiment that came there in '44 and the sixteen local hostages who were shot in retaliation for the death of two Nazis.

+ Bauer tells Giachetti to explain to the men that he won't give up and that his resort will bring the natives jobs and money—more than the evil spirits could do! Work picks up. The access road is nearing completion and Bauer begins to jeep up it.

— The workers stop again, staring fearfully up at the promontory. They threaten to quit entirely if he drives up to the top. Giachetti talks him into coming down—at least till the road's finished. Since he can't get through the rough, roadless terrain anyway, he gives up.

Crisis That night in his trailer, prematurely enjoying

the realization of his dream and his conviction of German superiority, he has a few drinks with Giachetti who patiently listens to his boasting about the New Europe that he and his kind are building. The access road is soon completed and equipment for the rest of the project arrives. His triumph is total!

Climax   Sullenly, the men take their pay, then turn their backs on Bauer and don't answer him when he tells them to come back to work tomorrow. Giachetti explains that their attitude has to do with their superstitious fear of the promontory, the haunted "place to avoid." To ridicule their ignorance and exhibit his own courage and superiority, Bauer drives his jeep all the way up. Victoriously he waves at the men below until . . . the jeep explodes!

Anti-climax   The work boss tells Giachetti that the Germans left many mines throughout the area—everywhere, in the lowlands and in the mountains where partisans used to hide out. Many Italian civilians have been killed by these Nazi mines since the war. When Giachetti says to the *capo*, "You knew but you didn't warn him?" the latter replies, "He was warned."

Premises   Do not underestimate others or overestimate yourself. Pride goeth before a fall. When in a foreign country you should learn everything you can about it and try to be *simpatico* instead of arrogant and hostile.

The following analysis of Lew Wallace's *Ben Hur* is an example of a crisscross of the first two plot types: Purpose Achieved from the hero's viewpoint and Biter-Bit from the point of view of the villain. Included is the third plot,

Decision, from the viewpoint of a minor character. The more different kinds of story threads credibly plaited, the better!

From the viewpoint of Judah Ben-Hur (Purpose Achieved)

Protagonist and his Purpose	Judah Ben-Hur wants to live peacefully and let live.

— Romans dominate his land, and his people are quarreling among themselves and rebelling against Roman tyranny.

+ The new Roman Tribunal is Messala, his life-long friend who has always loved him, his sister, and his mother. Surely this will mean peace and fairer treatment for his nation and his family.

— Messala is interested only in advancing politically. He asks Ben-Hur to become an informer and betray his people. When he refuses, Messala makes an example of the Ben-Hurs when tile from their roof accidentally falls on the Roman governor. Ben-Hur is sent to the galleys and his mother and sister to prison.

+ Ben-Hur survives three years as a galley slave and attracts the admiration of Roman Consul Arrius whose life he saves when pirates sink their ship. Arrius takes him to Rome, trains him to be his charioteer, and adopts him as his son.

— Even though Ben-Hur now outranks Messala, he cannot find his family. He renounces his Roman citizenship, and keeps searching.

+ He returns home to find loyal Esther and her father waiting. He gets a chance to race

Messala when a Roman-hating Arab hires him
to race his chariot and fine horses.

Crisis   Messala's unfair, dirty tricks almost defeat
and kill Ben-Hur. But he finally wins, only to
be tormented by Messala with the knowledge
that his mother and sister are worse than
dead . . . lepers.

Climax   Ben-Hur rushes to the Valley of the Lepers,
takes his dying sister and mother to the
Nazarene who cures them. They are all reunited in health and faith.

Premise   Love and Faith work miracles.

From Messala's viewpoint (*Biter Bit or Villain Foiled*)

Protagonist   Messala wants power, position, success with
and his   the Roman Emperor.
Purpose

—   He feels inferior. Receives the almost impossible assignment to pacify rebellious Jerusalem.

+   Even though he is a Roman Tribunal, he is
welcomed warmly by his friend, Judah Ben-
Hur, whose help he needs to squelch the
rebels.

—   Ben-Hur won't be bribed—loving integrity
more than reward.

+   A dislodged tile from Ben-Hur's roof injures
the Roman governor. Messala advances his
prestige by sending Judah to the galleys and
Judah's mother and sister to prison.

—   Judah survives the galley, rescues Roman
Consul Arrius who adopts him and gives him
Roman rank superior to Messala's.

Crisis   Ben-Hur seeks his mother and sister. Messala
evacuates them to a leper colony and plans to
destroy Ben-Hur in the Chariot race.

Climax   Messala is defeated. Dying, he enjoys Ben-
Hur's torment when he tells him his mother
and sister are worse then dead. But Messala
suffers a posthumous defeat: In contrast to his
hate and ambition, love and faith cure his
victims.

Premise   Hatred destroys the hater; Ambition corrodes
character.

From the viewpoint of Esther

Protagonist   Esther wants love, happiness, and freedom.
and her
Purpose

—   She is a slave, the daughter of a slave in the
Ben-Hur family.

+   Benevolent Judah Ben-Hur gives her freedom
when she receives a marriage proposal from
an Antioch merchant.

—   The Ben-Hur family is destroyed by Messala.
Her father is tortured for not revealing the
whereabouts of his master's wealth and she
gives up marriage to care for him.

+   Ben-Hur (thought dead) returns from galleys.
They declare love.

—   Thinking the Romans have killed his family,

he is embittered, vengeful, and without the
faith and love he used to have.

+   The women return but with leprosy. Esther
serves them by taking food to the Valley of the
Lepers and by respecting their pleas to tell
Judah they died so he won't trace them and
learn the hideous truth.

Crisis   Judah does find out and is angry with her.
Their love is threatened.

Climax   She appeases him, then persuades him to
believe in the Nazarene who has power to heal
all who have faith. The women are cured and
the family is reunited in joy.

Premise   Loyalty, love, and nobility of character are as
important as nobility of birth. Virtue is its own
reward.

3. *Decision*

The above is a *Decision* plot. Esther has many decisions; to
remain a slave in Ben-Hur's family or accept a marriage
proposal from an Antioch merchant and be a free citizen. She
decides on the latter course of action. Before her marriage,
however, the Romans try to destroy the Ben-Hurs, sending
Judah to the galleys and his mother and sister to prison. They
also torture her father for not giving them his master's wealth.
She *decides* to forego marriage to care for her father. When
Ben-Hur returns, she *decides* to accept his love and give up all
men for him. When she learns his mother and sister are lepers
and want her to keep this a secret from Judah, she *decides* to
obey them. As the Romans become more cruel and the times
more troubled, she *decides* to study and follow the new
religion introduced by the Nazarene. All of her *decisions* lead
to a happy ending.

Another Esther was the heroine of an earlier Decision

plot in the Bible. The most beautiful wife of the Persian King Ahasuerus, she has to *decide* whether to tell the King she is a Jewess and try to save her people who are to be killed because of the lies the ambitious villain Haman told the King. Esther's Uncle Mordecai's goal is to prevent the planned slaughter and to alert the King to Haman's evil ambitions. He tells Esther that she is the only person who can intercede with the King. Although it may mean her death for going to her husband unbidden, she *decides* to take the risk, is received, and *decides* to invite the King and Haman to a banquet. They come and the King promises to grant her request, which, of course, is to save her people and punish Haman. Realizing the truth, the King countermands the death order but has Haman hanged on the gallows he had built for Mordecai and the Jews.

This is just one example of how well the plot lines in Bible stories crisscross:

1. Purpose Achieved—Mordecai's viewpoint
2. Biter-Bit—Haman's viewpoint
3. Decision—Esther's viewpoint
4. Purpose Abandoned—King Ahasuerus abandons his initial attitude of trusting and believing Haman

4. Purpose Abandoned

In this fourth plot type, a sympathetic character has a negative goal, which, when he has a chance to achieve it, he voluntarily abandons. He gives up his goal because he wants to, not because he cannot attain it. The following analysis of "The Raffle" by E. J. Kahn, Jr., is a representative example of the Purpose Abandoned plot.

Protagonist and his Purpose	Unhappy husband has long been trying to figure out a decent way to get rid of his wife. He has the highest esteem for her, but they just don't seem to have any common interests and he is pretty bored with it all.
—	He isn't the violent type and divorce is out of the question since he has no real grounds; she

would probably drive a hard alimony bargain. Seems she is rather expensive.

+   He decides to raffle off his wife.

—   What if she objects? He hasn't yet told her about his idea.

+   He makes her share so enticing, she can't refuse. If a married man wins her, she will live in luxury and still have her share, and if a real creep wins her, she can buy him off.

—   The local fund-raising firm won't help him, but they want to buy tickets.

+   He has his own tickets printed up and sells them for $5.00 each. He plans to sell 200,000 tickets and they are going fast. He tells his wife about the plan and she is delighted, especially so when she finds out she may get as much as $683,000 with an absolute guarantee of $200,000 at worst.

Crisis   She wants to buy a chance on herself. He tells her it's not in the rules since only men can buy tickets in a raffle. He finally agrees to buy one ticket for her.

Climax   That ticket is the winning one and they take the proceeds and go to Tahiti—he by plane and she by chartered yacht. There they live happily ever after.

Premise   While money may not make you happy, it may make you less miserable. Habit is a chain that binds more strongly than any wish to break it. We may love what we think we hate.

5. Come to Realize

In the fifth possible plot, a sympathetic character is specifically unhappy in his life-situation until a crisis changes his attitude to make him appreciate the circumstances. Realization brings new joy. The following analysis of "Don't Ever Change" by R. W. Alexander (in *Good Housekeeping*) is just such a plot.

Protagonist and her Purpose	Newlywed Mary Dowling wants a happy marriage and a happy husband, Don.
—	She has burned many dinners standing at the living room window waiting for him to come home.
+	She breaks this habit. Stays in kitchen cooking, but with an eye on the clock.
—	He is so late tonight that she thinks something has happened to him.
+	He comes home safe and sound. Although he walks stiffly and slowly, hair untidily tossed, his shoes off, clothes damp and sagging, he tells her that he loves her.
—	He tells her what happened. A boy flagged down his car and told him his chum was drowning. Don went with him to the lake where the poor lad was dangerously submerged. The situation was grim.
+	Quickly Don dove in and pulled the boy out, saving his life. Mary is so proud that she kisses him and says, "Because of you a boy is alive." Don agrees that the boy is not only alive but well enough to have run away with his friend without proper thanks.

Crisis   When he takes off his damp clothes he discovers that his wallet has been stolen. He feels like a sucker and hates himself for having been taken in. His ego and self-respect are at a low ebb.

Climax   She reassures him that he did the right thing and it is because he is empathetic that she loves him. He plans to make a police report to stop such delinquency and save successors from the youths' con game. Although another dinner's burned, she's a good wife.

Premise   There's more to being a good wife than efficient cooking, housework, and other physical achievements. There's the psychological function of propping up your husband's ego and making him proud of his correct decisions especially when he is self-doubting.

Let's look at a Come-to-Realize plot line that crisscrosses with another one in the familiar clashing-goal situation of a husband wanting his wife to be a domestic stay-at-home, while she has other ideas. Ira Levin's *Critic's Choice* opens with the critic's frustration over his wife's ambition.

Protagonist and his Purpose   Drama critic Parker Ballantine wants his second wife Angela to be just a wife and mother to his son John.

—   Angela insists on writing a play and becoming a playwright.

+   He discourages her in a sarcastic article "Don't Write That Play." Tries to prove to her that she's no good at it.

—   Angela's play, *The Gingerbread World*, is

accepted by top producer S.P. Champlain and director Dion Kapakos.

+ As Dion grafts his Greek tragedy ideas and Champlain adds his own changes and cast troubles increase, the play will surely flop and Angela will come home meekly and be the housewifely gal he wants—especially after he pans it.

— His certainty of Angela is shaken by his first wife's nasty gossip about Angela and Dion in New Haven (gossip that Angela's own mother believes and blames on him). When he plans to ruin the play with an unfavorable review, Angela blackmails him into staying away from the theater and letting Harvey Rittenhouse review it. Ivy's (his first wife) high-voltage attempts to get him back and his awareness of having sold out are additional minuses at this point.

+ Even though Ivy has him thoroughly inebriated, Parker realizes his cowardice and lack of self-respect in letting Rittenhouse review the play. He rushes to the theater, is pleased to find the play as dreadful as he hoped it would be. He pans it with: ". . . Dr. Frankenstein is making monsters again. *This* time he's attached the arms and legs of Agamemnon to the torso of Rebecca of Sunnybrook Farm . . ." Parker's true to himself.

Crisis Instead of being chastised, Angela plans to leave him for Dion.

Climax This is shock therapy to make him see his mistakes in ignoring the fact that she has aspirations that are as important as his own. He promises to help her future plays—or any collaborations. Wins her back. Will be a more understanding husband from now on.

Premise   A man must realize and respect his wife's need for creative outlets and do what he can to help her in order to have a harmonious marriage with a fulfilled partner. A wife can be a perverse creature. As long as you block her, she'll oppose you. Give in, quit nagging, and go along with her plans, and she'll probably love you all the more; put marriage first and abandon any distractions.

Notice how beautifully Parker's plot line crisscrosses with that of Angela in the same play. Every plus for one is a minus for the other:

Protagonist   Angela Ballantine wants to fulfill herself by
and her   writing a hit play.
Purpose

—   Her drama-critic husband, Parker Ballantine, does not want her to become a playwright, insisting no amateur can write a good play. (His first wife, Ivy, was a career girl and an actress—and made him and their son John miserable. He wants Angela to be a homebody.)

+   Defying him, she starts writing a play based on her girlhood experiences and her wholesome Uncle Ben.

—   Parker speeds up his razzing by writing a biting article "Don't Write That Play," which he threatens to expand into a book. He pans her play, *The Gingerbread World.*

+   She plugs away, finishes it (the first thing in
    her life that she has finished). Play is accepted
    by top-Broadway producer S. P. Champlain
    and will be directed by the brilliant young
    director Dion Kapakos.

—   Instead of rejoicing, Parker continues his
    razzing and gloomy predictions of the play's
    failure. When Angela asks him to come up to
    New Haven to help them whip the play into
    shape, he refuses, saying that if he contributes
    to the play he cannot be objective. He insists
    on reviewing it honestly and detachedly, main-
    taining his integrity as a critic.

+   Feeling deserted and disparaged by her hus-
    band, Angela goes to New Haven without him,
    importing her crisply efficient mother (Char-
    lotte Orr) to care for Parker and John. Her
    ego, which has been squelched by her husband,
    is restored by the adoring director Dion. She
    uses strategy (almost blackmail) to keep pre-
    judiced Parker from reviewing the play.
    Forces him to let mild Harvey Rittenhouse
    review it (so she'll get good reviews).

Crisis   Ivy (Parker's first wife) tries to get Parker
    back by gossiping about Angela and Dion. At
    the last minute Parker goes to the theater,
    writes a slam-review that will finish the play.
    Furious, Angela plans to leave him.

Climax   In the blow-up climactic scene, Parker pro-
    claims his love, apologizes for not helping her
    with the play, promises to help her in future
    projects if she'll stay with him. He wants to be
    on her team forever and admits he was so
    concerned with his own self-respect that he

didn't realize he was highjacking hers. She stays, preferring a caress to a career.

Premise   Frustration is the shrieking of potentialities and when a wife is permitted to give vent to her creativity she'll value marriage more. Opposition can be a spur.

Angela's plot is a combination of Purpose Abandoned and Decision.

6. Doesn't Come to Realize

Some people are incapable of realization and insight like the two fatuous matrons in Katinka Loeser's "Messy and Windy" (*Redbook*) who criticize the younger generation, not realizing the part their phony values and stupidity play in youth's rebellion; or "The Kindness of Strangers" by Ruth Tracy Millard (analysis follows).

Protagonist and her Purpose   Wife wants to enjoy Europe with her husband.

— She and her husband are tired from rushing through London, Paris, Geneva, and Lucerne. She develops a vicious cold and sore throat.

+ She takes aspirin and cold pills, goes to bed early, and gets a good night's sleep.

— Her husband awakens with severe pains in his chest.

+ They visit a doctor who examines him and tells him his heart is in good condition.

Crisis   The next morning her husband doesn't get up. She finds him dead in bed.

Climax   Everyone around her is sympathetic and treats her kindly. They make all the arrangements, and the hotel manager even calls her brother long distance to tell him of the tragedy and to ask him to meet her at the airport. But she is miserable and self-pitying.

Premise   Some people don't realize that a friend in need is a friend indeed. This woman claims she has no one and will always be a lonely stranger. Her only friend was her husband because she has shared her life with him. She will never appreciate or accept the kindness of others.

7. *Character Regenerates*

In this plot, a person with negative traits overcomes them and rehabilitates. Most juvenile and confession stories follow this formula.

8. *Character Degenerates*

In reverse action to the above, this characterization toboggans downward to deterioration. There is an excellent crisscross of these two types in the classic "Miss Sadie Thompson" by Somerset Maugham (upon which the play and film *Rain* is based).

Protagonist and her Purpose   Sadie Thompson, a gay "wind-blown creature, the victim of her own good humor, fond of life and taking its rebuffs smiling," wants happiness.

—   Fleeing from troubles at home she takes a mailboat to Apia, but the rainy season causes the boat to be stranded at Pago Pago.

+   Sadie organizes a party for the few Marines there, cheering them up with a bottle of whiskey and a phonograph she brought from Hawaii.

— Mrs. Davidson, a missionary's wife in the group, objects to dancing on the Sabbath and her holier-than-thou husband, Rev. Davidson, denounces Sadie as a "Scarlet woman" whom he believes to be a refugee from Iweili, the recently raided red-light district of Honolulu. He presses a relentless campaign against Sadie and tries to have her evicted from the hotel.

+ O'Hara, a Marine, befriends Sadie and says if Rev. Davidson bars her way to Apia, she can stay with his friends in Sydney, Australia, Biff and Maggie and their two kids. She accepts.

— Rev. Davidson influences the Governor to deport her to the States, refusing permission for her to go on to Australia. She cannot go back to the U.S. because in San Francisco she was "framed" and will have to suffer a three year sentence in the penitentiary if she returns. She tells Davidson this and begs for mercy.

+ She accepts his offer, which he calls "the finest chance you have ever had" to repent. She prays with the Reverend for redemption and salvation. Even though O'Hara offers to marry her and help her escape to Sydney, she refuses him to continue praying and atoning for her past sins. Rev. Davidson says she is redeemed. She does not have to go back to San Francisco to be arrested.

Crisis After elevating Sadie from the carnal depths, the Reverend succumbs to temptation with her, shattering her faith. After spending the night with her, he commits suicide.

Climax Sadie thought Davidson's degradation of her was his joke on her. Now she realizes that he was weaker than she. She accepts O'Hara's proposal and plans to go to Sydney with his friends.

From Reverend Davidson's viewpoint

Protagonist and his Purpose Missionary Reverend Alfred Davidson "a tall, high-strung man with penetrating, relentless eyes and a deep voice," wants to save souls.

— He and his wife are on a mailboat to Apia when the rainy season strands them in Pago Pago.

+ A painted floozy in their party, Sadie Thompson, is a challenge to his spirituality, since obviously she is a scarlet woman needing redemption.

— All of his attacks on her immorality do not spur her to seek salvation, rather they antagonize her and she fights him viciously.

+ After he threatens to have her deported back to the U.S., she confesses that she is "wanted" in San Francisco and cannot return. She asks his help and agrees to pray with him and "get religion" to save her soul. She does pray steadily, sincerely. Surely he is succeeding.

— Spiritually exhausted by praying unceasingly for Sadie, he is troubled by strange dreams. He is unaware that his dreams of the "mountains of Nebraska" are sex symbols stirring in his unconscious.

Crisis   He interprets the dreams as holy. Heaven blesses his work in converting her and she is redeemed.

Climax   As he has regenerated her, he degenerates, succumbing to her physical magnetism . . . Disgraced by his own downfall, he ends his life.

Another example of a crisscross of plots seven and eight is *Days of Wine and Roses* in which the alcoholic husband regenerates and his wife degenerates into an alcoholic.

9. Purpose Lost

This plot type will yield a tragic, "quality" story. We are in such rapport with the sympathetic protagonist that we share his suffering in defeat, as we do deaf-mute John Singer's failure to find love and communication in Carson McCullers's *The Heart is a Lonely Hunter*. The following analysis of "I Will Keep Her Company" by Rhys Davies (in *New Yorker*) is another example of the Purpose Lost plot.

Protagonist and her Purpose   A Welsh social worker nurse tries to persuade an old man whose wife has just died to go back with her to town and enter a comfortable old folks' home. She finds great resistance among these stubborn old people to the institutionalized care offered by the state.

—   He refuses and insists upon staying with the body of his wife until they return to take her into town.

+   She persuades him to think over her suggestion.

—   A heavy snowstorm suddenly blankets the area and continues for a week. Nobody is able to get out to the old man in the farmhouse.

+   The nurse finally gets a helicopter to fly out to drop provisions to the old man.

—   The copter reports no sign of life near the house.

+   Nurse commandeers a snowplow and enlists the services of the vicar to go out with her as they break a way to the old man.

Crisis   They reach the house only to find it bitterly cold and apparently empty.

Climax   They go upstairs where they find the old man sitting, enveloped in woolens, in a chair by the bed of his dead wife, frozen to death.

Premise   Few, if any human beings are equipped to decide what is the best way for other people to live or die. No matter how hard you try to do what you think right for people, it may be a losing battle.

Most stories of yesterday rewarded virtue and punished villainy so consistently that Jack London's hard-hitting, true-to-life yarns were stark but honest in their realism. No matter how valiantly a man struggled against insurmountable odds, he wasn't rescued by a Hollywood happy ending in London's stories. This same stark realism has been used by a number of authors—Zola, Flaubert, Dreiser, W. D. Howells, Henry James, and Upton Sinclair, to name only a few. Although the plots of these authors are not easily reduced to any one plot type, they frequently fall within the classification of Purpose Lost.

10. *Villain Gets Away with It*

Several years ago Françoise Sagan shocked readers with her hard-hearted heroines who weren't punished for such "terrible" deeds as leading a married man into an affair or indirectly causing the death of someone. Today, these girls are softies compared to villains who act immorally without compunction or retribution.

Friedrich Duerrenmatt's villains always succeed with their nefarious plans. In *The Visit*, vengeful billionairess Claire Zachanassian offers to give the town of Gullen a billion marks if the citizens will kill popular Anton Schill (who once seduced her). They do and she wreaks a hideous revenge. In *The Physicists*, a sadistic woman doctor holds the world's greatest scientists prisoner in order to learn their total knowledge and use it to control them and gain power. Gogol's *Inspector-General* is an impersonator who preys on a town's guilt and escapes with fantastic loot just as crooks get away with ill-gotten gains in many movies like *Charlie Varrick, The Sting, The Godfather, Paper Moon* and hundreds of others.

Since there must be a victim or victims taken advantage of, this plot type often crisscrosses with a Purpose Lost story line. Sometimes there are many tragic victims as in the case of a dictator or sadistic Communist or Nazi, or a murderer like Jack the Ripper, or a charming conman like Emile Magis in Marceau's *The Egg*, who derives benefits from thievery, doublecrossing a friend, blackmail, and murder. Victorious villains are on the increase as fiction mirrors the moral decadence of society.

At least you'll improve your plot by crisscrossing before you start to write your story . . . long or short. The following analysis of Peter Benchley's *Jaws* is only one current example of the value of crisscrossing plots to achieve good fiction.

Main Characters

Police Chief Martin Brody	41, 6'1" tall, good-looking, but beginning to worry about his thickening middle and high blood-pressure, not realizing that it can be

aggravated by his quick temper and jealousy of his pretty wife Ellen. Basically honest, right-thinking, and dedicated, even though he's less than a two-fisted ultra-brave and active supercop.

Ellen Brody   36, but looks 30. Attractive but socially discontent with her less-than-glamorous life as wife and mother to three boys. More educated and better bred than her husband, she envies the jet setters who summer in Amity.

Mayor Lawrence P. Vaughan   Fiftyish, "with a body kept trim by exercise . . . he had made a great deal of money in real estate speculation and he was the senior partner in the most successful agency in town." Snobbish, ambitious, suave, smooth.

Harry Meadows   Editor of the Amity *Leader:* "He was in his late 40's, ate too much, chain-smoked cheap cigars, drank bonded bourbon and was, in the words of his doctor, the Western world's leading candidate for a huge coronary infarction."

Matt Hooper   Dedicated ichthyologist, sensitive, loves fish, even sharks. Handsome, tanned, hair bleached by the sun. Same height as Brody (6'1") but leaner. Belongs to the high society Ellen misses and yearns for.

Quint   A professional fisherman and shark-hater. As tough, sadistic and crude as Hooper is compassionate and sensitive. "About 50, he was 6'4" and very lean—perhaps 180 or 190 . . . His face, like the rest of him, was hard and sharp. It was ruled by a long, straight nose. When he looked down from the flying bridge, he seemed to aim his eyes . . . along the nose as if it were a rifle barrel."

Plot Blueprint from the Viewpoints of Each Main Character

Purpose gained

Police Chief Martin Brody wants to be good at his job, specifically to protect the people of Amity, Long Island, from harm. He also wants to enjoy his family (wife and three sons).

— Her uppercrust background and snobbish friends make him feel ill at ease and inferior.

+ For the first few years of their marriage Ellen was so busy with the boys and him that they didn't see her friends who only came to Amity during the summer season.

— After their last son started school, she became restless.

+ Her summer mood of discontent would always pass. They were really a happy family and he *had* achieved his long-time goal of becoming chief of police.

— A woman-swimmer, Christine Watkins, is reported missing, then found killed by a Great White Shark (rare in these waters).

+ Brody wants to protect the townspeople by publicizing the story and by closing the beaches.

— He is strongly opposed by Editor Harry Meadows and Mayor-Realtor Larry Vaughan who both talk him out of closing the beaches, since such a move would scare tourists away and ruin the town financially. Brody's own wife, Ellen, sides with the Mayor and Meadows.

+   He is persuaded to think the shark will go away (or has already left for good) since no killer sharks were ever in the vicinity before.

—   The shark does *not* go away, but kills a six-year-old boy. Brody is in agony: "He felt at once betrayed and betrayer, a criminal forced into crime. He had wanted to do the right thing. Larry Vaughan had forced him not to. But if he couldn't stand up to Vaughan what kind of cop was he? He should have closed the beaches." Other newsmen converge.

+   No one actually *saw* the shark kill the boy . . . maybe . . . (hope)

—   Brody's assistant, Hendricks, reports seeing the shark kill a sixty-five-year-old man.

+   Brody orders Hendricks to close the beaches.

—   The *Leader* finally prints news of the shark-killings of the man and boy, also mentioning the previous death and stating that Brody could have closed the beaches but didn't. The dead boy's mother attacks Brody, calling him a murderer.

+   He decides to try to kill the shark. Since he has no boat or police craft, he asks the Mayor for and gets a couple of hundred dollars to charter Ben Gardner's boat for a day or two.

— Next day, Brody and Hendricks see Ben's boat standing still instead of shark-hunting. They go out to it. No Ben. The boat has four ragged screw holes where a cleat had been. Embedded in the wood is a shark's tooth. Ben is victim number four. Brody calls his widow, Sally, with the grim news.

+ A shark expert, Matt Hooper, comes from Wood's Hole to help get the monster.

— Somehow Brody feels threatened by the younger man. His job is also threatened by the Mayor who insists he open the beaches for the Fourth of July weekend.

+ Realizing that Vaughan is pressured by mysterious, powerful partners, Brody asks Meadows to find out who they are . . . also to find a professional fisherman to help get the shark.

— Amity seems to be dying. At Ellen's dinner party, Brody is violently jealous of Hooper and his rapport with Ellen.

+ Things seem to smooth out. Next day she's OK and there are no more shark sightings or fatalities.

(A triple CRISIS)

— Certain that the shark is gone, the Mayor and selectmen pressure Brody into opening the beaches. He learns of Vaughan's Mafia connections: then the Brody's cat is murdered gangland style. Brody is increasingly suspicious of Ellen and Hooper since he couldn't reach either by phone all afternoon on Wednesday.

+ Heroically, Brody saves a boy-swimmer from the shark. Then, serious action is taken to kill the shark. Pro fisherman Quint and his boat are hired for $400 per day. Brody, Hooper, and Quint go out to get the leviathan with sure-fire gear.

— Discord aboard: Brody and Hooper quarrel. Also Hooper, who loves fish, fights with brutal Quint who plans to use an unborn baby dolphin as bait to catch the shark. Time drags on with no sign of the shark, just minor catches.

+ Great White Shark appears. He's fantastic. All are excited!

— More fighting between Hooper and Brody who demands to know where Matt was Wednesday afternoon. He says "motel . . .

+ with Daisy Wicker." Surely Ellen's innocent. He'll check later.

— Conflict between Quint and Matt when he wants to bring a shark cage aboard to take pictures of the shark.

+ Quint is persuaded to acquiesce. Shark reappears. Quint encircles boat, using lowered squid as bait. Shark eats a couple. Matt insists on going down in shark cage to photograph the Great White. He says he'll kill him with his underwater gun.

— Instead, the shark kills Matt. Even though Brody was jealous and suspicious of him, he's shocked by his death.

+ Bad weather and their exhaustion makes

Brody hope Quint will give up, or at least take a reprieve.

— He won't. Fanatically, he insists they continue to pursue the shark furiously and unceasingly. He's killed.

+ The shark attacks and sinks the boat, but is killed by Quint's harpoons before he can kill Brody, who escapes.

Come-to-realize

Ellen Brody wants fulfillment.

— Every summer she's tortured by thoughts of chances she's missed. Her former boarding school classmates come to Amity with their successful husbands whereas she's stuck year-round in Amity married to a mere policeman.

+ Martin's a good husband and father. Her life really isn't too bad. Mayor Larry Vaughan and his wife are their friends, representing the "class" she misses in ex-friends.

— As her discontent grows she rebuffs Martin's frequent attempts at lovemaking. Also takes sleeping pills.

+ She meets rich, handsome Matt Hooper at the post office. He recalls her former society life when she dated his brother.

— Wistfully she recalls a line from a song: "I'd trade all my tomorrows for a single yesterday." She's low.

+ She gives a dinner party, inviting Matt Hooper. It's fancy: butterfly lamb, gazpacho soup, etc. Matt gives her a tiger-shark tooth in a silver casing that he got in Macao.

— Jealous Martin acts like a boor all evening. She can't sleep.

+ Next day she invites Matt to meet her for lunch, then to a rendezvous—just to restore her spirits.

— Guilt when she returns home and Martin has been trying to reach her all afternoon to apologize for last night.

+ Larry Vaughan comes to say goodbye, admits he's always been attracted to her and they would have made a great couple. He says he would have given her "a life you would have loved." Now that he's washed up, she appreciates her own husband and his values.

— Martin's out after the shark. Doesn't return. She worries.

+ He returns safe. Joyous, she flings herself at him with new realization of his worth.

Character degeneration

Mayor Larry Vaughan wants prosperity for himself and Amity.

— The shark killing of a woman-swimmer threatens to keep summer crowds away. Town depends on them.

+ He decides to hush up the tragedy. Gets cooperation of Harry Meadows, editor of the Amity *Leader*.

— Police Chief Martin Brody insists on closing the beaches just before the seasonal rush and big Fourth of July.

+ Mayor Vaughan pulls rank, threatens Brody's job and wins.

— After a six-year-old boy and a sixty-five-year-old man are killed, the news is out. There are many cancellations and no new rentals. It is financial disaster for him and the town. Even worse for him for he's in hock to Mafia men.

+ He persuades the selectmen and even Brody to open the beaches, since the shark has disappeared.

— The Great White Shark returns, almost getting a boy swimmer, who is saved by Brody.

+ Mayor okays the hiring of pro fisherman Quint to get shark.

— Quint holds them up for $400 a day and demands a mate.

+ Shark expert Matt Hooper volunteers. These two should rid Amity of its three-ton curse.

— Nothing can extricate Vaughan from his debts and reputation-shattering involvement with his Mafia partners. In disgrace he leaves Amity to try for a new start.

Decision

Harry Meadows wants to run an interesting newspaper, the *Leader*.

—   Woman-swimmer is killed by a never-before-seen shark.

+   He decides not to run the story or summer vacationers will be afraid to come to Amity, which needs their business.

—   Police Chief Brody asks him to print it. Wants to close the beaches to protect the townspeople from the shark.

+   Pressured by advertisers and the paper's majority owner, Harry refuses. He pleases authorities and protects job.

—   Stubbornly, Brody insists he'll close the beaches, putting up signs of his own.

+   Brody is stopped by the Mayor. Meadows keeps it out of paper.

—   The shark story leaks out when out-of-town newsmen report a boy's death. This makes him look bad.

+   He stalls rivals, since no one *saw* shark kill boy.

—   Man is reportedly attacked and killed by the shark.

+   Meadows runs full story. Later helps Brody.

Sadistic, murderous Quint's plot line is a Biter-Bit.

WHAT ELSE YOUR STORY NEEDS

"Good art is like good cooking, it can be tasted but not explained" (Vlaminck). This may apply to the amateur in both fields, but the professional cook as well as the professional artist is aware of the ingredients that create a masterpiece.

Be sure your fiction includes these factors:

P = Premise. Persons with Probability.

L = Locale. Logical development.

O = Opposing Obstacles. Originality.

T = Technique Throughout all the way to a Tricky Twist.

Even Your Short Fiction Should Follow This Recipe

S = Suspenseful Situation. Setting. Sincerity.

H = Honesty (in your knowledge of subject and presentation of premise).

O = Obstacles. Oppositions.

R = Reader Rapport. Relevance.

T = Theme. Typical Traits of each character.

S = Style. Symbolism. Satisfactory Solution.

T = Timing. Tension. Twists.

O = Originality.

R = Reversals.

Y = YOU (the reader and his emotional involvement).
YOU (the author—your feelings and philosophy).
It is as Goethe wrote: "Every author in some way portrays himself in his works, even if it be against his will."

Index